ABOUT THIS PUBLICATION

FOR SERVICE ASSISTANCE

Customer Service Department
704.898.0770

North Carolina General Statues is published by The Muliti-Media Group of Greater Charlotte in Charlotte, North Carolina. Copyright 2015 by the Multi-Media Group of Greater Charlotte. This book or parts thereof may not be reproduced in any form, stored in a retrieval system, or transmitted in any form by any means—electronic, mechanical, photocopy, recording or otherwise—without prior written permission of the publisher, except as provided by United States of America copyright law.

The records required by U.S. Code 2257(a) through (c) and the pertinent regulations 28 C.F.R. Cli. 1, Part 75 with respect to this publication and all materials associated with such records are maintained by The Multi-Media Group of Greater Charlotte, Publisher and available for review by Attorney General.

www.visionbooks.org

Copyright © 2015 by MMGGC
All rights reserved!

TID: 5031768
ISBN (10) digit: 1502599023
ISBN (13) digit: 978-1502599025

123-4-56789-01239-Paperback
123-4-56789-01239-Hardback

First Edition

090520140547

Printed in the United States of America

2015 EDITION

North Carolina Criminal Law And Procedure-Pamphlet # 23

Printed In conjunction with the Administration of the Courts

North Carolina Criminal Law and Procedure
Pamphlet Reference Guide

Chapters	Pamphlet
Chapter 1 Civil Procedure	1
Chapter 1 Civil Procedure (Continue)	2
Chapter 1A Rules of Civil Procedure	2
Chapter 1B Contribution.	2
Chapter 1C Enforcement of Judgments.	2
Chapter 1D Punitive Damages.	2
Chapter 1E Eastern Band of Cherokee Indians.	2
Chapter 1F North Carolina Uniform Interstate Depositions and Discovery Act.	2
Chapter 2 - Clerk of Superior Court [Repealed and Transferred.]	3
Chapter 3 - Commissioners of Affidavits and Deeds [Repealed.]	3
Chapter 4 - Common Law	3
Chapter 5 - Contempt [Repealed.]	3
Chapter 5A - Contempt	3
Chapter 6 - Liability for Court Costs	3
Chapter 7 - Courts [Repealed and Transferred.]	3
Chapter 7A – Judicial Department	3
Chapter 7A – Continuation (Judicial Department)	4
Chapter 7A – Continuation (Judicial Department)	5
Chapter 7B - Juvenile Code	5
Chapter 8 - Evidence	6
Chapter 8A - Interpreters for Deaf Persons [Recodified.]	6
Chapter 8B - Interpreters for Deaf Persons	6
Chapter 8C - Evidence Code	6
Chapter 9 - Jurors	6
Chapter 10 - Notaries [Repealed.]	6
Chapter 10A - Notaries [Recodified.]	6
Chapter 10B - Notaries	6
Chapter 11 - Oaths	6
Chapter 12 - Statutory Construction	6
Chapter 13 - Citizenship Restored	6
Chapter 14 - Criminal Law	7
Chapter 14 –Criminal Law (Continuation)	8
Chapter 15 - Criminal Procedure	9
Chapter 15A - Criminal Procedure Act (Continuation)	10
Chapter 15A - Criminal Procedure Act (Continuation)	11
Chapter 15B - Victims Compensation	11
Chapter 15C - Address Confidentiality Program	11
Chapter 16 - Gaming Contracts and Futures	11
Chapter 17 - Habeas Corpus	11

Chapter 17A - Law-Enforcement Officers [Recodified.]	11
Chapter 17B - North Carolina Criminal Justice Education and Training System [Recodified.] Chapter 17C - North Carolina Criminal Justice Education and Training Standards Commission	11
Chapter 17D - North Carolina Justice Academy	11
Chapter 17E - North Carolina Sheriffs' Education and Training Standards Commission	11
Chapter 18 - Regulation of Intoxicating Liquors [Repealed.]	12
Chapter 18A - Regulation of Intoxicating Liquors [Repealed.]	12
Chapter 18B - Regulation of Alcoholic Beverages	12
Chapter 18C - North Carolina State Lottery	12
Chapter 19 - Offenses against Public Morals	12
Chapter 19A - Protection of Animals	12
Chapter 20 - Motor Vehicles	13
Chapter 20 - Motor Vehicles (Continuation)	14
Chapter 20 - Motor Vehicles (Continuation)	15
Chapter 20 - Motor Vehicles (Continuation)	16
Chapter 21 - Bills of Lading	17
Chapter 22 - Contracts Requiring Writing	17
Chapter 22A - Signatures	17
Chapter 22B - Contracts Against Public Policy	17
Chapter 22C - Payments to Subcontractors	17
Chapter 23 - Debtor and Creditor	17
Chapter 24 – Interest	17
Chapter 25 – Uniform Commercial Code	18
Chapter 25 – Uniform Commercial Code (Continuation)	19
Chapter 25A – Retail Installment Sales Act	20
Chapter 25B - Credit	20
Chapter 25C - Sales of Artwork	20
Chapter 26 - Suretyship	20
Chapter 27 - Warehouse Receipts [Repealed.]	20
Chapter 28 - Administration [Repealed.]	20
Chapter 28A - Administration of Decedents' Estates	20
Chapter 28B - Estates of Absentees in Military Service	20
Chapter 28C - Estates of Missing Persons	20
Chapter 29 - Intestate Succession	21
Chapter 30 - Surviving Spouses	21
Chapter 31 - Wills	21
Chapter 31A - Acts Barring Property Rights	21
Chapter 31B - Renunciation of Property and Renunciation of Fiduciary Powers Act	21
Chapter 31C - Uniform Disposition of Community Property Rights at Death Act	21
Chapter 32 - Fiduciaries	21
Chapter 32A - Powers of Attorney	21
Chapter 33 - Guardian and Ward [Repealed and Recodified.]	21

Chapter 33A - North Carolina Uniform Transfers to Minors Act	21
Chapter 33B - North Carolina Uniform Custodial Trust Act	21
Chapter 34 - Veterans' Guardianship Act	22
Chapter 35 - Sterilization Procedures	22
Chapter 35A - Incompetency and Guardianship	22
Chapter 36 - Trusts and Trustees [Repealed.]	22
Chapter 36A - Trusts and Trustees	22
Chapter 36B - Uniform Management of Institutional Funds Act [Repealed.]	22
Chapter 36C - North Carolina Uniform Trust Code	22
Chapter 36D - North Carolina Community Third Party Trusts, Pooled Trusts	23
Chapter 36E - Uniform Prudent Management of Institutional Funds Act	23
Chapter 37 - Allocation of Principal and Income [Repealed.]	23
Chapter 37A - Uniform Principal and Income Act	23
Chapter 38 - Boundaries	23
Chapter 38A - Landowner Liability	23
Chapter 38B - **Trespasser Responsibility**	23
Chapter 39 - Conveyances	23
Chapter 39A - Transfer Fee Covenants Prohibited	23
Chapter 40 - Eminent Domain [Repealed.]	23
Chapter 40A - Eminent Domain	23
Chapter 41 - Estates	23
Chapter 41A - State Fair Housing Act	23
Chapter 42 - Landlord and Tenant	23
Chapter 42A - Vacation Rental Act	23
Chapter 43 - Land Registration	23
Chapter 44 - Liens	24
Chapter 44A - Statutory Liens and Charges	24
Chapter 45 - Mortgages and Deeds of Trust	24
Chapter 45A - Good Funds Settlement Act	24
Chapter 46 - Partition	24
Chapter 47 - Probate and Registration	25
Chapter 47A - Unit Ownership	25
Chapter 47B - Real Property Marketable Title Act	25
Chapter 47C - North Carolina Condominium Act	25
Chapter 47D - Notice of Settlement Act [Expired.]	25
Chapter 47E - Residential Property Disclosure Act	25
Chapter 47F - North Carolina Planned Community Act	25
Chapter 47G - Option to Purchase Contracts	25
Chapter 47H - Contracts for Deed	25
Chapter 48 - Adoptions +	26
Chapter 48A - Minors	26
Chapter 49 - Bastardy	26
Chapter 49A - Rights of Children	26
Chapter 50 - Divorce and Alimony	26

Chapter 50A - Uniform Child-Custody Jurisdiction and Enforcement Act	26
Chapter 50B - Domestic Violence	26
Chapter 50C - Civil No-Contact Orders	26
Chapter 51 - Marriage	26
Chapter 52 - Powers and Liabilities of Married Persons	27
Chapter 52A - Uniform Reciprocal Enforcement of Support Act [Repealed.]	27
Chapter 52B - Uniform Premarital Agreement Act	27
Chapter 52C - Uniform Interstate Family Support Act	27
Chapter 53 - Banks	27
Chapter 53A - Business Development Corporations and North Carolina Capital Resource Corporations	28
Chapter 53B - Financial Privacy Act	28
Chapter 54 - Cooperative Organizations	28
Chapter 54A - Capital Stock Savings and Loan Associations [Repealed.]	28
Chapter 54B - Savings and Loan Associations	29
Chapter 54C - Savings Banks	29
Chapter 55 - North Carolina Business Corporation Act	30
Chapter 55A - North Carolina Nonprofit Corporation Act	31
Chapter 55B - Professional Corporation Act	31
Chapter 55C - Foreign Trade Zones	31
Chapter 55D - Filings, Names, and Registered Agents for Corporations, Nonprofit Corporations, and Partnerships	31
Chapter 56 - Electric, Telegraph and Power Companies [Repealed.]	31
Chapter 57 - Hospital, Medical and Dental Service Corporations [Recodified.]	31
Chapter 57A - Health Maintenance Organization Act [Recodified.]	31
Chapter 57B - Health Maintenance Organization Act [Recodified.]	31
Chapter 57C - North Carolina Limited Liability Company Act.	31
Chapter 58 - Insurance.	32
Chapter 58 - Insurance (Continuation)	33
Chapter 58 - Insurance (Continuation)	34
Chapter 58 - Insurance (Continuation)	35
Chapter 58 - Insurance (Continuation)	36
Chapter 58 - Insurance (Continuation)	37
Chapter 58 - Insurance (Continuation)	38
Chapter 58A - North Carolina Health Insurance Trust Commission [Recodified.]	38
Chapter 59 - Partnership.	39
Chapter 59B - Uniform Unincorporated Nonprofit Association Act.	39
Chapter 60 - Railroads and Other Carriers [Repealed and Transferred.]	39
Chapter 61 - Religious Societies	39
Chapter 62 - Public Utilities	39

Chapter 62 - Public Utilities (Continuation)	40
Chapter 62A - Public Safety Telephone Service And Wireless Telephone Service	40
Chapter 63 - Aeronautics	40
Chapter 63A - North Carolina Global TransPark Authority	40
Chapter 64 - Aliens	40
Chapter 65 – Cemeteries	40
Chapter 66 - Commerce and Business	41
Chapter 67 - Dogs	41
Chapter 68 - Fences and Stock Law	41
Chapter 69 - Fire Protection	41
Chapter 70 - Indian Antiquities, Archaeological Resources and Unmarked Human Skeletal Remains Protection	42
Chapter 71 - Indians [Repealed.]	42
Chapter 71A - Indians	42
Chapter 72 - Inns, Hotels and Restaurants	42
Chapter 73 - Mills	42
Chapter 74 - Mines and Quarries	42
Chapter 74A - Company Police [Repealed.]	42
Chapter 74B - Private Protective Services Act [Repealed.]	42
Chapter 74C - Private Protective Services	42
Chapter 74D - Alarm Systems	42
Chapter 74E - Company Police Act	42
Chapter 74F - Locksmith Licensing Act	42
Chapter 74G - Campus Police Act	42
Chapter 75 - Monopolies, Trusts and Consumer Protection	42
Chapter 75A - Boating and Water Safety	43
Chapter 75B - Discrimination in Business	43
Chapter 75C - Motion Picture Fair Competition Act	43
Chapter 75D - Racketeer Influenced and Corrupt Organizations	43
Chapter 75E - Unlawful Activities in Connection With Certain Corporate Transactions	43
Chapter 76 - Navigation	43
Chapter 76A - Navigation and Pilotage Commissions	43
Chapter 77 - Rivers, Creeks, and Coastal Waters	43
Chapter 78 - Securities Law [Repealed.]	43
Chapter 78A - North Carolina Securities Act	43
Chapter 78B - Tender Offer Disclosure Act [Repealed.]	43
Chapter 78C - Investment Advisers	43
Chapter 78D - Commodities Act	43
Chapter 79 - Strays [Repealed.]	43
Chapter 80 - Trademarks, Brands, etc.	44
Chapter 81 - Weights and Measures [Recodified.]	44
Chapter 81A - Weights and Measures Act of 1975.	44
Chapter 82 - Wrecks [Repealed.]	44
Chapter 83 - Architects [Recodified.]	44

Chapter 83A - Architects	44
Chapter 84 - Attorneys-at-Law	44
Chapter 84A - Foreign Legal Consultants	44
Chapter 85 - Auctions and Auctioneers [Repealed.]	44
Chapter 85A - Bail Bondsmen and Runners [Recodified.]	44
Chapter 85B - Auctions and Auctioneers	44
Chapter 85C - Bail Bondsmen and Runners [Recodified.]	44
Chapter 86 - Barbers [Recodified.]	44
Chapter 86A - Barbers	44
Chapter 87 - Contractors	44
Chapter 88 - Cosmetic Art [Repealed.]	44
Chapter 88A - Electrolysis Practice Act	44
Chapter 88B - Cosmetic Art	45
Chapter 89 - Engineering and Land Surveying [Recodified.]	45
Chapter 89A - Landscape Architects	45
Chapter 89B - Foresters	45
Chapter 89C - Engineering and Land Surveying	45
Chapter 89D - Landscape Contractors	45
Chapter 89E - Geologists Licensing Act	45
Chapter 89F - North Carolina Soil Scientist Licensing Act	45
Chapter 89G - Irrigation Contractors	45
Chapter 90 - Medicine and Allied Occupations	45
Chapter 90 - Medicine and Allied Occupations (Continuation)	46
Chapter 90 - Medicine and Allied Occupations (Continuation)	47
Chapter 90 - Medicine and Allied Occupations (Continuation)	48
Chapter 90A - Sanitarians and Water and Wastewater Treatment Facility Operators	48
Chapter 90B - Social Worker Certification and Licensure Act	48
Chapter 90C - North Carolina Recreational Therapy Licensure Act	48
Chapter 90D - Interpreters and Transliterators	48
Chapter 91 - Pawnbrokers [Repealed.]	48
Chapter 91A - Pawnbrokers Modernization Act of 1989	48
Chapter 92 - Photographers [Deleted.]	48
Chapter 93 - Certified Public Accountants	48
Chapter 93A - Real Estate License Law	49
Chapter 93B - Occupational Licensing Boards	49
Chapter 93C - Watchmakers [Repealed.]	49
Chapter 93D - North Carolina State Hearing Aid Dealers and Fitters Board.	49
Chapter 93E - North Carolina Appraisers Act	49
Chapter 94 - Apprenticeship	49
Chapter 95 - Department of Labor and Labor Regulations	49
Chapter 95 - Department of Labor and Labor Regulations (Continuation)	50
Chapter 96 - Employment Security	50
Chapter 97 - Workers' Compensation Act	50
Chapter 97 - Workers' Compensation Act (Continuation)	51

Chapter 98 - Burnt and Lost Records	51
Chapter 99 - Libel and Slander	51
Chapter 99A - Civil Remedies for Criminal Actions	51
Chapter 99B - Products Liability	51
Chapter 99C - Actions Relating to Winter Sports Safety and Accidents	51
Chapter 99D - Civil Rights	51
Chapter 99E - Special Liability Provisions	51
Chapter 100 - Monuments, Memorials and Parks	51
Chapter 101 - Names of Persons	51
Chapter 102 - Official Survey Base	51
Chapter 103 - Sundays, Holidays and Special Days	51
Chapter 104 - United States Lands	51
Chapter 104A - Degrees of Kinship	51
Chapter 104B - Hurricanes or Other Acts of Nature	51
Chapter 104C - Atomic Energy, Radioactivity and Ionizing Radiation [Repealed and Recodified.]	51
Chapter 104D - Southern States Energy Compact	51
Chapter 104E - North Carolina Radiation Protection Act	51
Chapter 104F - Southeast Interstate Low-Level Radioactive Waste Management Compact [Repealed]	51
Chapter 104G - North Carolina Low-Level Radioactive Waste Management Authority Act of 1987 [Repealed]	51
Chapter 105 - Taxation	51
Chapter 105 - Taxation (Continuation)	52
Chapter 105 - Taxation (Continuation)	53
Chapter 105 - Taxation (Continuation)	54
Chapter 105A - Setoff Debt Collection Act	55
Chapter 105B - Defaulted Student Loan Recovery Act	55
Chapter 106 - Agriculture	55
Chapter 106 - Agriculture (Continue)	56
Chapter 106 - Agriculture (Continue)	57
Chapter 107 - Agricultural Development Districts [Repealed.]	57
Chapter 108 - Social Services [Repealed and Recodified.]	57
Chapter 108A - Social Services	57
Chapter 108B - Community Action Programs	58
Chapter 108C Medicaid and Health Choice Provider Requirements.	58
Chapter 108D Medicaid Managed Care for Behavioral Health Services.	58
Chapter 109 - Bonds [Recodified.]	58
Chapter 110 - Child Welfare	58
Chapter 111 - Aid to the Blind	58
Chapter 112 - Confederate Homes and Pensions [Repealed.]	58
Chapter 113 - Conservation and Development	58
Chapter 113 - Conservation and Development (Continuation)	59

Chapter 113A - Pollution Control and Environment	59
Chapter 113A - Pollution Control and Environment (Continuation)	60
Chapter 113B - North Carolina Energy Policy Act of 1975	60
Chapter 114 - Department of Justice	60
Chapter 115 - Elementary and Secondary Education [Repealed.]	60
Chapter 115A - Community Colleges, Technical Institutes, and Industrial Education Centers [Repealed.]	60
Chapter 115B - Tuition and Fee Waivers	60
Chapter 115C - Elementary and Secondary Education	60
Chapter 115C - Elementary and Secondary Education (Continuation)	61
Chapter 115C - Elementary and Secondary Education (Continuation)	62
Chapter 115C - Elementary and Secondary Education (Continuation)	63
Chapter 115D - Community Colleges	63
Chapter 115E - Private Educational Facilities Finance Act [Recodified]	63
Chapter 116 - Higher Education	63
Chapter 116 - Higher Education (Continuation)	63
Chapter 116A - Escheats and Abandoned Property [Repealed.]	64
Chapter 116B - Escheats and Abandoned Property	64
Chapter 116C - Continuum of Education Programs	64
Chapter 116D - Higher Education Bonds	64
Chapter 117 - Electrification	64
Chapter 118 - Firemen's and Rescue Squad Workers' Relief and Pension Funds [Recodified.]	64
Chapter 118A - Firemen's Death Benefit Act [Repealed.]	64
Chapter 118B - Members of a Rescue Squad Death Benefit Act [Repealed.]	64
Chapter 119 - Gasoline and Oil Inspection and Regulation	64
Chapter 120 - General Assembly	65
Chapter 120 - General Assembly (Continuation)	66
Chapter 120 - General Assembly (Continuation)	67
Chapter 120C - Lobbying	67
Chapter 121 - Archives and History	67
Chapter 122 - Hospitals for the Mentally Disordered [Repealed.]	67
Chapter 122A - North Carolina Housing Finance Agency	67
Chapter 122B - North Carolina Agricultural Facilities Finance Act [Repealed.]	67
Chapter 122C - Mental Health, Developmental Disabilities, and Substance Abuse Act of 1985	67
Chapter 122C - Mental Health, Developmental Disabilities, and Substance Abuse Act of 1985 (Continuation)	68
Chapter 122D - North Carolina Agricultural Finance Act	68

Chapter 122E - North Carolina Housing Trust and Oil Overcharge Act	68
Chapter 123 - Impeachment	69
Chapter 123A - Industrial Development [Repealed.]	69
Chapter 124 - Internal Improvements	69
Chapter 125 - Libraries	69
Chapter 126 - State Personnel System	69
Chapter 127 - Militia [Repealed.]	69
Chapter 127A - Militia	69
Chapter 127B - Military Affairs	69
Chapter 127C - Advisory Commission on Military Affairs	69
Chapter 128 - Offices and Public Officers	69
Chapter 128 - Offices and Public Officers (Continuation)	70
Chapter 129 - Public Buildings and Grounds	70
Chapter 130 - Public Health [Repealed.]	70
Chapter 130A - Public Health	70
Chapter 130A - Public Health (Continuation)	71
Chapter 130A - Public Health (Continuation)	72
Chapter 130B - Hazardous Waste Management Commission [Repealed.]	72
Chapter 131 - Public Hospitals [Repealed.]	72
Chapter 131A - Health Care Facilities Finance Act	72
Chapter 131B - Licensing of Ambulatory Surgical Facilities [Repealed.]	72
Chapter 131C - Charitable Solicitation Licensure Act [Repealed.]	72
Chapter 131D - Inspection and Licensing of Facilities	72
Chapter 131E - Health Care Facilities and Services	72
Chapter 131E - Health Care Facilities and Services (Continuation)	73
Chapter 131F - Solicitation of Contributions	73
Chapter 132 - Public Records	73
Chapter 133 - Public Works	74
Chapter 134 - Youth Development [Recodified.]	74
Chapter 134A - Youth Services [Repealed.]	74
Chapter 135 - Retirement System for Teachers and State Employees; Social Security; Health Insurance Program for Children	74
Chapter 135 - Retirement System for Teachers and State Employees; Social Security; Health Insurance Program for Children	75
Chapter 136 - Transportation	75
Chapter 136 - Transportation (Continuation)	76
Chapter 137 - Rural Rehabilitation [Repealed.]	76
Chapter 138 - Salaries, Fees and Allowances	76
Chapter 138A - State Government Ethics Act	76
Chapter 139 - Soil and Water Conservation Districts	76

Chapter 140 - State Art Museum; Symphony and Art Societies	76
Chapter 140A - State Awards System	76
Chapter 141 - State Boundaries	76
Chapter 142 - State Debt	76
Chapter 143 - State Departments, Institutions, and Commissions	77
Chapter 143 - State Departments, Institutions, and Commissions (Continuation)	78
Chapter 143 - State Departments, Institutions, and Commissions (Continuation)	79
Chapter 143 - State Departments, Institutions, and Commissions (Continuation)	80
Chapter 143A - State Government Reorganization	80
Chapter 143B - Executive Organization Act of 1973	80
Chapter 143B - Executive Organization Act of 1973 (Continuation)	81
Chapter 143B - Executive Organization Act of 1973 (Continuation)	82
Chapter 143C - State Budget Act	83
Chapter 143D - The State Governmental Accountability and Internal Control Act	83
Chapter 144 - State Flag, Official Governmental Flags, Motto, and Colors	83
Chapter 145 - State Symbols and Other Official Adoptions.	83
Chapter 146 - State Lands	83
Chapter 147 - State Officers	83
Chapter 148 - State Prison System	84
Chapter 149 - State Song and Toast	84
Chapter 150 - Uniform Revocation of Licenses [Repealed.]	84
Chapter 150A - Administrative Procedure Act [Recodified.]	84
Chapter 150B - Administrative Procedure Act	84
Chapter 151 - Constables [Repealed.]	84
Chapter 152 - Coroners	84
Chapter 152A - County Medical Examiner [Repealed.]	84
Chapter 152A - County Medical Examiner [Repealed.] (Continuation)	85
Chapter 153 - Counties and County Commissioners [Repealed.]	85
Chapter 153A - Counties	85
Chapter 153B - Mountain Resources Planning Act	85
Chapter 153C - Uwharrie Regional Resources Act	85
Chapter 154 - County Surveyor [Repealed.]	85
Chapter 155 - County Treasurer [Repealed.]	85
Chapter 156 - Drainage	85
Chapter 156 – Drainage (Continuation)	86

Chapter 157 - Housing Authorities and Projects	86
Chapter 157A - Historic Properties Commissions [Transferred.]	86
Chapter 158 - Local Development	86
Chapter 159 - Local Government Finance	86
Chapter 159 - Local Government Finance (Continuation)	87
Chapter 159A - Pollution Abatement and Industrial Facilities Financing Act [Unconstitutional.]	87
Chapter 159B - Joint Municipal Electric Power and Energy Act	87
Chapter 159C - Industrial and Pollution Control Facilities Financing Act	87
Chapter 159D - The North Carolina Capital Facilities Financing Act	87
Chapter 159E - Registered Public Obligations Act	87
Chapter 159F - North Carolina Energy Development Authority [Repealed.]	87
Chapter 159G - Water Infrastructure	87
Chapter 159H - [Reserved.]	87
Chapter 159I - Solid Waste Management Loan Program and Local Government Special Obligation Bonds	87
Chapter 160 - Municipal Corporations [Repealed And Transferred.]	87
Chapter 160A - Cities and Towns	88
Chapter 160A - Cities and Towns (Continuation)	89
Chapter 160B - Consolidated City-County Act	89
Chapter 160C - Baseball Park Districts [Repealed.]	90
Chapter 161 - Register of Deeds	90
Chapter 162 - Sheriff	90
Chapter 162A - Water and Sewer Systems	90
Chapter 162B Continuity of Local Government in Emergency.	90
Chapter 163 Elections and Election Laws.	90
Chapter 163 Elections and Election Laws. (Continuation)	91
Chapter 164 Concerning the General Statutes of North Carolina.	92
Chapter 165 Veterans.	92
Chapter 166 Civil Preparedness Agencies [Repealed.]	92
Chapter 166A North Carolina Emergency Management Act.	92
Chapter 167 State Civil Air Patrol [Repealed.]	92
Chapter 168 Persons with Disabilities.	92
Chapter 168A Persons With Disabilities Protection Act.	92

Chapter 36D

North Carolina Community Third Party Trusts, Pooled Trusts.

§ 36D-1. Title; findings.

(a) This Chapter shall be known and may be cited as the "North Carolina Community Third Party Trusts, Pooled Trusts Act."

(b) The General Assembly finds that it is in the public interest to encourage activities by voluntary associations and private citizens that will supplement and augment those services provided by local, State, and federal government agencies in discharge of their responsibilities toward individuals with severe chronic disabilities. The General Assembly further finds that, as a result of changing social, economic, and demographic trends, families of persons with severe chronic disabilities are increasingly aware of the need for a vehicle by which they can assure ongoing individualized personal concern for a family member with a disability who may survive his or her parents or other family members, and provide for the efficient management of trust funds to be used for the benefit of that person with a disability. In a number of other states, voluntary associations have established foundations or trusts intended to be responsive to these concerns. Therefore, the General Assembly finds that North Carolina will benefit by the enactment of enabling legislation expressly authorizing the formation of Community Third Party Trusts and Pooled Trusts in accordance with 42 U.S.C. § 1396p(d)(4) and criteria set forth by statute and administered by the Secretary of State under Chapter 55A of the General Statutes.

(c) This Chapter shall be liberally construed and applied to promote its underlying purposes and policies, which are, among others, to:

(1) Repealed by Session Laws 2010-118, s. 1, effective July 20, 2010.

(2) Ensure that Community Third Party or Pooled Trusts for the benefit of persons with severe chronic disabilities are established and administered properly and that the managing boards of the trusts are free from conflicts of interest.

(3) Facilitate sound administration of trust funds for persons with severe chronic disabilities by allowing family members, persons with disabilities, and others to pool resources in order to make professional management investment more efficient.

(4) Provide parents of persons with severe chronic disabilities peace of mind in knowing that a means exists to ensure that the interests of their children who have severe chronic disabilities are properly looked after and managed after the parents die or become incapacitated.

(5) Assist in making guardians available for persons with severe chronic disabilities who are incompetent, when no other family member is available for this purpose.

(6) Encourage the availability of private resources to purchase for persons with severe chronic disabilities goods and services that are not available through any governmental or charitable program and to conserve these resources by limiting purchases to those that are not available from other sources.

(7) Encourage the inclusion, as beneficiaries of Community Third Party or Pooled Trusts, of persons who lack resources and whose families are indigent, in a way that does not diminish the resources available to other beneficiaries whose families have contributed to the trust.

(8) Remove the disincentives that discourage parents and others from setting aside funds for the future protection of persons with severe chronic disabilities by ensuring that the interest of beneficiaries of trusts that meet the rules set forth by the Department are not considered assets or income that would disqualify them from any governmental or charitable entitlement program with an economic means test.

(9) Require, pursuant to 42 U.S.C. § 1396p(d)(4), the payback of monies from Pooled Trusts up to an amount equal to the total amount of assistance paid for by the Department on behalf of or to the beneficiary from any funds remaining in the beneficiary's individual trust account upon the death of the individual or the termination of the individual trust account.

(d) Nothing in this Chapter shall affect the establishment, interpretation, or construction of Pooled Trust instruments which do not conform with the provisions of this Chapter, nor shall this Chapter impair the State's authority to be paid from or seek reimbursement from any Pooled Trust which does not conform with the provisions of this Chapter or to deem the principal or income of any nonconforming 36D Trust an available resource under any program of government benefits or assistance. (1991 (Reg. Sess., 1992), c. 768, s. 1; 2005-192, s. 3; 2010-118, s. 1.)

§ 36D-2. Definitions.

As used in this Chapter, unless the context clearly requires otherwise:

(1)   Beneficiary. - Any of the following persons:

a.   Any person of any age with a severe chronic disability who has qualified as a member of the Community Third Party Trust, funded with assets of a third party or by will.

b.   Any person who meets the definition of disability as defined in 42 U.S.C. § 1382c(a)(3) on whose behalf an individual Medicaid Pooled Trust subaccount was established by the parent, grandparent, or legal guardian of the individual, by the individual, or by a court.

(2)   Community Third Party Trust. - A trust funded with the assets of a third party for the benefit of a person of any age with severe chronic disabilities, that is administered by a nonprofit corporation that offers the following services:

a.   Administration of trust funds for persons with severe chronic disabilities.

b.   Follow along services.

c.   Guardianship for persons with severe chronic disabilities who are incompetent, when no other family member or immediate friend is available for this purpose.

d.   Information and referral services to persons who have been appointed as individual guardians of the persons or estates of persons with severe chronic disabilities.

(2a)   Department. - The Department of Health and Human Services.

(2b)   Family members. - Persons who are related by blood or marriage within the sixth degree to the beneficiary.

(3)   Follow-along services. - Includes the following: (i) those services offered by Community Third Party or Pooled Trusts that are designed to ensure that the needs of each beneficiary are being met for as long as may be required and may include periodic visits to the beneficiary and to the places where the beneficiary receives services, (ii) participation in the development of

individualized plans being made by service providers for the beneficiary, and (iii) other similar services consistent with the purposes of this Chapter.

(3a)   Medicaid Pooled Trust, pooled trust, or umbrella pooled trust. - A trust pursuant to 42 U.S.C. § 1396p(d)(4)(C) and the rules set forth for pooled trusts by the Department that meets all of the following requirements:

a.   The trust is irrevocable.

b.   The trust contains a separate subaccount for each beneficiary of the trust, but the funds in the accounts are pooled for the purpose of investment and management of funds. Investment of funds pursuant to this subdivision shall be in accord with G.S. 32-71, the Prudent Person rule.

c.   The beneficiary is disabled as defined by 42 U.S.C. § 1382c(a)(3).

d.   The trust is established solely for the benefit of the beneficiary by a parent, grandparent, legal guardian, by the beneficiary, or by a court.

e.   The trust was created on or after April 1, 1994.

f.   The trust provides that upon the death of the beneficiary the State will receive all amounts remaining in the beneficiary's account up to the total amount of medical assistance paid on behalf of the beneficiary as set forth in G.S. 36D-6.

g.   Trust language governing each Medicaid Pooled Trust shall be approved by the Department.

h.   A Medicaid Pooled Trust shall be established by a nonprofit corporation that offers any of the following:

1.   Administration of trust funds for persons with a disability as defined in 42 U.S.C. § 1382c(a)(3).

2.   Follow-along services.

3.   Guardianship for individuals with a disability pursuant to 42 U.S.C. § 1382c(a)(3) who are incompetent, when no other family member or immediate friend is available for this purpose.

4. Information and referral services to persons who have been appointed as individual guardians of the persons or estates of persons with a disability pursuant to 42 U.S.C. § 1382c(a)(3).

(4) Severe chronic disability. - A disability which impairs one or more areas of independent functioning.

(5), (6) Repealed by Session Laws 2010-118, s. 1, effective July 20, 2010.

(7) Sole benefit. - No individual other than the beneficiary benefits from the trust, either directly or indirectly.

(8) Surplus trust funds. - All funds remaining in the trust upon termination of the trust, whether by death of the beneficiary or otherwise.

(9) Trustee. - An original, additional, or successor trustee, and a cotrustee, whether or not appointed or confirmed by a court. The term does not include trustees in mortgages and deeds of trust.

(10) 36D Trust. - Any trust governed by this Chapter. (1991 (Reg. Sess., 1992), c. 768, s. 1; 2005-192, s. 3; 2010-118, s. 1.)

§ 36D-3. Scope.

This Chapter applies to every Community Third Party Trust or Medicaid Pooled Trust established in this State. In addition to meeting the other requirements of this Chapter, every board that administers a Community Third Party Trust or Medicaid Pooled Trust shall incorporate as a nonprofit corporation under Chapter 55A of the General Statutes. Except as otherwise provided in this Chapter, Chapter 55A of the General Statutes applies to all trusts governed by this Chapter. Article 9 of Chapter 36C of the General Statutes, the Uniform Trust Code, applies to 36D Trusts in the same manner that it applies to trusts under the Uniform Trust Code, with the exception of the following: the trustee of a pooled trust is liable to the Department to the extent the trustee administers the trust in a way that is not for the sole benefit of the beneficiary, regardless of the terms of the trust. The terms of the trust shall not contradict the meaning of "sole benefit" as defined in G.S. 36D-2(7). (1991 (Reg. Sess., 1992), c. 768, s. 1; 2005-192, s. 3; 2010-118, s. 1.)

§ 36D-4. Administration of Community Third Party and Pooled Trusts; powers and duties.

(a) Every Community Third Party or Pooled Trust shall be administered by a board. The board shall be comprised of no less than nine and no more than 21 members, at least one-third of whom are parents or relatives of persons with severe chronic disabilities. No board member shall be a provider of habilitative, health, social, or educational services to persons with severe chronic disabilities or an employee of such a service provider. The board may, however, allow service providers to serve on the board in an advisory capacity. Board members shall be selected, to the maximum extent possible, from geographic areas throughout the area served by the trust.
The certificate of incorporation filed with the Secretary of State under Chapter 55A of the General Statutes shall, in addition to the requirements set forth in that Chapter, demonstrate that the requirements of this section have been met.

(b) Notwithstanding any other law, no trustee may be compensated for services provided as a member of the board of a Community Third Party or Pooled Trust. No fees or commissions shall be paid to these trustees; however, a trustee may be paid for necessary expenses incurred by the trustee and may receive indemnification as permitted under Chapter 55A of the General Statutes as it applies to nonprofit organizations.

(c) For every Community Third Party or Pooled Trust incorporated under this Chapter, the corporation itself is considered the trustee of any funds administered by it. No individual board member is considered to be trustee of any fund deposited on behalf of any individual beneficiary with severe chronic disabilities.

(d) The board shall adopt bylaws that include a declaration delineating the primary geographic area serviced by the trust and the principal services to be provided. The board shall file the bylaws with the Secretary of State.

(e) The board may retain paid staff as it considers necessary to provide follow along services to the extent required by each beneficiary.

(e1) The Community Third Party or Pooled Trust may authorize the expenditure of funds for any goods or services, including recreational services, which will promote the well-being and is for the sole benefit of the beneficiary. The Community Third Party or Pooled Trust may pay for the reasonable burial expenses of any beneficiary; however, if the beneficiary receives SSI benefits, burial expenses may be paid for only as allowed by Social Security Administration regulations. The Community Third Party or Pooled Trust however, may not expend funds for any goods or services of comparable quality to those available to any particular beneficiary through any governmental or charitable program, insurance, or other sources. The Community Third Party or Pooled Trust may expend funds to meet the reasonable costs of administering the Community Third Party or Pooled Trust.

(f)   The Community Third Party or Pooled Trust is not required to provide services to a beneficiary who is a competent adult and who has refused to accept the services. Further, the Community Third Party or Pooled Trust shall not provide services of a nature or in a manner that would be contrary to the public policy of this State at the time the services are to be provided. In either case, the Community Third Party or Pooled Trust may offer alternate services that are consistent with the purposes of this Chapter and in keeping with the best interests of the beneficiary.

(g)   The Community Third Party or Pooled Trust may accept appointment as guardian of the person, guardian of the estate, or guardian of both on behalf of any beneficiary. If the Community Third Party or Pooled Trust accepts appointment as guardian of the person of an individual, it shall assign a staff member to carry out its responsibilities as the guardian. The Community Third Party or Pooled Trust may, upon request, offer consultative and professional assistance to an individual, private or public guardian of any of its beneficiaries.

(h)   The Community Third Party or Pooled Trust may accept contributions, devises, and designations under life insurance policies to the Community Third Party or Pooled Trust on behalf of individuals with severe chronic disabilities for the purpose of qualifying them as beneficiaries.

(i)   At the time a contribution, devise, or assignment of insurance proceeds is made to a Community Third Party Trust, or to a beneficiary of a Pooled Trust, the trustor shall receive a written statement of the services to be provided to the beneficiary. The statement shall include a starting date for the delivery of services or the condition precedent, such as the death of the trustor, which shall determine the starting date. The statement shall describe the frequency with which services shall be provided and their duration, and the criteria or procedures for modifying the program of services from time to time in the best interests of the beneficiary. In addition, there shall be a properly executed trust agreement between the Community Third Party or Pooled Trust and the trustor.

(j) No trustee, board member, or paid staff member of a Community Third Party or Pooled Trust shall undertake legal representation or other professional services on behalf of the trust or its beneficiaries.

(k) The Department shall be given a minimum of 30 days notice if there is to be a change in trustee. (1991 (Reg. Sess., 1992), c. 768, s. 1; 2005-192, s. 3; 2010-118, s. 1; 2011-284, s. 46(a), (b).)

§ 36D-5. Community Third Party and Pooled Trust accountability.

(a) Along with the annual report filed with the Secretary of State under Chapter 55A of the General Statutes, the Community Third Party or Pooled Trust shall file an itemized statement that shows the funds collected for the year, income earned, salaries, other expenses incurred, and the opening and final trust balances. A copy of the annual individual accounting statement of each beneficiary's subaccount shall be made available by the trustee, upon request, to the Department, any beneficiary, guardian, trustor, or designee of the trustor. In addition, once annually, each trustor or the trustor's designee shall receive a detailed individual statement of the services provided to the trustor's beneficiary during the previous 12 months and the services to be provided during the following 12 months. The Community Third Party or Pooled Trust shall make a copy of the individual statement available to any beneficiary, upon request.

(b) The Department or its agents may perform annual audits of any Community Third Party or Pooled Trusts existing in the State. (1991 (Reg. Sess., 1992), c. 768, s. 1; 2005-192, s. 3; 2010-118, s. 1.)

§ 36D-6. Gifts, Community Third Party or Pooled Trust surplus trust funds.

(a) Community Third Party and Pooled Trusts may accept gifts and use surplus trust funds to meet reasonable start-up costs and reduce the charges to the trust for the cost of administration and for the purpose of qualifying as beneficiary any indigent person whose family members lack the resources to make a full contribution on that person's behalf. A maximum of fifty percent (50%) of the surplus trust funds may be retained in the Community Third Party or Pooled Trust account for this purpose as well as to cover administrative costs. Gifts made to the Community Third Party or Pooled Trust for an unspecified purpose shall be used by the trust either to qualify indigent persons whose families lack the means to qualify them as beneficiaries of the trust or to meet any reasonable start-up or administrative costs that the trust incurs.

(b)   For Community Third Party Trusts, remaining surplus trust funds may be distributed to additional beneficiaries as specified in the Trust Agreement.

(c)   For Medicaid Pooled Trusts, upon termination of an individual trust account, the surplus trust funds remaining in the individual account shall be used to satisfy any claims or liens of the Department, up to an amount equal to the total medical assistance paid on behalf of or to the disabled individual by the Department. The amount retained by the trust shall be determined on a sliding scale calculation, based upon the number of years the disabled individual received services from the nonprofit corporation, but in no instance shall the trust retain more than fifty percent (50%) of the surplus trust funds, unless the claims or liens of the Department are less than fifty percent (50%) of the surplus trust funds.

(d)   A Medicaid Pooled Trust may not distribute surplus trust funds to any remaindermen identified in the trust document unless there are funds remaining after all claims or liens of the Department have been satisfied, nor shall it use surplus trust funds to make any charitable contribution on behalf of any beneficiary or any group or class of beneficiaries. (1991 (Reg. Sess., 1992), c. 768, s. 1; 2005-192, s. 3; 2010-118, s. 1.)

§ 36D-7. Special requests on behalf of beneficiary.

The Community Third Party Trust may agree to fulfill any special requests made on behalf of a beneficiary as long as the requests are consistent with this Chapter and provided that an adequate contribution has been made for this purpose on behalf of a beneficiary. The Medicaid Pooled Trust may only disburse subaccount trust funds if such disbursement is in the sole benefit of the beneficiary. (1991 (Reg. Sess., 1992), c. 768, s. 1; 2005-192, s. 3; 2010-118, s. 1.)

§ 36D-8: Repealed by Session Laws 2010-118, s. 1, effective July 20, 2010.

§ 36D-9. Beneficiary's interest in trust not asset for income eligibility determination.

The beneficiary's interest in any 36D Trust is not considered to be an asset for the purpose of determining income eligibility for any publicly operated program, nor shall that interest be reached in satisfaction of a claim for support and maintenance of the beneficiary. The Department shall not reduce the benefits or services available to any individual because that person is the beneficiary of a 36D Trust. The Department may authorize termination of an individual's eligibility for medical assistance or impose sanctions as necessary for failure of a purported 36D Trust to comply with the requirements of this Chapter and any rules adopted by the Department pursuant to this Chapter. The Department may authorize termination of an individual's eligibility for medical assistance or impose sanctions as necessary for failure of the trustee to administer the 36D Trust in a manner consistent with this Chapter, the rules adopted by the Department pursuant to this Chapter, and federal law and policy. (1991 (Reg. Sess., 1992), c. 768, s. 1; 2005-192, s. 3; 2010-118, s. 1.)

§ 36D-10. Trust not subject to law against perpetuities; restraints on alienation.
A 36D Trust shall not be subject to or held to be in violation of any principle of law against perpetuities or restraints on alienation or perpetual accumulations of trusts. (1991 (Reg. Sess., 1992), c. 768, s. 1; 2005-192, s. 3; 2010-118, s. 1.)
§ 36D-11. Settlement; trustee limitations.

(a) The trustee of a Medicaid Pooled Trust shall provide a final disbursement and accounting for an individual Pooled Trust subaccount to the Division of Medical Assistance, Third Party Recovery Section, within 30 days of the receipt of an accounting of charges from Medicaid, after the death of the beneficiary or other termination of the trust. An individual Pooled Trust subaccount shall terminate upon the death of the beneficiary and the satisfaction of all outstanding charges.
(b) At any time before the settlement of the final account, the Community Third Party or Pooled Trust, the Secretary of State, or the Attorney General may bring an action for the dissolution of a nonprofit corporation in the superior court for the purpose of terminating the trust or merging it with another charitable trust.
(c) No trustee or any private individual is entitled to share in the distribution of any of the trust assets upon dissolution, merger, or settlement of the Community Third Party or Pooled Trust. Upon dissolution, merger, or settlement, the superior court shall distribute all of the remaining net assets of the Community Third Party or Pooled Trust in a manner that is consistent with the purposes of this Chapter. (1991 (Reg. Sess., 1992), c. 768, s. 1; 2005-192, s. 3; 2010-118, s. 1.)

§ 36D-12. Administrative rules.
The Department shall adopt rules pursuant to Chapter 150B of the General Statutes governing the eligibility of beneficiaries for State medical assistance and State-County Special Assistance, and to supplement and expand upon the general requirements set forth in this Chapter, including, but not limited to, rules that may be more restrictive than the general requirements of this Chapter. With

respect to Medicaid Pooled Trusts, a subaccount is irrevocable. The State shall be paid an amount up to the total medical assistance paid on behalf of the beneficiary by the Department from funds remaining in the individual trust subaccount upon the death of the beneficiary or termination of the trust as described in this Chapter. If the pooled trust is to be funded with the proceeds of a settlement of a lawsuit against a third party, the settlement proceeds are subject to the Department's subrogated rights of recovery as set forth in G.S. 108A-57, and all such subrogated rights of recovery shall be satisfied in full prior to execution and judicial approval of the trust, or both. (2010-118, s. 1.)

Chapter 36E.

Uniform Prudent Management of Institutional Funds Act.

§ 36E-1. Short title.

This Chapter may be cited as the Uniform Prudent Management of Institutional Funds Act. (1985, c. 98, s. 1; 2009-8, s. 2.)

§ 36E-2. Definitions.

The following definitions apply in this Chapter:

(1) Charitable purpose. - The relief of poverty, the advancement of education or religion, the promotion of health, scientific, benevolent, literary, governmental, or municipal purposes, or any other purpose the achievement of which is beneficial to the community.

(2) Endowment fund. - An institutional fund or part thereof that, under the terms of a gift instrument, is not wholly expendable by the institution on a current basis. The term does not include assets that an institution designates as an endowment fund for its own use.

(3) Gift instrument. - A record or records, including an institutional solicitation or a response to an institutional solicitation, under which property is granted to, transferred to, or held by an institution as an institutional fund.

(4) Institution. - Any of the following:

a. A person, other than an individual, organized and operated exclusively for charitable purposes;

b. A government or governmental subdivision, agency, or instrumentality, to the extent that it holds funds exclusively for a charitable purpose; or

c. A trust that had both charitable and noncharitable interests, after all noncharitable interests have terminated.

(5) Institutional fund. - A fund held by an institution exclusively for charitable purposes. The term includes tangible assets but does not include:

a. Program-related assets;

b. A fund held for an institution by a trustee that is not an institution; or

c. A fund in which a beneficiary that is not an institution has an interest, other than an interest that could arise only upon violation or failure of the purposes of the fund.

(6) Person. - An individual, corporation, business trust, estate, trust, partnership, limited liability company, association, joint venture, public corporation, government or governmental subdivision, agency, or instrumentality, or any other legal or commercial entity.

(7) Program-related asset. - An asset held by an institution not primarily for investment.

(8) Record. - Information that is inscribed on a tangible medium or that is stored in an electronic or other medium and is retrievable in perceivable form. (1985, c. 98, s. 1; 1991, c. 39, s. 1; 2009-8, s. 2.)

§ 36E-3. Standard of conduct in managing and investing institutional fund.

(a) Subject to the intent of a donor expressed in a gift instrument, an institution, in managing and investing an institutional fund, shall consider the charitable purposes of the institution and the purposes of the institutional fund.

(b) In addition to complying with the duty of loyalty imposed by law other than this Chapter, each person responsible for managing and investing an institutional fund shall manage and invest the fund in good faith and with the care an ordinarily prudent person in a like position would exercise under similar circumstances.

(c)   In managing and investing an institutional fund, an institution:

(1)   May incur only costs that are appropriate and reasonable in relation to the assets, the purposes of the institution, and the skills available to the institution; and

(2)   Shall make a reasonable effort to verify facts relevant to the management and investment of the fund.

(d)   An institution may pool two or more institutional funds for purposes of management and investment.

(e)   Except as otherwise provided by a gift instrument, the following rules apply:

(1)   In managing and investing an institutional fund, the following factors, if relevant, must be considered:

a.   General economic conditions;

b.   The possible effect of inflation or deflation;

c.   The expected tax consequences, if any, of investment decisions or strategies;

d.   The role that each investment or course of action plays within the overall investment portfolio of the fund;

e.   The expected total return from income and the appreciation of investments;

f.   Other resources of the institution;

g.   The needs of the institution and the fund to make distributions and to preserve capital; and

h.   An asset's special relationship or special value, if any, to the charitable purposes of the institution.

(2) Management and investment decisions about an individual asset must be made not in isolation but rather in the context of the institutional fund's portfolio of investments as a whole and as a part of an overall investment strategy having risk and return objectives reasonably suited to the institutional fund and to the institution.

(3) Except as otherwise provided by law other than this Chapter, an institution may invest in any kind of property or type of investment consistent with this section.

(4) An institution shall diversify the investments of an institutional fund unless the institution reasonably determines that, because of special circumstances, the purposes of the fund are better served without diversification.

(5) Within a reasonable time after receiving property, an institution shall make and carry out decisions concerning the retention or disposition of the property or to rebalance a portfolio in order to bring the institutional fund into compliance with the purposes, terms, and distribution requirements of the institution as necessary to meet other circumstances of the institution and the requirements of this Chapter.

(6) A person that has special skills or expertise, or is selected in reliance upon the person's representation that the person has special skills or expertise, has a duty to use those skills or that expertise in managing and investing institutional funds. This subdivision does not apply to a volunteer who is not compensated beyond reimbursement for expenses. (1985, c. 98, s. 1; 2009-8, s. 2.)

§ 36E-4. Appropriation for expenditure or accumulation of endowment fund; rules of construction.

(a) Subject to the intent of a donor expressed in the gift instrument, an institution may appropriate for expenditure or accumulate so much of an endowment fund as the institution determines is prudent for the uses, benefits, purposes, and duration for which the endowment fund is established. Unless stated otherwise in the gift instrument, the assets in an endowment fund are donor-restricted assets until appropriated for expenditure by the institution. In making a determination to appropriate or accumulate, the institution shall act in good faith, with the care that an ordinarily prudent person in a like position would exercise under similar circumstances, and shall consider, if relevant, the following factors:

(1)   The duration and preservation of the endowment fund;

(2)   The purposes of the institution and the endowment fund;

(3)   General economic conditions;

(4)   The possible effect of inflation or deflation;

(5)   The expected total return from income and the appreciation of investments;

(6)   Other resources of the institution; and

(7)   The investment policy of the institution.

(b)   To limit the authority to appropriate for expenditure or accumulate under subsection (a) of this section, a gift instrument must specifically state the limitation.

(c)   Terms in a gift instrument designating a gift as an endowment, or a direction or authorization in the gift instrument to use only "income," "interest," "dividends," or "rents, issues, or profits," or "to preserve the principal intact," or words of similar import:

(1)   Create an endowment fund of permanent duration unless other language in the gift instrument limits the duration or purpose of the fund; and

(2)   Do not otherwise limit the authority to appropriate for expenditure or accumulate under subsection (a) of this section. (1985, c. 98, s. 1; 2009-8, s. 2.)

§ 36E-5. Delegation of management and investment functions.

(a)   Subject to any specific limitation set forth in a gift instrument or in law other than this Chapter, an institution may delegate to an external agent the management and investment of an institutional fund to the extent that an institution could prudently delegate under the circumstances. An institution shall act in good faith, with the care that an ordinarily prudent person in a like position would exercise under similar circumstances, in:

(1)   Selecting an agent;

(2)   Establishing the scope and terms of the delegation, consistent with the purposes of the institution and the institutional fund; and

(3)   Periodically reviewing the agent's actions in order to monitor the agent's performance and compliance with the scope and terms of the delegation.

(b)   In performing a delegated function, an agent owes a duty to the institution to exercise reasonable care to comply with the scope and terms of the delegation.

(c)   An institution that complies with subsection (a) of this section is not liable for the decisions or actions of an agent to which the function was delegated.

(d)   By accepting delegation of a management or investment function from an institution that is subject to the laws of this State, an agent submits to the jurisdiction of the courts of this State in all proceedings arising from or related to the delegation or the performance of the delegated function.

(e)   An institution may delegate management and investment functions to its committees, officers, or employees as authorized by law of this State other than this Chapter. (1985, c. 98, s. 1; 2009-8, s. 2.)

§ 36E-6. Release or modification of restrictions on management, investment, or purpose.

(a)   If the donor consents in a record, an institution may release or modify, in whole or in part, a restriction contained in a gift instrument on the management, investment, or purpose of an institutional fund. A release or modification may not allow a fund to be used for a purpose other than a charitable purpose of the institution.

(b)   The superior court, upon application of an institution, may modify a restriction contained in a gift instrument regarding the management or investment of an institutional fund if the restriction has become impracticable or wasteful, if it impairs the management or investment of the fund, or if, because of circumstances not anticipated by the donor, a modification of the restriction will further the purposes of the fund. The institution shall notify the Attorney General of the application, and the Attorney General must be given an opportunity to be heard. To the extent practicable, any modification must be made in accordance with the donor's probable intention.

(c) If a particular charitable purpose or restriction contained in a gift instrument on the use of an institutional fund becomes unlawful, impracticable, impossible to achieve, or wasteful, the superior court, upon application of an institution, may modify the purpose of the fund or the restriction on the use of the fund in a manner consistent with the charitable purposes expressed in the gift instrument. The institution shall notify the Attorney General of the application, and the Attorney General must be given an opportunity to be heard.

(d) If an institution determines that a restriction contained in a gift instrument on the management, investment, or purpose of an institutional fund is unlawful, impracticable, impossible to achieve, or wasteful, the institution may release or modify the restriction, in whole or part, if:

(1) The institutional fund subject to the restriction has a total value of less than one hundred thousand dollars ($100,000);

(2) More than 10 years have elapsed since the fund was established; and

(3) The institution uses the property in a manner consistent with the charitable purposes expressed in the gift instrument.

The institution must provide written notice of the proposed release or modification of the restriction to the Attorney General not less than 60 days before releasing or modifying the restriction. The Attorney General may make application to the superior court to contest the institution's determination that the restriction should be released or modified within 60 days of receipt of the institution's written notice. (1985, c. 98, s. 1; 2009-8, s. 2.)
§ 36E-7. Reviewing compliance.

Compliance with this Chapter is determined in light of the facts and circumstances existing at the time a decision is made or action is taken, and not by hindsight. (2009-8, s. 2.)

§ 36E-8. Application to existing institutional funds.

This Chapter applies to institutional funds existing on or established after March 19, 2009. As applied to institutional funds existing on March 19, 2009, this Chapter governs only decisions made or actions taken on or after that date. (2009-8, s. 2.)

§ 36E-9. Relation to Electronic Signatures in Global and National Commerce Act.

This Chapter modifies, limits, and supersedes the Electronic Signatures in Global and National Commerce Act, 15 U.S.C. § 7001, et seq., but does not modify, limit, or supersede section 101 of that act, 15 U.S.C. § 7001(c), or authorize electronic delivery of any of the notices described in section 103 of that act, 15 U.S.C. § 7003(b). (2009-8, s. 2.)

§ 36E-10. Conflict with other law; exemptions.

(a) To the extent that the provisions of this Chapter are inconsistent with the provisions of Chapter 36C, Chapter 36D, Chapter 37A, or Chapter 55A of the General Statutes, the provisions of this Chapter shall control.

(b) The provisions of this Chapter do not apply to funds, other than endowment funds, held by a government or governmental subdivision, agency, or instrumentality. (1985, c. 98, s. 1; 1991, c. 39, s. 1; 2007-106, s. 1.3; 2009-8, s. 2.)

§ 36E-11. Uniformity of application and construction.

In applying and construing this Chapter, consideration may be given to promoting uniformity of interpretation with respect to its subject matter among the states that enact it. (1985, c. 98, s. 1; 2009-8, s. 2.)

Chapter 37.

Allocation of Principal and Income.

Article 1.

Uniform Principal and Income Act.

§§ 37-1 through 37-15. Repealed by Session Laws 1973, c. 729, s. 3.

Article 2.

Principal and Income Act of 1973.

§§ 37-16 through 37-40: Repealed by Session Laws 2003-232, s. 1, effective January 1, 2004, and applicable to every trust or decedent's estate existing on that date or coming into existence after that date, except as otherwise expressly provided in the will or terms of the trust or in provisions of Chapter 37A of the General Statutes.

Chapter 37A.

Uniform Principal and Income Act.

Article 1.

Definitions and Fiduciary Duties; Conversion to Unitrust; Judicial Control of Discretionary Power.

Part 1. Definitions.

§ 37A-1-101. Short title.

This Chapter may be cited as the Uniform Principal and Income Act. (2003-232, s. 2.)

§ 37A-1-102. Definitions.

The following definitions apply in this Chapter:

(1) "Accounting period" means a calendar year unless another 12-month period is selected by a fiduciary. The term includes a portion of a calendar year or other 12-month period that begins when an income interest begins or ends when an income interest ends.

(2) "Beneficiary" includes, in the case of a decedent's estate, an heir and devisee and, in the case of a trust, an income beneficiary and a remainder beneficiary.

(3) "Fiduciary" means a personal representative or a trustee. The term includes an executor, administrator, successor personal representative, special administrator, and a person performing substantially the same function.

(4) "Income" means money or property that a fiduciary receives as current return from a principal asset. The term includes a portion of receipts from a sale, exchange, or liquidation of a principal asset, to the extent provided in Article 4 of this Chapter.

(5) "Income beneficiary" means a person to whom net income of a trust is or may be payable.

(6) "Income interest" means the right of an income beneficiary to receive all or part of net income, whether the terms of the trust require it to be distributed or authorize it to be distributed in the trustee's discretion.

(7) "Mandatory income interest" means the right of an income beneficiary to receive net income that the terms of the trust require the fiduciary to distribute.

(8) "Net income" means the total receipts allocated to income during an accounting period minus the disbursements made from income during the period, plus or minus transfers under this Chapter to or from income during the period.

(9) "Person" means an individual, corporation, business trust, estate, trust, partnership, limited liability company, association, joint venture, or government; governmental subdivision, agency, or instrumentality; public corporation, or any other legal or commercial entity.

(10) "Principal" means property held in trust for distribution to a remainder beneficiary when the trust terminates.

(11) "Remainder beneficiary" means a person entitled to receive principal when an income interest ends.

(12) "Terms of a trust" means the manifestation of the intent of a settlor or decedent with respect to the trust, expressed in a manner that admits of its proof in a judicial proceeding, whether by written or spoken words or by conduct.

(13) "Trustee" includes an original, additional, or successor trustee, whether or not appointed or confirmed by a court. (2003-232, s. 2; 2011-284, s. 47.)

§ 37A-1-103. Fiduciary duties; general principles.

(a) In allocating receipts and disbursements to or between principal and income, and with respect to any matter within the scope of Articles 2 and 3 of this Chapter, a fiduciary:

(1) Shall administer a trust or estate in accordance with the terms of the trust or the will, even if there is a different provision in this Chapter;

(2) May administer a trust or estate by the exercise of a discretionary power of administration given to the fiduciary by the terms of the trust or the will, even if the exercise of the power produces a result different from a result required or permitted by this Chapter;

(3) Shall administer a trust or estate in accordance with this Chapter if the terms of the trust or the will do not contain a different provision or do not give the fiduciary a discretionary power of administration; and

(4) Shall add a receipt or charge a disbursement to principal to the extent that the terms of the trust and this Chapter do not provide a rule for allocating the receipt or disbursement to or between principal and income.

(b) In exercising the power to adjust under G.S. 37A-1-104(a), any discretionary power in connection with the conversion or administration of a unitrust under Part 2 of this Article, or a discretionary power of administration regarding a matter within the scope of this Chapter, whether granted by the terms of a trust, a will, or this Chapter, a fiduciary shall administer a trust or estate impartially, based on what is fair and reasonable to all of the beneficiaries, except to the extent that the terms of the trust or the will clearly manifest an intention that the fiduciary shall or may favor one or more of the beneficiaries. A determination in accordance with this Chapter is presumed to be fair and reasonable to all of the beneficiaries.

(c) The exercise of powers of allocation of receipts and expenditures contained or incorporated by reference to G.S. 32-27(29) in wills dated prior to January 1, 2004, shall continue to be valid. (2003-232, s. 2.)

§ 37A-1-104. Trustee's power to adjust.

(a) A trustee may adjust between principal and income to the extent the trustee considers necessary if the trustee invests and manages trust assets as a prudent investor, the terms of the trust describe the amount that may or shall be distributed to a beneficiary by referring to the trust's income, and the trustee determines, after applying the rules in G.S. 37A-1-103(a), that the trustee is unable to comply with G.S. 37A-1-103(b). In lieu of exercising the power to adjust, the trustee may convert the trust to a unitrust as permitted under Part 2 of this Article, in which case the unitrust amount shall become the net income of the trust.

(b) In deciding whether and to what extent to exercise the power conferred by subsection (a) of this section, a trustee shall consider all factors relevant to the trust and its beneficiaries, including the following factors to the extent they are relevant:

(1) The nature, purpose, and expected duration of the trust;

(2) The intent of the grantor or settlor;

(3) The identity and circumstances of the beneficiaries;

(4) The needs for liquidity, regularity of income, and preservation and appreciation of capital;

(5) The assets held in the trust; the extent to which they consist of financial assets, interests in closely held enterprises, tangible and intangible personal property, or real property; the extent to which an asset is used by a beneficiary; and whether an asset was purchased by the trustee or received from the settlor;

(6) The net amount allocated to income under the other sections of this Chapter and the increase or decrease in the value of the principal assets, which the trustee may estimate as to assets for which market values are not readily available;

(7) Whether and to what extent the terms of the trust give the trustee the power to invade principal or accumulate income or prohibit the trustee from invading principal or accumulating income, and the extent to which the trustee has exercised a power from time to time to invade principal or accumulate income;

(8) The actual and anticipated effect of economic conditions on principal and income and effects of inflation and deflation; and

(9) The anticipated tax consequences of an adjustment.

(c) A trustee shall not make an adjustment:

(1) That diminishes the income interest in a trust that requires all of the income to be paid at least annually to a spouse and for which an estate tax or gift tax marital deduction would be allowed, in whole or in part, if the trustee did not have the power to make the adjustment;

(2) That reduces the actuarial value of the income interest in a trust to which a person transfers property with the intent to qualify for a gift tax exclusion;

(3) That changes the amount payable to a beneficiary as a fixed annuity or a fixed fraction of the value of the trust assets;

(4) From any amount that is permanently set aside for charitable purposes under a will or the terms of a trust unless both income and principal are so set aside;

(5) If possessing or exercising the power to make an adjustment causes an individual to be treated as the owner of all or part of the trust for income tax purposes and the individual would not be treated as the owner if the trustee did not possess the power to make an adjustment;

(6) If possessing or exercising the power to make an adjustment causes all or part of the trust assets to be included for estate tax purposes in the estate of an individual who has the power to remove a trustee or appoint a trustee, or both, and the assets would not be included in the estate of the individual if the trustee did not possess the power to make an adjustment;

(7) If the trustee is a beneficiary of the trust;

(8) If the trustee is not a beneficiary but the adjustment would benefit the trustee directly or indirectly, except that a trustee may make an adjustment that also benefits a beneficiary even if the terms of the trust provide for trustee compensation as a percentage of the trust's income; or

(9) If the trust has been converted to, and is then operating as, a unitrust under Part 2 of this Article.

(d) If subdivision (5), (6), (7), or (8) of subsection (c) of this section applies to a trustee and there is more than one trustee, a cotrustee to whom the provision does not apply may make the adjustment unless the exercise of the power by the remaining trustee or trustees is not permitted by the terms of the trust.

(e) A trustee may renounce the entire power conferred by subsection (a) of this section or may renounce only the power to adjust from income to principal or the power to adjust from principal to income if the trustee is uncertain about whether possessing or exercising the power will cause a result described in subdivisions (1) through (6) or subdivision (8) of subsection (c) of this section or if the trustee determines that possessing or exercising the power will or may deprive the trust of a tax benefit or impose a tax burden not described in subsection (c) of this section. The renunciation may be permanent or for a specified period, including a period measured by the life of an individual.

(f) Terms of a trust that limit the power of a trustee to make an adjustment between principal and income do not affect the application of this section unless it is clear from the terms of the trust that the terms are intended to deny the trustee the power of adjustment conferred by subsection (a) of this section. (2003-232, s. 2; 2007-106, s. 44.)

Part 2. Conversion to Unitrust.

§ 37A-1-104.1. Definitions.

The following definitions apply to this Part:

(1) Code. - The Internal Revenue Code of 1986, as amended from time to time, and any statutory enactment successor to the Code; reference to a specific section of the Code in this Part shall be considered a reference also to any successor provision dealing with the subject matter of that section of the Code.

(2) Repealed by Session Laws 2007-106, s. 45, effective October 1, 2007.

(3) Disinterested person. - A person who is not a related or subordinate party with respect to the person then acting as trustee of the trust and excludes the settlor of the trust and any interested trustee.

(4) Repealed by Session Laws 2007-106, s. 45, effective October 1, 2007.

(5) Income trust. - A trust, created by either an inter vivos or a testamentary instrument, which directs or permits the trustee to distribute the net income of the trust to one or more persons, either in fixed proportions or in amounts or proportions determined by the trustee, and regardless of whether the trust directs or permits the trustee to distribute principal of the trust to one or more of those persons.

(6) Interested distributee. - A living beneficiary who is a distributee or permissible distributee of trust income or principal who has the power to remove the existing trustee and designate as successor a person who may be a related or subordinate party with respect to that distributee.

(7) Interested trustee. - Any of the following:

a. An individual trustee who is a qualified beneficiary.

b. Any trustee who may be removed and replaced by an interested distributee.

c. An individual trustee whose legal obligation to support a beneficiary may be satisfied by distributions of income and principal of the trust.

(7a) Legal disability. - A person under a legal disability is a person who is a minor, an incompetent, or an unborn individual, or whose identity or location is unknown.

(7b) Qualified beneficiary. - A qualified beneficiary as defined in G.S. 36C-1-103(15).

(8) Related or subordinate party. - A related or subordinate party as defined in section 672(c) of the Code.

(8a) Representative. - A person who may represent and bind another as provided in Article 3 of Chapter 36C of the General Statutes, the provisions of which shall apply for purposes of this Article.

(8b) Settlor. - An individual, including a testator, who creates a trust.

(9) Total return unitrust. - An income trust that has been converted under and meets the provisions of this Part.

(9a) Treasury regulations. - The regulations, rulings, procedures, notices, or other administrative pronouncements issued by the Internal Revenue Service, as amended from time to time.

(10) Trustee. - Any person acting as trustee of the trust, except as otherwise expressly provided in this Part, whether acting in that person's discretion or on the direction of one or more persons acting in a fiduciary capacity.

(11) Unitrust amount. - An amount computed as a percentage of the fair market value of the trust. (2003-232, s. 2; 2005-244, ss. 1, 2; 2007-106, s. 45.)

§ 37A-1-104.2. Conversion in trustee's discretion without court approval.

(a) Any trustee, other than an interested trustee, or, where two or more persons are acting as trustees, a majority of the trustees who are not interested trustees (in either case hereafter "trustee"), may, in the trustee's sole discretion and without court approval, (i) convert an income trust to a total return unitrust, (ii) reconvert a total return unitrust to an income trust, or (iii) change the percentage used to calculate the unitrust amount or the method used to determine the fair market value of the trust if all of the following apply:

(1) The trustee adopts a written policy for the trust providing (i) in the case of a trust being administered as an income trust, that future distributions from the trust will be unitrust amounts rather than net income, (ii) in the case of a trust being administered as a total return unitrust, that future distributions from the trust will be net income rather than unitrust amounts, or (iii) that the percentage used to calculate the unitrust amount or the method used to determine the fair market value of the trust will be changed as stated in the policy.

(2) The trustee gives written notice of its intention to take the action, including copies of the written policy and this Part, to (i) the settlor of the trust, if living, and (ii) all persons who are the qualified beneficiaries of the trust at the time the notice is given. If a qualified beneficiary is under a legal disability, notice shall be given to the representative of the qualified beneficiary if a representative is available without court order.

(3) There is at least (i) one qualified beneficiary described in G.S. 36C-1-103(15)a. or b. who is not under a legal disability or a representative of a qualified beneficiary so described and (ii) one qualified beneficiary described in G.S. 36C-1-103(15)c. who is not under a legal disability or a representative of a qualified beneficiary so described.

and

(4) No person receiving notice of the trustee's intention to take the proposed action objects to the action within 60 days after notice has been given. The objection shall be by written instrument delivered to the trustee.

(b) If there is no trustee of the trust other than an interested trustee, the interested trustee or, where two or more persons are acting as trustee and are interested trustees, a majority of the interested trustees may, in its sole discretion and without court approval, (i) convert an income trust to a total return unitrust, (ii) reconvert a total return unitrust to an income trust, or (iii) change the percentage used to calculate the unitrust amount or the method used to determine the fair market value of the trust if all of the following apply:

(1) The trustee adopts a written policy for the trust providing (i) in the case of a trust being administered as an income trust, that future distributions from the trust will be unitrust amounts rather than net income as determined under this Chapter, (ii) in the case of a trust being administered as a total return unitrust, that future distributions from the trust will be net income as determined under this Chapter rather than unitrust amounts, or (iii) that the percentage used to calculate the unitrust amount or the method used to determine the fair market value of the trust will be changed as stated in the policy.

(2) The trustee appoints a disinterested person who, in its sole discretion but acting in a fiduciary capacity, determines for the trustee (i) the percentage to be used to calculate the unitrust amount, (ii) the method to be used in determining the fair market value of the trust, and (iii) which assets, if any, are to be excluded in determining the unitrust amount.

(3) The trustee gives written notice of its intention to take the action, including copies of the written policy and this Part, and the determinations of the disinterested person to (i) the settlor of the trust, if living, and (ii) all persons who are the qualified beneficiaries of the trust at the time of the giving of the notice. If a qualified beneficiary is under a legal disability, notice shall be given to the

representative of the qualified beneficiary if a representative is available without court order.

(4)   There is at least one (i) qualified beneficiary described in G.S. 36C-1-103(15)a. or b. or a representative of a beneficiary so described and (ii) one qualified beneficiary described in G.S. 36C-1-103(15)c. or a representative of a qualified beneficiary so described.

(5)   No person receiving notice of the trustee's intention to take the proposed action of the trustee objects to the action or to the determination of the disinterested person within 60 days after notice has been given. The objection must be by written instrument delivered to the trustee.

(c)   A trustee may act under subsection (a) or (b) of this section with respect to a trust for which both income and principal have been set aside permanently for charitable purposes under the governing instrument and for which a federal estate or gift tax deduction has been taken, provided that all of the following apply:

(1)   Instead of sending written notice to the persons described in subdivisions (2) and (3) of subsection (a) of this section or subdivisions (3) and (4) of subsection (b) of this section, as the case may be, the trustee shall send written notice to each charitable organization expressly designated to receive the income of the trust under the governing instrument and, if no charitable organization is expressly designated to receive all of the income of the trust under the governing instrument, to the Attorney General of this State.

(2)   Subdivision (4) of subsection (a) of this section or subdivision (5) of subsection (b) of this section, as the case may be, shall not apply to this action.

(3)   In each taxable year, the trustee shall distribute the greater of the unitrust amount or the amount required by section 4942 of the Code.

(d)   The provisions of G.S. 36C-1-109 regarding notices and the sending of documents to persons under Chapter 36C of the General Statutes shall apply for purposes of notices and the sending of documents under this section. (2003-232, s. 2; 2005-244, s. 3; 2007-106, s. 46.)

§ 37A-1-104.3. Conversion with court approval.

(a) If any trustee desires to (i) convert an income trust to a total return unitrust, (ii) reconvert a total return unitrust to an income trust, or (iii) change the percentage used to calculate the unitrust amount or the method used to determine the fair market value of the trust but does not have the ability to or elects not to do it under G.S. 37A-1-104.2, the trustee may petition the court for an order as the trustee considers appropriate. In the event, however, there is only one trustee of the trust and the trustee is an interested trustee or in the event there are two or more trustees of the trust and a majority of them are interested trustees, the court, in its own discretion or on the petition of the trustee or trustees or any person interested in the trust, may appoint a disinterested person who, acting in a fiduciary capacity, shall present information to the court as shall be necessary to enable the court to make its determinations under this Part.

(b) A qualified beneficiary or a representative of a qualified beneficiary may request the trustee to (i) convert an income trust to a total return unitrust, (ii) reconvert a total return unitrust to an income trust, or (iii) change the percentage used to calculate the unitrust amount or the method used to determine the fair market value of the trust. If the trustee does not take the action requested, the qualified beneficiary or a representative of the qualified beneficiary may petition the court to order the trustee to take the action.

(c) All proceedings under this section shall be conducted as provided in Article 2 of Chapter 36C of the General Statutes. (2003-232, s. 2; 2007-106, s. 47.)

§ 37A-1-104.4. Determination of unitrust amount.

(a) The fair market value of the trust shall be determined at least annually, using a valuation date selected by the trustee in its discretion. The trustee, in its discretion, may use an average of the fair market value on the same valuation date for the current fiscal year and not more than three preceding fiscal years, if the use of this average appears desirable to reduce the impact of fluctuations in market value on the unitrust amount. Assets for which a fair market value cannot be readily ascertained shall be valued using valuation methods as are considered reasonable and appropriate by the trustee. Assets, such as a residence or tangible personal property, used by the trust beneficiary may be excluded from the fair market value for computing the unitrust amount.

(b) The percentage to be used in determining the unitrust amount shall be a reasonable current return from the trust, in any event not less than three percent

(3%) nor more than five percent (5%), taking into account the intentions of the settlor of the trust as expressed in the governing instrument, the needs of the beneficiaries, general economic conditions, projected current earnings and appreciation for the trust, and projected inflation and its impact on the trust.

(c)   Repealed by Session Laws 2005-244, s. 4, effective July 30, 2005. See notes for applicability language.

(d)   Following the conversion of an income trust to a total return unitrust, the trustee:

(1)   Shall consider the unitrust amount as paid from net accounting income determined as if the trust were not a unitrust;

(2)   Shall then consider the unitrust amount as paid from ordinary income not allocable to net accounting income;

(3)   May, in the trustee's discretion, consider the unitrust amount as paid from net short-term gain described in section 1222(5) of the Code and then from net long-term capital gain described in section 1222(7) of the Code so long as the discretionary power is exercised consistently and in a reasonable and impartial manner, but the amount so paid from net capital gains may not be greater than the excess of the unitrust amount over the amount of distributable net income as defined in section 643(a) of the Code without regard to section 1.643(a)-3(b) of the Treasury Regulations, as amended from time to time; and

(4)   Shall then consider the unitrust amount as coming from the principal of the trust. (2003-232, s. 2; 2005-244, s. 4; 2007-106, ss. 48, 49.)

§ 37A-1-104.5. Matters in trustee's discretion.

In administering a total return unitrust, the trustee may, in its sole discretion but subject to the provisions of the governing instrument, determine:

(1)   The effective date of the conversion;

(2)   The timing of distributions, including provisions for prorating a distribution for a short year in which a beneficiary's right to payments commences or ceases;

(3) Whether distributions are to be made in cash or in kind or partly in cash and partly in kind;

(4) If the trust is reconverted to an income trust, the effective date of the reconversion; and

(5) Any other administrative issues as may be necessary or appropriate to carry out the purposes of this Part. (2003-232, s. 2.)

§ 37A-1-104.6. No effect on principal distributions.

Conversion to a total return unitrust under this Part shall not affect any other provision of the governing instrument, if any, regarding distributions of principal. For purposes of this Part, the distribution of a unitrust amount is considered a distribution of income and not of principal. (2003-232, s. 2.)

§ 37A-1-104.7: Repealed by Session Laws 2007-106, s. 49.1, effective October 1, 2007.

§ 37A-1-104.8. No liability on part of trustee or disinterested person acting in good faith.

No trustee or disinterested person who in good faith takes or fails to take any action under this Part shall be liable to any person affected by the action or inaction, regardless of whether the person received written notice as provided in this Part and regardless of whether the person was under a legal disability at the time of the delivery of the notice. The exclusive remedy for any person affected by an action or inaction shall be to obtain an order of the court directing the trustee (i) to convert an income trust to a total return unitrust, (ii) to reconvert from a total return unitrust to an income trust, or (iii) to change the percentage used to calculate the unitrust amount. (2003-232, s. 2.)

§ 37A-1-104.9. Applicability.

This Part shall apply to all trusts in existence on, or created after January 1, 2004, unless (i) the governing instrument contains a provision clearly expressing the settlor's intention that the current beneficiary or beneficiaries are to receive an amount other than a reasonable current return from the trust, (ii) the trust is a trust described in section 170(f)(2)(B), section 664(d), section 2702(a)(3), or section 2702(b) of the Code, (iii) the trust is a trust under which any amount is, or has been in the past, set aside permanently for charitable purposes unless the income from the trust also is devoted permanently to charitable purposes, or (iv) the governing instrument expressly prohibits use of this Part by specific reference to this Part, or expressly states the settlor's intent that net income not be calculated as a unitrust amount. A provision in the governing instrument that "the provisions of Part 2 of Article 1 of Chapter 37A of the General Statutes or any corresponding provision of future law, shall not be used in the administration of this trust." or "the trustee shall not determine the distributions to the income beneficiary as a unitrust amount." or similar words reflecting that intent is sufficient to preclude the use of this Part. (2003-232, s. 2; 2005-244, s. 5; 2007-106, s. 50.)

Part 2A. Express Total Return Unitrusts.

§ 37A-1-104.21. Definitions.

(a) An "express total return unitrust" means a trust that has a governing instrument requiring the distribution at least annually of a unitrust amount equal to a fixed percentage of not less than three percent (3%) nor more than five percent (5%) per year of the net fair market value of the trust's assets, valued at least annually.

(b) "Code" means the Internal Revenue Code as described in G.S. 37A-1-104.1(1).

(c) "Treasury regulations" means the treasury regulations described in G.S. 37A-1-104.1(9a). (2005-244, s. 6.)

§ 37A-1-104.22. Determination of unitrust amount.

(a) The unitrust amount to be distributed by the express total return unitrust may be determined in the governing instrument by reference to the net fair market value of the trust's assets determined annually or averaged on a multiple year basis.

(b) The terms of the governing instrument of an express total return unitrust may provide that:

(1) Assets for which a fair market value cannot be readily ascertained shall be valued using valuation methods that the trustee considers reasonable and appropriate.

(2) Assets, such as a residence property or tangible personal property, used by the trust beneficiary entitled to the unitrust amount may be excluded from the net fair market value for computing the unitrust amount. (2005-244, s. 6.)

§ 37A-1-104.23. Effect of distribution of unitrust amount.

The distribution from an express total return unitrust of the fixed percentage of not less than three percent (3%) nor more than five percent (5%) reasonably apportions between the income beneficiaries and remaindermen the total return of an express total return unitrust. (2005-244, s. 6.)

§ 37A-1-104.24. Change or conversion of unitrust amount.

(a) The terms of the governing instrument of an express total return unitrust may provide the method similar to the method provided under G.S. 37A-1-104.2(a) for changing the unitrust percentage or for converting from a unitrust to an income trust or for a reconversion of an income trust to a unitrust, or for all of these actions.

(b) If the terms of the governing instrument of an express total return unitrust do not specifically or by reference to G.S. 37A-1-104.2 grant a power to the trustee to change the unitrust percentage or change to an income trust, the trustee shall not have that power. (2005-244, s. 6.)

§ 37A-1-104.25. Determination of character of unitrust amount.

Unless the terms of the governing instrument of the express total return unitrust specifically provide otherwise, the trustee:

(1) Shall consider the unitrust amount as paid from net accounting income determined as if the trust were not a unitrust;

(2) Shall then consider the unitrust amount as paid from ordinary income not allocable to net accounting income;

(3) May, in the trustee's discretion, consider the unitrust amount as paid from net short-term gain described in section 1222(5) of the Code and then from net long-term capital gain described in section 1222(7) of the Code so long as this discretionary power is exercised consistently and in a reasonable and impartial manner, but the amount so paid from net capital gains may not be greater than the excess of the unitrust amount over the amount of distributable net income as defined in section 643(a) of the Code without regard to section 1.643(a)-3(b) of the treasury regulations; and

(4) Shall then consider the unitrust amount as coming from the principal of the trust. (2005-244, s. 6.)

§ 37A-1-104.26. Unitrust amount in excess of a five percent payout.

A trust that provides for a fixed percentage payout in excess of five percent (5%) per year is considered an express total return unitrust that pays out a fixed percentage of five percent (5%) per year and pays out principal to the extent that the fixed percentage payout exceeds five percent (5%) per year. (2005-244, s. 6.)

Part 3. Judicial Control of Discretionary Power.

§ 37A-1-105. Judicial control of discretionary power.

(a) The court shall not order a fiduciary to change a decision to exercise or not to exercise a discretionary power conferred by this Chapter unless it determines that the decision was an abuse of the fiduciary's discretion. A fiduciary's decision is not an abuse of discretion merely because the court would have exercised the power in a different manner or would not have exercised the power.

(b) The decisions to which subsection (a) of this section applies include:

(1) A decision under G.S. 37A-1-104(a) as to whether and to what extent an amount should be transferred from principal to income or from income to principal.

(2) A decision regarding the factors that are relevant to the trust and its beneficiaries, the extent to which the factors are relevant, and the weight, if any,

to be given to those factors in deciding whether and to what extent to exercise the discretionary power conferred by G.S. 37A-1-104(a).

(c)   If the court determines that a fiduciary has abused the fiduciary's discretion, the court may place the income and remainder beneficiaries in the positions they would have occupied if the discretion had not been abused, according to the following rules:

(1)   To the extent that the abuse of discretion has resulted in no distribution to a beneficiary or in a distribution that is too small, the court shall order the fiduciary to distribute from the trust to the beneficiary an amount that the court determines will restore the beneficiary, in whole or in part, to the beneficiary's appropriate position.

(2)   To the extent that the abuse of discretion has resulted in a distribution to a beneficiary that is too large, the court shall place the beneficiaries, the trust, or both, in whole or in part, in their appropriate positions by ordering the fiduciary to withhold an amount from one or more future distributions to the beneficiary who received the distribution that was too large or ordering that beneficiary to return some or all of the distribution to the trust.

(3)   To the extent that the court is unable, after applying subdivisions (1) and (2) of this subsection, to place the beneficiaries, the trust, or both in the positions they would have occupied if the discretion had not been abused, the court may order the fiduciary to pay an appropriate amount from its own funds to one or more of the beneficiaries or the trust or both.

(d)   Upon petition by the fiduciary, the court having jurisdiction over a trust or estate shall determine whether a proposed exercise or nonexercise by the fiduciary of a discretionary power conferred by this Chapter will result in an abuse of the fiduciary's discretion. If the petition describes the proposed exercise or nonexercise of the power and contains sufficient information to inform the beneficiaries of the reasons for the proposal, the facts upon which the fiduciary relies, and an explanation of how the income and remainder beneficiaries will be affected by the proposed exercise or nonexercise of the power, a beneficiary who challenges the proposed exercise or nonexercise has the burden of establishing that it will result in an abuse of discretion. (2003-232, s. 2.)

Article 2.

Decedent's Estate or Terminating Income Interest.

§ 37A-2-201. Determination and distribution of net income.

After a decedent dies, in the case of an estate, or after an income interest in a trust ends, the following rules apply:

(1) A fiduciary of an estate or of a terminating income interest shall determine the amount of net income and net principal receipts received from property specifically given to a beneficiary under the rules in Articles 3 through 5 of this Chapter that apply to trustees and the rules in subdivision (5) of this section. The fiduciary shall distribute the net income and net principal receipts to the beneficiary who is to receive the specific property.

(2) A fiduciary shall determine the remaining net income of a decedent's estate or a terminating income interest under the rules in Articles 3 through 5 of this Chapter that apply to trustees and by:

a. Including in net income all income from property used to discharge liabilities;

b. Paying from income or principal, in the fiduciary's discretion, fees of attorneys, accountants, and fiduciaries; court costs and other expenses of administration; and interest on death taxes, but the fiduciary may pay those expenses from income of property passing to a trust for which the fiduciary claims an estate tax marital or charitable deduction only to the extent that the payment of those expenses from income will not cause the reduction or loss of the deduction; and

c. Paying from principal all other disbursements made or incurred in connection with the settlement of a decedent's estate or the winding up of a terminating income interest, including debts, funeral expenses, disposition of remains, family allowances, and death taxes and related penalties that are apportioned to the estate or terminating income interest by the will, the terms of the trust, or applicable law.

(3) Unless the will or trust instrument otherwise provides, or the court otherwise directs, a fiduciary shall distribute to a beneficiary who receives a pecuniary amount outright interest, computed as provided in G.S. 24-1 from the date that is one year following the date of death of the person whose death

gives rise to the payment of the pecuniary devise or the happening of the contingency that causes the income interest to end, from net income determined under subdivision (2) of this section or from principal to the extent that net income is insufficient. However, this subdivision shall not apply to a pecuniary devise:

a. To or for the benefit of a decedent's surviving spouse that is or can be qualified for the federal estate tax marital deduction; or

b. To or for the benefit of charitable organizations that are qualified for the federal estate tax charitable deduction, including a charitable remainder trust.

(4) A fiduciary shall distribute the net income remaining after distributions required by subdivision (3) of this section in the manner described in G.S. 37A-2-202 to all other beneficiaries, including a beneficiary who receives a pecuniary amount in trust, even if the beneficiary holds an unqualified power to withdraw assets from the trust or other presently exercisable general power of appointment over the trust.

(5) A fiduciary shall not reduce principal or income receipts from property described in subdivision (1) of this section because of a payment described in G.S. 37A-5-501 or G.S. 37A-5-502 to the extent that the will, the terms of the trust, or applicable law requires the fiduciary to make the payment from assets other than the property or to the extent that the fiduciary recovers or expects to recover the payment from a third party. The net income and principal receipts from the property are determined by including all of the amounts the fiduciary receives or pays with respect to the property, whether those amounts accrued or became due before, on, or after the date of a decedent's death or an income interest's terminating event, and by making a reasonable provision for amounts that the fiduciary believes the estate or terminating income interest may become obligated to pay after the property is distributed. (2003-232, s. 2; 2011-284, s. 48.)

§ 37A-2-202. Distribution to residuary and remainder beneficiaries.

(a) Each beneficiary described in G.S. 37A-2-201(4) is entitled to receive a portion of the net income equal to the beneficiary's fractional interest in undistributed principal assets, using values as of the distribution date. If a fiduciary makes more than one distribution of assets to beneficiaries to whom this section applies, each beneficiary, including one who does not receive part of the distribution, is entitled, as of each distribution date, to the net income the fiduciary has received after the date of death or terminating event or earlier distribution date but has not distributed as of the current distribution date.

(b) In determining a beneficiary's share of net income, the following rules apply:

(1) The beneficiary is entitled to receive a portion of the net income equal to the beneficiary's fractional interest in the undistributed principal assets immediately before the distribution date, including assets that later may be sold to meet principal obligations.

(2) The beneficiary's fractional interest in the undistributed principal assets shall be calculated without regard to property specifically given to a beneficiary and property required to pay pecuniary amounts not in trust to which G.S. 37A-2-201(3) applies.

(3) The beneficiary's fractional interest in the undistributed principal assets shall be calculated on the basis of the aggregate value of those assets as of the distribution date without reducing the value by any unpaid principal obligation.

(4) The distribution date for purposes of this section may be the date as of which the fiduciary calculates the value of the assets if that date is reasonably near the date on which assets are actually distributed.

(c) If a fiduciary does not distribute all of the collected but undistributed net income to each person as of a distribution date, the fiduciary shall maintain appropriate records showing the interest of each beneficiary in that net income.

(d) A fiduciary may apply the rules in this section, to the extent that the fiduciary considers it appropriate, to net gain or loss realized after the date of death or terminating event or earlier distribution date from the disposition of a principal asset if this section applies to the income from the asset. (2003-232, s. 2; 2006-259, s. 13(p).)

Article 3.

Apportionment at Beginning and End of Income Interest.

§ 37A-3-301. When right to income begins and ends.

(a) An income beneficiary is entitled to net income from the date on which the income interest begins. An income interest begins on the date specified in the terms of the trust or, if no date is specified, on the date an asset becomes subject to a trust or successive income interest.

(b) An asset becomes subject to a trust:

(1) On the date it is transferred to the trust in the case of an asset that is transferred to a trust during the transferor's life;

(2) On the date of a testator's death in the case of an asset that becomes subject to a trust by reason of a will, even if there is an intervening period of administration of the testator's estate; or

(3) On the date of an individual's death in the case of an asset that is transferred to a fiduciary by a third party because of the individual's death.

(c) An asset becomes subject to a successive income interest on the day after the preceding income interest ends, as determined under subsection (d) of this section, even if there is an intervening period of administration to wind up the preceding income interest.

(d) An income interest ends on the day before an income beneficiary dies or another terminating event occurs or on the last day of a period during which there is no beneficiary to whom a trustee may distribute income. (2003-232, s. 2.)

§ 37A-3-302. Apportionment of receipts and disbursements when decedent dies or income interest begins.

(a) A trustee shall allocate an income receipt or disbursement, other than one to which G.S. 37A-2-201(1) applies to principal, if its due date occurs before a decedent dies in the case of an estate or before an income interest begins in the case of a trust or successive income interest.

(b) A trustee shall allocate an income receipt or disbursement to income if its due date occurs on or after the date on which a decedent dies or an income interest begins and it is a periodic due date. An income receipt or disbursement shall be treated as accruing from day to day if its due date is not periodic or it has no due date. The portion of the receipt or disbursement accruing before the date on which a decedent dies or an income interest begins shall be allocated to principal, and the balance shall be allocated to income.

(c) An item of income or an obligation is due on the date the payer is required to make a payment. If a payment date is not stated, there is no due date for the purposes of this Chapter. Distributions to shareholders or other owners from an entity to which G.S. 37A-4-401 applies are considered to be due on the date fixed by the entity for determining who is entitled to receive the distribution or, if no date is fixed, on the declaration date for the distribution. A due date is periodic for receipts or disbursements that shall be paid at regular intervals under a lease or an obligation to pay interest or if an entity customarily makes distributions at regular intervals. (2003-232, s. 2.)

§ 37A-3-303. Apportionment when income interest ends.

(a) In this section, "undistributed income" means net income received before the date on which an income interest ends. The term does not include an item of income or expense that is due or accrued or net income that has been added or is required to be added to principal under the terms of the trust.

(b) When a mandatory income interest ends, the trustee shall pay to a mandatory income beneficiary who survives that date, or to the estate of a deceased mandatory income beneficiary whose death causes the interest to end, the beneficiary's share of the undistributed income that is not disposed of under the terms of the trust unless the beneficiary has an unqualified power to revoke more than five percent (5%) of the trust immediately before the income interest ends. In the latter case, the undistributed income from the portion of the trust that may be revoked shall be added to principal.

(c) When a trustee's obligation to pay a fixed annuity or a fixed fraction of the value of the trust's assets ends, the trustee shall prorate the final payment if and to the extent required by applicable law to accomplish a purpose of the trust or its settlor relating to income, gift, estate, or other tax requirements. (2003-232, s. 2.)

Article 4.

Allocation of Receipts During Administration of Trust.

Part 1. Receipts From Entities.

§ 37A-4-401. Character of receipts.

(a) In this section, "entity" means a corporation, partnership, limited liability company, regulated investment company, real estate investment trust, common trust fund, or any other organization in which a trustee has an interest other than a trust or estate to which G.S. 37A-4-402 applies, a business or activity to which G.S. 37A-4-403 applies, or an asset-backed security to which G.S. 37A-4-415 applies.

(b) Except as otherwise provided in this section, a trustee shall allocate to income money received from an entity.

(c) A trustee shall allocate the following receipts from an entity to principal:

(1) Property other than money;

(2) Money received in one distribution or a series of related distributions in exchange for part or all of a trust's interest in the entity;

(3) Money received in total or partial liquidation of the entity; and

(4) Money received from an entity that is a regulated investment company or a real estate investment trust if the money distributed is a capital gain dividend for federal income tax purposes.

(d) Money is received in partial liquidation:

(1) To the extent that the entity, at or near the time of a distribution, indicates that it is a distribution in partial liquidation; or

(2) If the total amount of money and property received in a distribution or series of related distributions is greater than twenty percent (20%) of the entity's gross assets, as shown by the entity's year-end financial statements immediately preceding the initial receipt.

(e) Money is not received in partial liquidation, nor may it be taken into account under subdivision (2) of subsection (d) of this section, to the extent that it does not exceed the amount of income tax that a trustee or beneficiary shall pay on taxable income of the entity that distributes the money.

(f) A trustee may rely upon a statement made by an entity about the source or character of a distribution if the statement is made at or near the time of distribution by the entity's board of directors or other person or group of persons authorized to exercise powers to pay money or transfer property comparable to those of a corporation's board of directors. (2003-232, s. 2.)

§ 37A-4-402. Distribution from trust or estate.

A trustee shall allocate to income an amount received as a distribution of income from a trust or an estate in which the trust has an interest other than a purchased interest and shall allocate to principal an amount received as a distribution of principal from the trust or estate. If a trustee purchases an interest in a trust that is an investment entity, or a decedent or donor transfers an interest in a trust to a trustee, G.S. 37A-4-401 or G.S. 37A-4-415 applies to a receipt from the trust. (2003-232, s. 2.)
§ 37A-4-403. Business and other activities conducted by trustee.

(a) If a trustee who conducts a business or other activity determines that it is in the best interest of all the beneficiaries to account separately for the business or activity instead of accounting for it as part of the trust's general accounting records, the trustee may maintain separate accounting records for its transactions, whether or not its assets are segregated from other trust assets.

(b) A trustee who accounts separately for a business or other activity may determine the extent to which its net cash receipts shall be retained for working capital, the acquisition or replacement of fixed assets, and other reasonably foreseeable needs of the business or activity, and the extent to which the remaining net cash receipts are accounted for as principal or income in the trust's general accounting records. If a trustee sells assets of the business or other activity, other than in the ordinary course of the business or activity, the trustee shall account for the net amount received as principal in the trust's general accounting records to the extent the trustee determines that the amount received is no longer required in the conduct of the business.

(c) Activities for which a trustee may maintain separate accounting records include:

(1) Retail, manufacturing, service, and other traditional business activities;

(2) Farming;

(3) Raising and selling livestock and other animals;

(4) Management of rental properties;

(5) Extraction of minerals and other natural resources;

(6) Timber operations; and

(7) Activities to which G.S. 37A-4-414 applies. (2003-232, s. 2.)

Part 2. Receipts Not Normally Apportioned.

§ 37A-4-404. Principal receipts.

A trustee shall allocate to principal:

(1) To the extent not allocated to income under this Chapter, assets received from a transferor during the transferor's lifetime, a decedent's estate, a trust with a terminating income interest, or a payer under a contract naming the trust or its trustee as beneficiary;

(2) Money or other property received from the sale, exchange, liquidation, or change in form of a principal asset, including realized profit, subject to this Article;

(3) Amounts recovered from third parties to reimburse the trust because of disbursements described in G.S. 37A-5-502(a)(7) or for other reasons to the extent not based on the loss of income;

(4) Proceeds of property taken by eminent domain, but a separate award made for the loss of income with respect to an accounting period during which a current income beneficiary had a mandatory income interest is income;

(5) Net income received in an accounting period during which there is no beneficiary to whom a trustee may or shall distribute income; and

(6) Other receipts as provided in Part 3 of this Article. (2003-232, s. 2.)

§ 37A-4-405. Rental property.

To the extent that a trustee accounts for receipts from rental property under this section, the trustee shall allocate to income an amount received as rent of real or personal property, including an amount received for cancellation or renewal of a lease. An amount received as a refundable deposit, including a security deposit or a deposit that is to be applied as rent for future periods, shall be added to principal and held subject to the terms of the lease and is not available for distribution to a beneficiary until the trustee's contractual obligations have been satisfied with respect to that amount. (2003-232, s. 2.)

§ 37A-4-406. Obligation to pay money.

(a)   An amount received as interest, whether determined at a fixed, variable, or floating rate, on an obligation to pay money to the trustee, including an amount received as consideration for prepaying principal, shall be allocated to income without any provision for amortization of premium.

(b)   A trustee shall allocate to principal an amount received from the sale, redemption, or other disposition of an obligation to pay money to the trustee more than one year after it is purchased or acquired by the trustee, including an obligation whose purchase price or value when it is acquired is less than its value at maturity. If the obligation matures within one year after it is purchased or acquired by the trustee, an amount received in excess of its purchase price or its value when acquired by the trust shall be allocated to income.

(c)   This section does not apply to an obligation to which G.S. 37A-4-409, 37A-4-410, 37A-4-411, 37A-4-412, 37A-4-414, or 37A-4-415 applies. (2003-232, s. 2.)

§ 37A-4-407. Insurance policies and similar contracts.

(a)   Except as otherwise provided in subsection (b) of this section, a trustee shall allocate to principal the proceeds of a life insurance policy or other contract in which the trust or its trustee is named as beneficiary, including a contract that insures the trust or its trustee against loss for damage to, destruction of, or loss of title to a trust asset. The trustee shall allocate dividends on an insurance policy to income if the premiums on the policy are paid from income and to principal if the premiums are paid from principal.

(b) A trustee shall allocate to income proceeds of a contract that insures the trustee against loss of occupancy or other use by an income beneficiary, loss of income, or, subject to G.S. 37A-4-403, loss of profits from a business.

(c) This section does not apply to a contract to which G.S. 37A-4-409 applies. (2003-232, s. 2.)

Part 3. Receipts Normally Apportioned.

§ 37A-4-408. Insubstantial allocations not required.

If a trustee determines that an allocation between principal and income required by G.S. 37A-4-409, 37A-4-410, 37A-4-411, 37A-4-412, or 37A-4-415 is insubstantial, the trustee may allocate the entire amount to principal unless one of the circumstances described in G.S. 37A-1-104(c) applies to the allocation. This power may be exercised by a cotrustee in the circumstances described in G.S. 37A-1-104(d) and may be released for the reasons and in the manner described in G.S. 37A-1-104(e). An allocation is presumed to be insubstantial if:

(1) The amount of the allocation would increase or decrease net income in an accounting period, as determined before the allocation, by less than ten percent (10%); or

(2) The value of the asset producing the receipt for which the allocation would be made is less than ten percent (10%) of the total value of the trust's assets at the beginning of the accounting period. (2003-232, s. 2.)

§ 37A-4-409. Deferred compensation, annuities, and similar payments.

(a) In this section:

(1) "Payment" means a payment that a trustee may receive over a fixed number of years or during the life of one or more individuals because of services rendered or property transferred to the payer in exchange for future payments. The term includes a payment made in money or property from the payer's general assets or from a separate fund created by the payer. For purposes of subsections (d), (d1), (d2), and (d3) of this section, the term also includes any payment from any separate fund, regardless of the reason for the payment.

(2) "Separate fund" includes a private or commercial annuity, an individual retirement account, and a pension, profit sharing, stock-bonus, or stock-ownership plan.

(b) To the extent that a payment is characterized as interest, a dividend, or a payment made in lieu of interest or a dividend, a trustee shall allocate the payment to income. The trustee shall allocate to principal the balance of the payment and any other payment received in the same accounting period that is not characterized as interest, a dividend, or an equivalent payment.

(c) If no part of a payment is characterized as interest, a dividend, or an equivalent payment, and all or part of the payment is required to be made, a trustee shall allocate to income ten percent (10%) of the part that is required to be made during the accounting period and the balance to principal. If no part of a payment is required to be made or the payment received is the entire amount to which the trustee is entitled, the trustee shall allocate the entire payment to principal. For purposes of this subsection, a payment is not "required to be made" to the extent that it is made because the trustee exercises a right of withdrawal.

(d) Except as otherwise provided in subsection (d1) of this section, subsections (d2) and (d3) of this section apply, and subsections (b) and (c) of this section do not apply in determining the allocation of a payment from a separate fund to:

(1) A trust to which an election to qualify for a marital deduction under section 2056(b)(7) of the Internal Revenue Code has been made, or

(2) A trust that qualifies for the marital deduction under section 2056(b)(5) of the Internal Revenue Code.

(d1) Subsections (d), (d2), and (d3) of this section do not apply if and to the extent that the series of payments would, without the application of subsection (d) of this section, qualify for the marital deduction under section 2056(b)(7)(C) of the Internal Revenue Code.

(d2) A trustee shall determine the internal income of each separate fund for the accounting period as if the separate fund were a trust subject to this section. Upon request of the surviving spouse, the trustee shall demand that the person administering the separate fund distribute the internal income to the trust. The trustee shall allocate a payment from the separate fund to income to the extent of the internal income of the separate fund and distribute that amount to the surviving spouse. The trustee shall allocate the balance of the payment to principal. Upon request of the surviving spouse, the trustee shall allocate principal to income to the extent that the internal income of the separate fund exceeds payments made from the separate fund to the trust during the accounting period.

(d3)   If a trustee cannot determine the internal income of a separate fund but can determine the value of the separate fund, the internal income of the separate fund is deemed to equal four percent (4%) of the fund's value, according to the most recent statement of value preceding the beginning of the accounting period. If the trustee can determine neither the internal income of the separate fund nor the fund's value, the internal income of the fund is deemed to equal the product of the interest rate and the present value of the expected future payments, as determined under section 7520 of the Internal Revenue Code for the month preceding the accounting period for which the computation is made.

(e)   This section does not apply to payments to which G.S. 37A-4-410 applies. (2003-232, s. 2; 2010-181, s. 3.)

§ 37A-4-410. Liquidating asset.

(a)   In this section, "liquidating asset" means an asset whose value will diminish or terminate because the asset is expected to produce receipts for a period of limited duration. The term includes a leasehold, patent, copyright, royalty right, and right to receive payments during a period of more than one year under an arrangement that does not provide for the payment of interest on the unpaid balance. The term does not include a payment subject to G.S. 37A-4-409, resources subject to G.S. 37A-4-411, timber subject to G.S. 37A-4-412, an activity subject to G.S. 37A-4-414, an asset subject to G.S. 37A-4-415, or any asset for which the trustee establishes a reserve for depreciation under G.S. 37A-5-503.

(b)   A trustee shall allocate to income ten percent (10%) of the receipts from a liquidating asset and the balance to principal. (2003-232, s. 2.)

§ 37A-4-411. Minerals, water, and other natural resources.

(a) To the extent that a trustee accounts for receipts from an interest in minerals or other natural resources under this section, the trustee shall allocate them as follows:

(1) If received as nominal delay rental or nominal annual rent on a lease, a receipt shall be allocated to income.

(2) If received from a production payment, a receipt shall be allocated to income if and to the extent that the agreement creating the production payment provides a factor for interest or its equivalent. The balance shall be allocated to principal.

(3) If an amount received as a royalty, shut-in-well payment, take-or-pay payment, bonus, or delay rental is more than nominal, ninety percent (90%) shall be allocated to principal and the balance to income.

(4) If an amount is received from a working interest or any other interest not provided for in subdivision (1), (2), or (3) of this subsection, ninety percent (90%) of the net amount received shall be allocated to principal and the balance to income.

(b) An amount received on account of an interest in water that is renewable shall be allocated to income. If the water is not renewable, ninety percent (90%) of the amount shall be allocated to principal and the balance to income.

(c) This Chapter applies whether or not a decedent or donor was extracting minerals, water, or other natural resources before the interest became subject to the trust.

(d) If a trust owns an interest in minerals, water, or other natural resources on January 1, 2004, the trustee may allocate receipts from the interest as provided in this Chapter or in the manner used by the trustee before January 1, 2004. If the trust acquires an interest in minerals, water, or other natural resources after January 1, 2004, the trustee shall allocate receipts from the interest as provided in this Chapter. (2003-232, s. 2.)

§ 37A-4-412. Timber.

(a) To the extent that a trustee accounts for receipts from the sale of timber and related products pursuant to this section, the trustee shall allocate the net receipts:

(1) To income to the extent that the amount of timber removed from the land does not exceed the rate of growth of the timber during the accounting periods in which a beneficiary has a mandatory income interest;

(2) To principal to the extent that the amount of timber removed from the land exceeds the rate of growth of the timber or the net receipts are from the sale of standing timber;

(3) To or between income and principal if the net receipts are from the lease of timberland or from a contract to cut timber from land owned by a trust, by determining the amount of timber removed from the land under the lease or contract and applying the rules in subdivisions (1) and (2) of this subsection; or

(4) To principal to the extent that advance payments, bonuses, and other payments are not allocated pursuant to subdivision (1), (2), or (3) of this subsection.

(b) In determining net receipts to be allocated pursuant to subsection (a) of this section, a trustee shall deduct and transfer to principal a reasonable amount for depletion.

(c) This Chapter applies whether or not a decedent or transferor was harvesting timber from the property before it becomes subject to the trust.

(d) If a trust owns an interest in timberland on January 1, 2004, the trustee may allocate net receipts from the sale of timber and related products as provided in this Chapter or in the manner used by the trustee before January 1, 2004. If the trust acquires an interest in timberland after January 1, 2004, the trustee shall allocate net receipts from the sale of timber and related products as provided in this Chapter. (2003-232, s. 2.)

§ 37A-4-413. Property not productive of income.

(a) If a marital deduction is allowed for all or part of a trust whose assets consist substantially of property that does not provide the spouse with sufficient income from or use of the trust assets, and if the amounts that the trustee transfers from principal to income under G.S. 37A-1-104 and distributes to the spouse from principal under the terms of the trust are insufficient to provide the spouse with the beneficial enjoyment required to obtain the marital deduction, the spouse may require the trustee to make property productive of income, convert property within a reasonable time, or exercise the power conferred by G.S. 37A-1-104(a). The trustee may decide which action or combination of actions to take.

(b) In cases not governed by subsection (a) of this section, proceeds from the sale or other disposition of an asset are principal without regard to the amount of income the asset produces during any accounting period. (2003-232, s. 2.)

§ 37A-4-414. Derivatives and options.

(a) In this section, "derivative" means a contract or financial instrument or a combination of contracts and financial instruments that gives a trust the right or obligation to participate in some or all changes in the price of a tangible or intangible asset or group of assets or changes in a rate, an index of prices or rates, or other market indicator for an asset or a group of assets.

(b) To the extent that a trustee does not account under G.S. 37A-4-403 for transactions in derivatives, the trustee shall allocate to principal receipts from and disbursements made in connection with those transactions.

(c) If a trustee grants an option to buy property from the trust, whether or not the trust owns the property when the option is granted, grants an option that permits another person to sell property to the trust, or acquires an option to buy property for the trust or an option to sell an asset owned by the trust, and the trustee or other owner of the asset is required to deliver the asset if the option is exercised, an amount received for granting the option shall be allocated to principal. An amount paid to acquire the option shall be paid from principal. A gain or loss realized upon the exercise of an option, including an option granted to a settlor of the trust for services rendered, shall be allocated to principal. (2003-232, s. 2.)

§ 37A-4-415. Asset-backed securities.

(a) In this section, "asset-backed security" means an asset whose value is based upon the right it gives the owner to receive distributions from the proceeds of financial assets that provide collateral for the security. The term includes an asset that gives the owner the right to receive from the collateral financial assets only the interest or other current return or only the proceeds other than interest or current return. The term does not include an asset to which G.S. 37A-4-401 or G.S. 37A-4-409 applies.

(b) If a trust receives a payment from interest or other current return and from other proceeds of the collateral financial assets, the trustee shall allocate to income the portion of the payment the payer identifies as being from interest or other current return and shall allocate the balance of the payment to principal.

(c) If a trust receives one or more payments in exchange for the trust's entire interest in an asset-backed security in one accounting period, the trustee shall allocate the payments to principal. If a payment is one of a series of payments that will result in the liquidation of the trust's interest in the security over more than one accounting period, the trustee shall allocate ten percent (10%) of the payment to income and the balance to principal. (2003-232, s. 2.)

Article 5.

Allocation of Disbursements During Administration of Trust.

§ 37A-5-501. Disbursements from income.

A trustee shall make the following disbursements from income to the extent that they are not disbursements to which G.S. 37A-2-201(2)b. or G.S. 37A-2-201(2)c. applies:

(1) One-half of the regular compensation of the trustee and of any person providing investment advisory or custodial services to the trustee;

(2) One-half of all expenses for accountings, judicial proceedings, or other matters that involve both the income and remainder interests;

(3) All of the other ordinary expenses incurred in connection with the administration, management, or preservation of trust property and the distribution of income, including interest, ordinary repairs, regularly recurring taxes assessed against principal, and expenses of a proceeding or other matter that concerns primarily the income interest; and

(4) Recurring premiums on insurance covering the loss of a principal asset or the loss of income from or use of the asset. (2003-232, s. 2.)

§ 37A-5-502. Disbursements from principal.

(a) A trustee shall make the following disbursements from principal:

(1) The remaining one-half of the disbursements described in G.S. 37A-5-501(1) and G.S. 37A-5-501(2);

(2) All of the trustee's compensation calculated on principal as a fee for acceptance, distribution, or termination and disbursements made to prepare property for sale;

(3) Payments on the principal of a trust debt;

(4) Expenses of a proceeding that concerns primarily principal, including a proceeding to construe the trust or to protect the trust or its property;

(5) Premiums paid on a policy of insurance not described in G.S. 37A-5-501(4) of which the trust is the owner and beneficiary;

(6) Estate, inheritance, and other transfer taxes, including penalties, apportioned to the trust; and

(7) Disbursements related to environmental matters, including reclamation, assessing environmental conditions, remedying and removing environmental contamination, monitoring remedial activities and the release of substances, preventing future releases of substances, collecting amounts from persons liable or potentially liable for the costs of those activities, penalties imposed under environmental laws or regulations and other payments made to comply with those laws or regulations, statutory or common-law claims by third parties, and defending claims based on environmental matters.

(b) If a principal asset is encumbered with an obligation that requires income from that asset to be paid directly to the creditor, the trustee shall transfer from principal to income an amount equal to the income paid to the creditor in reduction of the principal balance of the obligation. (2003-232, s. 2.)

§ 37A-5-503. Transfers from income to principal for depreciation.

(a) In this section, "depreciation" means a reduction in value due to wear, tear, decay, corrosion, or gradual obsolescence of a fixed asset having a useful life of more than one year.

(b) A trustee may transfer to principal a reasonable amount of the net cash receipts from a principal asset that is subject to depreciation, but may not transfer any amount for depreciation:

(1) Of that portion of real property used or available for use by a beneficiary as a residence or of tangible personal property held or made available for the personal use or enjoyment of a beneficiary;

(2) During the administration of a decedent's estate; or

(3) Under this section if the trustee is accounting under G.S. 37A-4-403 for the business or activity in which the asset is used.

(c) An amount transferred to principal under this section need not be held as a separate fund. (2003-232, s. 2.)

§ 37A-5-504. Transfers from income to reimburse principal.

(a) If a trustee makes or expects to make a principal disbursement described in this section, the trustee may transfer an appropriate amount from income to principal in one or more accounting periods to reimburse principal or to provide a reserve for future principal disbursements.

(b) Principal disbursements to which subsection (a) of this section applies include the following, but only to the extent that the trustee has not been and does not expect to be reimbursed by a third party:

(1) An amount chargeable to income but paid from principal because it is unusually large, including extraordinary repairs;

(2) A capital improvement to a principal asset, whether in the form of changes to an existing asset or the construction of a new asset, including special assessments;

(3) Disbursements made to prepare property for rental, including tenant allowances, leasehold improvements, and broker's commissions;

(4) Periodic payments on an obligation secured by a principal asset to the extent that the amount transferred from income to principal for depreciation is less than the periodic payments; and

(5) Disbursements described in G.S. 37A-5-502(a)(7).

(c) If the asset whose ownership gives rise to the disbursements becomes subject to a successive income interest after an income interest ends, a trustee may continue to transfer amounts from income to principal as provided in subsection (a) of this section. (2003-232, s. 2.)

§ 37A-5-505. Income taxes.

(a) A tax required to be paid by a trustee based on receipts allocated to income shall be paid from income.

(b) A tax required to be paid by a trustee based on receipts allocated to principal shall be paid from principal, even if the tax is called an income tax by the taxing authority.

(c) A tax required to be paid by a trustee on the trust's share of an entity's taxable income shall be paid:

(1) From income to the extent that receipts from the entity are only allocated to income;

(2) From principal to the extent receipts from the entity are only allocated to principal;

(3) Proportionately from principal and income to the extent that receipts from the entity are allocated to both income and principal; and

(4) From principal to the extent that the tax exceeds the total receipts from the entity.

(d) After applying subsections (a) through (c) of this section, the trustee shall adjust income or principal receipts to the extent that the trust's taxes are reduced because the trust receives a deduction for payments made to a beneficiary. (2003-232, s. 2; 2010-181, s. 4.)

§ 37A-5-506. Adjustments between principal and income because of taxes.

(a) A fiduciary may make adjustments between principal and income to offset the shifting of economic interests or tax benefits between income beneficiaries and remainder beneficiaries that arise from:

(1) Elections and decisions, other than those described in subsection (b) of this section, that the fiduciary makes from time to time regarding tax matters;

(2) An income tax or any other tax that is imposed upon the fiduciary or a beneficiary as a result of a transaction involving or a distribution from the estate or trust; or

(3) The ownership by an estate or trust of an interest in an entity whose taxable income, whether or not distributed, is includable in the taxable income of the estate or trust or a beneficiary.

(b) If the amount of an estate tax marital deduction or charitable contribution deduction is reduced because a fiduciary deducts an amount paid from principal for income tax purposes instead of deducting it for estate tax purposes, and as a result estate taxes paid from principal are increased and income taxes paid by an estate, trust, or beneficiary are decreased, each estate, trust, or beneficiary that benefits from the decrease in income tax shall reimburse the principal from which the increase in estate tax is paid. The total reimbursement shall equal the increase in the estate tax to the extent that the principal used to pay the increase would have qualified for a marital deduction or charitable contribution deduction but for the payment. The proportionate share of the reimbursement for each estate, trust, or beneficiary whose income taxes are reduced shall be the same as its proportionate share of the total decrease in income tax. An estate or trust shall reimburse principal from income. (2003-232, s. 2.)

Article 6.

Miscellaneous Provisions.

§ 37A-6-601. Uniformity of application and construction.

In applying and construing this Chapter, consideration shall be given to the need to promote uniformity of the law with respect to its subject matter among states that enact it. (2003-232, s. 2.)

§ 37A-6-602. Severability clause.

If any provision of this Chapter or its application to any person or circumstance is held invalid, the invalidity does not affect other provisions or applications of this Chapter that can be given effect without the invalid provision or application, and to this end the provisions of this Chapter are severable. (2003-232, s. 2.)

Chapter 38.

Boundaries.

§ 38-1. Special proceeding to establish.

The owner of land, any of whose boundary lines are in dispute, may establish any of such lines by special proceedings in the superior court of the county in which the land or any part thereof is situated. (1893, c. 22; Rev., s. 325; C.S., s. 361.)

§ 38-2. Occupation sufficient ownership.

The occupation of land constitutes sufficient ownership for the purposes of this Chapter. (1893, c. 22; 1903, c. 21; Rev., s. 326; C.S., s. 362.)

§ 38-3. Procedure.

(a) Petition; Summons; Hearing. - The owner shall file his petition under oath stating therein facts sufficient to constitute the location of such line as claimed by him and making defendants all adjoining owners whose interest may be affected by the location of said line. The clerk shall thereupon issue summons to the defendants as in other cases of special proceedings. If the defendants fail to answer, judgment shall be given establishing the line according to petition. If the answer deny the location set out in the petition, the clerk shall issue an order to the county surveyor or, if cause shown, to any competent surveyor to survey said line or lines according to the contention of both parties, and make report of the same with a map at a time to be fixed by the clerk, not more than 30 days from date of order; to which time the cause shall be continued. The cause shall then be heard by the clerk upon the location of said line or lines and judgment given determining the location thereof.

(b)   Appeal to Session. - Either party may within 10 days after such determination by the clerk serve notice of appeal from the ruling of the clerk determining the said location. When notice of appeal is served it shall be the duty of the clerk to transmit the issues raised before him to the next session of the superior court of the county for trial by a jury, when the question shall be heard de novo.

(c)   Survey after Judgment. - When final judgment is given in the proceeding the court shall issue an order to the surveyor to run and mark the line or lines as determined in the judgment. The surveyor shall make report including a map of the line as determined, which shall be filed with the judgment roll in the cause and entered with the judgment on the special proceedings docket.

(d)   Procedure as in Special Proceedings. - The procedure under this Chapter, the jurisdiction of the court, and the right of appeal shall, in all respects, be the same as in special proceedings except as herein modified. (1893, c. 22; 1903, c. 21; Rev., s. 326; C.S., s. 363; 1971, c. 528, s. 35.)

§ 38-4. Surveys in disputed boundaries.

(a)   When in any action or special proceeding pending in the superior court the boundaries of lands are drawn in question, the court may, if deemed necessary, order a survey of the lands in dispute, in accordance with the boundaries and lines expressed in each party's titles, and such other surveys as shall be deemed useful.

(b)   Surveys pursuant to this section shall be made by one surveyor appointed by the court, unless the court, in its discretion, determines that additional surveyors are necessary. The surveyor or surveyors shall proceed according to the order of the court, and make the surveys and as many plats thereof as shall be ordered.

(c) Upon the request of any party to the action or special proceeding, the court shall call such surveyor or surveyors as the court's witness, and any party to such action or proceeding shall have the privilege of direct examination, cross-examination, and impeachment of such witness. The fact that such witness is called by the court shall not change the weight, effect or admissibility of the testimony of such witness, and upon the request of any party to the suit, the court shall so instruct the jury.

(d) The court shall make an allowance for the fees of the surveyor or surveyors and they shall be taxed as a part of the costs. The court may, in its discretion, require the parties to make a deposit to secure the payment of such fees, and may, in its discretion, provide for the payment of such fees prior to the termination of the suit. (1779, c. 157; 1786, c. 252; R.C., c. 31, s. 119; Code, s. 939; Rev., s. 1504; C.S., s. 364; 1967, c. 33.)

Chapter 38A.

Landowner Liability.

§ 38A-1. Purpose.

The purpose of this Chapter is to encourage owners of land to make land and water areas available to the public at no cost for educational and recreational purposes by limiting the liability of the owner to persons entering the land for those purposes. (1995, c. 308, s. 1.)

§ 38A-2. Definitions.

The following definitions shall apply throughout this Chapter, unless otherwise specified:

(1) "Charge" means a price or fee asked for services, entertainment, recreation performed, or products offered for sale on land or in return for an invitation or permission to enter upon land, except as otherwise excluded in this Chapter.

(2) "Educational purpose" means any activity undertaken as part of a formal or informal educational program, and viewing historical, natural, archaeological, or scientific sites.

(3) "Land" means real property, land, and water, but does not mean a dwelling and the property immediately adjacent to and surrounding such dwelling that is generally used for activities associated with occupancy of the dwelling as a living space.

(4) "Owner" means any individual or nongovernmental legal entity that has any fee, leasehold interest, or legal possession, and any employee or agent of such individual or nongovernmental legal entity.

(5) "Recreational purpose" means any activity undertaken for recreation, exercise, education, relaxation, refreshment, diversion, or pleasure or sport, including equestrian recreation as defined in G.S. 99E-1. (1995, c. 308, s. 1; 2013-265, s. 3.1.)

§ 38A-3. Exclusions.

For purposes of this Chapter, the term "charge" does not include:

(1) Any contribution in kind, services or cash contributed by a person, legal entity, nonprofit organization, or governmental entity other than the owner, whether or not sanctioned or solicited by the owner, the purpose of which is to (i) remedy damage to land caused by educational or recreational use; (ii) provide warning of hazards on, or remove hazards from, land used for educational or recreational purposes; or (iii) pay expenses related to the use of land for a recreational or educational purpose.

(2) Unless otherwise agreed in writing or otherwise provided by the State or federal tax codes, any property tax abatement or relief received by the owner from the State or local taxing authority in exchange for the owner's agreement to open the land for educational or recreational purposes.

(3) Dues or fees charged by an individual, group, club, partnership, corporation, or governmental entity sponsoring the educational or recreational use when (i) the sponsor is operating as a nonprofit or in a nonprofit capacity and (ii) the dues or fees are used to pay expenses relating to the educational or recreational use or to raise funds to support the sponsor's mission. (1995, c. 308, s. 1; 2013-265, s. 3.4.)

§ 38A-4. Limitation of liability.

(a) Except as specifically recognized by or provided for in this Chapter, an owner of land who either directly or indirectly invites or permits without charge any person to use such land for educational or recreational purposes owes the person the same duty of care that he owes a trespasser, except nothing in this Chapter shall be construed to limit or nullify the doctrine of attractive nuisance and the owner shall inform direct invitees of artificial or unusual hazards of which the owner has actual knowledge. This section does not apply to an owner who invites or permits any person to use land for a purpose for which the land is regularly used and for which a price or fee is usually charged even if it is not charged in that instance, or to an owner whose purpose in extending an invitation or granting permission is to promote a commercial enterprise.

(b) Nothing in this section shall be construed to conflict with or render ineffectual a liability release, indemnification, assumption, or acknowledgment of risk agreement between the landowner and a person who uses the land for educational or recreational purposes. (1995, c. 308, s. 1; 2013-265, s. 3.5.)

Chapter 38B.

Trespasser Responsibility.

§ 38B-1. Title.

This Chapter may be cited as the Trespasser Responsibility Act. (2011-283, s. 3.2; 2011-317, s. 1.1.)

§ 38B-2. General rule.

A possessor of land, including an owner, lessee, or other occupant, does not owe a duty of care to a trespasser and is not subject to liability for any injury to a trespasser. (2011-283, s. 3.2; 2011-317, s. 1.1.)

§ 38B-3. Exceptions.

Notwithstanding G.S. 38B-2, a possessor of land may be subject to liability for physical injury or death to a trespasser in the following situations:

(1) Intentional harms. - A possessor may be subject to liability if the trespasser's bodily injury or death resulted from the possessor's willful or wanton conduct, or was intentionally caused by the possessor, except that a possessor may use reasonable force to repel a trespasser who has entered the land or a building with the intent to commit a crime.

(2) Harms to trespassing children caused by artificial condition. - A possessor may be subject to liability for bodily injury or death to a child trespasser resulting from an artificial condition on the land if all of the following apply:

a. The possessor knew or had reason to know that children were likely to trespass at the location of the condition.

b. The condition is one the possessor knew or reasonably should have known involved an unreasonable risk of serious bodily injury or death to such children.

c. The injured child did not discover the condition or realize the risk involved in the condition or in coming within the area made dangerous by it.

d. The utility to the possessor of maintaining the condition and the burden of eliminating the danger were slight as compared with the risk to the child involved.

e. The possessor failed to exercise reasonable care to eliminate the danger or otherwise protect the injured child.

(3) Position of peril. - A possessor may be subject to liability for physical injury or death to a trespasser if the possessor discovered the trespasser in a position of peril or helplessness on the property and failed to exercise ordinary care not to injure the trespasser. (2011-283, s. 3.2; 2011-317, s. 1.1.)

§ 38B-4. Definitions.

The following definitions shall apply in this Chapter:

(1) Child trespasser. - A trespasser who is less than 14 years of age or who has the level of mental development found in a person less than 14 years of age.

(2) Possessor. - A person in lawful possession of land, including an owner, lessee, or other occupant, or a person acting on behalf of such a lawful possessor of land.

(3) Trespasser. - A person who enters on the property of another without permission and without an invitation, express or implied. (2011-283, s. 3.2; 2011-317, s. 1.1.)

Chapter 39.

Conveyances.

Article 1.

Construction and Sufficiency.

§ 39-1. Fee presumed, though word "heirs" omitted.

When real estate is conveyed to any person, the same shall be held and construed to be a conveyance in fee, whether the word "heir" is used or not, unless such conveyance in plain and express words shows, or it is plainly intended by the conveyance or some part thereof, that the grantor meant to convey an estate of less dignity. (1879, c. 148; Code, s. 1280; Rev., s. 946; C.S., s. 991.)

§ 39-1.1. In construing conveyances court shall give effect to intent of the parties.

(a) In construing a conveyance executed after January 1, 1968, in which there are inconsistent clauses, the courts shall determine the effect of the instrument on the basis of the intent of the parties as it appears from all of the provisions of the instrument.

(b) The provisions of subsection (a) of this section shall not prevent the application of the rule in Shelley's case. (1967, c. 1182.)

§ 39-2. Vagueness of description not to invalidate.

No deed or other writing purporting to convey land or an interest in land shall be declared void for vagueness in the description of the thing intended to be granted by reason of the use of the word "adjoining" instead of the words "bounded by," or for the reason that the boundaries given do not go entirely around the land described: Provided, it can be made to appear to the satisfaction of the jury that the grantor owned at the time of the execution of such deed or paper-writing no other land which at all corresponded to the description contained in such deed or paper-writing. (1891, c. 465, s. 2; Rev., s. 948; C.S., s. 992.)

§ 39-3. Repealed by Session Laws 1961, c. 52.

§ 39-4. Conveyances by infant trustees.

When an infant is seized or possessed of any estate in trust, whether by way of mortgage or otherwise, for another person who may be entitled in law to have a conveyance of such estate, or may be declared to be seized or possessed, in the course of any proceeding in the superior court, the court may decree that the infant shall convey and assure such estate, in such manner as it may direct, to such other person; and every conveyance and assurance made in pursuance of such decree shall be as effectual in law as if made by a person of full age. (1821, c. 1116, ss. 1, 2; R.C., c. 37, s. 27; Code, s. 1265; Rev., s. 1036; C.S., s. 994.)

§ 39-5. Official deed, when official selling or empowered to sell is not in office.

When a sheriff, coroner, or tax collector, in virtue of his office, sells any real or personal property and goes out of office before executing a proper deed therefor, he may execute the same after his term of office has expired; and when he dies or removes from the State before executing the deed, his successor in office shall execute it. When a sheriff or tax collector dies having a tax list in his hands for collection, and his personal representative or surety, in collecting the taxes, makes sale according to law, his successor in office shall execute the conveyance for the property to the person entitled. (R.C., c. 37, s. 30; Code, s. 1267; 1891, c. 242; Rev., ss. 950, 951; C.S., s. 995; 1971, c. 528, s. 36.)

§ 39-6. Revocation of deeds of future interests made to persons not in esse.

The grantor in any voluntary conveyance in which some future interest in real estate is conveyed or limited to a person not in esse may, at any time before he comes into being, revoke by deed such interest so conveyed or limited. This deed of revocation shall be registered as other deeds; and the grantor of like interest for a valuable consideration may, with the joinder of the person from whom the consideration moved, revoke said interest in like manner. The grantor, maker or trustor who has heretofore created or may hereafter create a voluntary trust estate in real or personal property for the use and benefit of himself or of any other person or persons in esse with a future contingent interest to some person or persons not in esse or not determined until the happening of a future event may at any time, prior to the happening of the contingency vesting the future estates, revoke the grant of the interest to such person or persons not in esse or not determined by a proper instrument to that effect; and the grantor of like interest for a valuable consideration may, with the joinder of the person from whom the consideration moved, revoke said interest in like manner: Provided, that in the event the instrument creating such estate has been recorded, then the deed of revocation of such estate shall be likewise recorded before it becomes effective: Provided, further, that this section shall not apply to any instrument hereafter executed creating such a future contingent interest when said instrument shall expressly state in effect that the grantor, maker, or trustor may not revoke such interest: Provided, further, that this section shall not apply to any instrument heretofore executed whether or not such instrument contains express provisions that it is irrevocable unless the grantor, maker, or trustor shall within six months after the effective date of this proviso either revoke such future interest, or file with the trustee an instrument stating or declaring that it is his intention to retain the power to revoke under this section: Provided, further, that in the event the instrument creating such estate has been recorded, then the revocation or declaration shall likewise be recorded before it becomes effective. (1893, c. 498; Rev., s. 1045; C.S., s. 996; 1929, c. 305; 1941, c. 264; 1943, c. 437.)

§ 39-6.1. Validation of deeds of revocation of conveyances of future interests to persons not in esse.

All deeds or instruments heretofore executed, revoking any conveyance of future interest made to persons not in esse, are hereby validated insofar as any such deed of revocation may be in conflict with the provisions of G.S. 39-6.

All such deeds of revocation heretofore executed are hereby validated and no such deed of revocation shall be held to be invalid by reason of not having been executed within the six-month period prescribed in the third proviso of G.S. 39-6. (1947, c. 62.)

§ 39-6.2. Creation of interest or estate in personal property.

Any interest or estate in personal property which may be created by last will and testament may also be created by a written instrument of transfer. (1953, c. 198.)

§ 39-6.3. Inter vivos and testamentary conveyances of future interests permitted.

(a) The conveyance, by deed or will, of an existing future interest shall not be ineffective on the sole ground that the interest so conveyed is future or contingent. All future interests in real or personal property, including all reversions, executory interests, vested and contingent remainders, rights of entry both before and after breach of condition and possibilities of reverter may be conveyed by the owner thereof, by an otherwise legally effective conveyance, inter vivos or testamentary, subject, however, to all conditions and limitations to which such future interest is subject.

(b) The power to convey as provided in subsection (a), can be exercised by any form of conveyance, inter vivos or testamentary, which is otherwise legally effective in this State at the date of such conveyance to transfer a present estate of the same duration in the property.

(c) This section shall apply only to conveyances which become operative to transfer title on or after October 1, 1961. (1961, c. 435.)

§ 39-6.4. Creation of easements, restrictions, and conditions.

(a) The holder of legal or equitable title of an interest in real property may create, grant, reserve, or declare valid easements, restrictions, or conditions of record burdening or benefiting the same interest in real property.

(b) Subsection (a) of this section shall not affect the application of the doctrine of merger after the severance and subsequent reunification of title to all of the benefited or burdened real property or interests therein. (1997-333, s. 1.)

§ 39-6.5. Elimination of seal.

The seal of the signatory shall not be necessary to effect a valid conveyance of an interest in real property; provided, that this section shall not affect the requirement for affixing a seal of the officer taking an acknowledgment of the instrument. (1999-221, s. 2.)

§ 39-6.6. Subordination agreements.

(a) A subordination agreement shall be given effect in accordance with its terms and is not required to state any interest rate, principal amount secured, or other financial terms.

(b) The trustee of a deed of trust shall not be a necessary party to a subordination agreement unless the deed of trust provides otherwise.

(c) For purposes of G.S. 1-47, a subordination agreement is deemed a conveyance of an interest in real property.

(d) This section is not exclusive. No subordination agreement that is otherwise valid shall be invalidated by this section.

(e) This section applies to a subordination agreement regardless of when the agreement was signed by the party or parties thereto, except that this section does not apply to an agreement that (i) is the subject of litigation pending on the effective date of this subsection, and (ii) was filed or recorded before October 1, 2003.

(f) In this section:

(1) "Interest in real property" includes all rights, title, and interest in and to land, buildings, and other improvements of an owner, tenant, subtenant, secured lender, materialman, judgment creditor, lienholder, or other person, whether the interest in real property is evidenced by a deed, easement, lease, sublease, deed of trust, mortgage, assignment of leases and rents, judgment, claim of lien, or any other record, instrument, document, or entry of court.

(2) "Subordination agreement" means a written commitment or agreement to subordinate or that subordinates an interest in real property signed by a person entitled to priority. (2003-219, s. 1; 2005-212, s. 1.)

§ 39-6.7. Construction of conveyances to or by trusts.

(a) A deed, will, beneficiary designation, or other instrument that purports to convey, devise, or otherwise transfer any ownership or security interest in real or personal property to a trust shall be deemed to be a transfer to the trustee or trustees of that trust.

(b) A deed or other instrument which purports to convey or otherwise transfer any ownership or security interest in real or personal property by a trust shall be deemed to be a transfer by the trustee or trustees of that trust. This rule of construction shall apply:

(1) Regardless of whether the instrument is signed by the trustee or trustees as such, or by the trustee or trustees purportedly for or on behalf of the trust; and

(2) Regardless of whether the instrument by which the trustee or trustees acquired title transferred that title to the trustee or trustees as such, or purportedly to the trust.

(c) A deed or other instrument by which the trustee or trustees of a trust convey or otherwise transfer any ownership or security interest in real or personal property shall be deemed sufficient:

(1) Regardless of whether the instrument is signed by the trustee or trustees as such, or by the trustee or trustees purportedly for or on behalf of the trust; and

(2) Regardless of whether the instrument by which the trustee or trustees acquired title transferred that title to the trustee or trustees as such, or purportedly to the trust.

(d) The trustee or trustees of a trust may convey or otherwise transfer any ownership or security interest in real or personal property as trustee or trustees even though the deed or instrument by which the trustee or trustees acquired title purported to convey or transfer that title to the trust.

(e) Nothing in this section shall be construed to limit the manner in which title to real or personal property may be conveyed or transferred to or by trustees. (2007-106, s. 53.)

Article 2.

Conveyances by Husband and Wife.

§ 39-7. Instruments affecting married person's title; joinder of spouse; exceptions.

(a) In order to waive the elective life estate of either husband or wife as provided for in G.S. 29-30, every conveyance or other instrument affecting the estate, right or title of any married person in lands, tenements or hereditaments must be executed by such husband or wife, and due proof or acknowledgment thereof must be made and certified as provided by law.

(b) A married person may bargain, sell, lease, mortgage, transfer and convey any of his or her separate real estate without joinder or other waiver by his or her spouse if such spouse is incompetent and a guardian or trustee has been appointed as provided by the laws of North Carolina, and if the appropriate instrument is executed by the married person and the guardian or trustee of the incompetent spouse and is probated and registered in accordance with law, it shall convey all the estate and interest as therein intended of the married person in the land conveyed, free and exempt from the elective life estate as provided in G.S. 29-30 and all other interests of the incompetent spouse.

(c) Subsection (a) shall not be construed to require the spouse's joinder or other waiver of the elective life estate of such spouse as provided for in G.S. 29-30 where a different provision is made or provided for in the General Statutes including, but not limited to, G.S. 39-13, 39-13.3, 39-13.4, 31A-1(d), and 52-10. (C.C.P., s. 429; subsec. 6; 1868-9, c. 277, s. 15; Code, s. 1256; 1899, c. 235, s. 9; Rev., s. 952; C.S., s. 997; 1945, c. 73, s. 4; 1957, c. 598, s. 3; 1965, c. 855.)

§ 39-7.1. Certain instruments affecting married woman's title not executed by husband validated.

No conveyance, power of attorney, or other instrument affecting the estate, right or title of any married woman in lands, tenements or hereditaments which was executed by such married woman prior to June 8, 1965, shall be invalid for the reason that the instrument was not also executed by the husband of such married woman. (1965, c. 857; 1973, c. 853, s. 1.)

§ 39-8. Acknowledgment at different times and places; before different officers; order immaterial.

In all cases of deeds, or other instruments executed by husband and wife and requiring registration, the probate of such instruments as to the husband and due proof or acknowledgment of the wife may be taken before different officers authorized by law to taken probate of deeds, and at different times and places, whether both of said officials reside in this State or only one in this State and the other in another state or country. And in taking the probate of such instruments executed by husband and wife, it is immaterial whether the execution of the instrument was proven as to or acknowledged by the husband before or after due proof as to or acknowledgment of the wife. (1895, c. 136; 1899, c. 235, s. 9; Rev., s. 953; C.S., s. 998; 1945, c. 73, s. 5.)

§ 39-9. Absence of wife's acknowledgment does not affect deed as to husband.

When an instrument purports to be signed by a husband and wife the instrument may be ordered registered, if the acknowledgment of the husband is duly taken, but no such instrument shall be the act or deed of the wife unless proven or acknowledged by her according to law. (1889, c. 235, s. 8; 1901, c. 637; Rev., s. 954; C.S., s. 999; 1945, c. 73, s. 6.)

§ 39-10: Repealed by Session Laws 1977, c. 375, s. 16.

§ 39-11. Certain conveyances not affected by fraud if acknowledgment or privy examination regular.

No deed conveying lands nor any instrument required or allowed by law to be registered, executed by husband and wife since the eleventh of March, 1889, if the acknowledgment or private examination of the wife is thereto certified as prescribed by law, shall be invalid because its execution or acknowledgment was procured by fraud, duress or undue influence, unless it is shown that the grantee or person to whom the instrument was made participated in the fraud, duress or undue influence, or had notice thereof before the delivery of the instrument. Where such participation or notice is shown, an innocent purchaser for value under the grantee or person to whom the instrument was made shall not be affected by such fraud, duress or undue influence. (1889, c. 389; 1899, c. 235, s. 10; Rev., s. 956; C.S., s. 1001; 1945, c. 73, s. 7.)

§ 39-12. Power of attorney of married person.

Every competent married person of lawful age is authorized to execute, without the joinder of his or her spouse, instruments creating powers of attorney affecting the real and personal property of such married person naming either third parties or, subject to the provisions of G.S. 52-10 or 52-10.1, his or her spouse as attorney-in-fact. When such a married person executes a power of attorney authorized by the preceding sentence naming his or her spouse as attorney in fact the acknowledgment by the spouse of the grantor is not necessary. Such instruments may confer upon the attorney, and the attorney may exercise, any and all powers which lawfully can be conferred upon an attorney-in-fact, including, but not limited to, the authority to join in conveyances of real property for the purpose of waiving or quitclaiming any rights which may be acquired as a surviving spouse under the provisions of G.S. 29-30. (1798, c. 510; R.C., c. 37, s. 11; Code, s. 1257; Rev., s. 957; C.S., s. 1002; 1965, c. 856; 1977, c. 375, s. 7; 1979, c. 528, s. 8.)

§ 39-13. Spouse need not join in purchase-money mortgage.

The purchaser of real estate who does not pay the whole of the purchase money at the time when he or she takes a deed for title may make a mortgage or deed of trust for securing the payment of such purchase money, or such part thereof as may remain unpaid, which shall be good and effectual against his or her spouse as well as the purchaser, without requiring the spouse to join in the execution of such mortgage or deed of trust. (1868-9, c. 204; Code, s. 1272; Rev., s. 958; 1907, c. 12; C.S., s. 1003; 1965, c. 852.)

§ 39-13.1. Validation of certain deeds, etc., executed by married women without private examination.

(a) No deed, contract, conveyance, leasehold or other instrument executed since the seventh day of November, 1944, shall be declared invalid because of the failure to take the private examination of any married woman who was a party to such deed, contract, conveyance, leasehold or other instrument.

(b) Any deed, contract, conveyance, lease or other instrument executed prior to February 7, 1945, which is in all other respects regular except for the failure to take the private examination of a married woman who is a party to such deed, contract, conveyance, lease or other instrument is hereby validated and confirmed to the same extent as if such private examination had been taken, provided that this section shall not apply to any instruments now involved in any pending litigation. (1945, c. 73, s. 21 1/2; 1969, c. 1008, s. 1.)

§ 39-13.2. Married persons under 18 made competent as to certain transactions; certain transactions validated.

(a) Any married person under 18 years of age is authorized and empowered and shall have the same privileges as are conferred upon married persons 18 years of age or older to:

(1) Waive, release or renounce by deed or other written instrument any right or interest which he or she may have in the real or personal property (tangible or intangible) of the other spouse; or

(2) Jointly execute with his or her spouse, if such spouse is 18 years of age or older, any note, contract of insurance, deed, deed of trust, mortgage, lien of whatever nature or other instrument with respect to real or personal property (tangible or intangible) held with such other spouse either as tenants by the entirety, joint tenants, tenants in common, or in any other manner.

(b) Any transaction between a husband and wife pursuant to this section shall be subject to the provisions of G.S. 52-10 or 52-10.1 whenever applicable.

(c) No renunciation of dower or curtesy or of rights under G.S. 29-30(a) by a married person under the age of 21 years after June 30, 1960, and until April 7, 1961, shall be invalid because such person was under such age. No written assent by a husband under the age of 21 years to a conveyance of the real property of his wife after June 30, 1960, and until April 7, 1961, shall be invalid because such husband was under such age. (1951, c. 934, s. 1; 1955, c. 376; 1961, c. 184; 1965, c. 851; c. 878, s. 2; 1971, c. 1231, s. 1; 1977, c. 375, s. 8.)

§ 39-13.3. Conveyances between husband and wife.

(a) A conveyance from a husband or wife to the other spouse of real property or any interest therein owned by the grantor alone vests such property or interest in the grantee.

(b) A conveyance of real property, or any interest therein, by a husband or a wife to such husband and wife vests the same in the husband and wife as tenants by the entirety unless a contrary intention is expressed in the conveyance.

(c) A conveyance from a husband or a wife to the other spouse of real property, or any interest therein, held by such husband and wife as tenants by the entirety dissolves such tenancy in the property or interest conveyed and vests such property or interest formerly held by the entirety in the grantee.

(d) The joinder of the spouse of the grantor in any conveyance made by a husband or a wife pursuant to the foregoing provisions of this section is not necessary.

(e) Any conveyance authorized by this section is subject to the provisions of G.S. 52-10 or 52-10.1, except that acknowledgment by the spouse of the grantor is not necessary. (1957, c. 598, s. 1; 1965, c. 878, s. 3; 1977, c. 375, s. 9.)

§ 39-13.4. Conveyances by husband or wife under deed of separation.

Any conveyance of real property, or any interest therein, by the husband or wife who have previously executed a valid and lawful deed of separation which authorizes said husband or wife to convey real property or any interest therein without the consent and joinder of the other and which deed of separation or a memorandum of the deed of separation setting forth such authorization is recorded in the county where the land lies, shall be valid to pass such title as the conveying spouse may have to his or her grantee and shall pass such title free and clear of all rights in such property and free and clear of such interest in property that the other spouse might acquire solely as a result of the marriage, including any rights arising under G.S. 29-30, unless an instrument in writing canceling the deed of separation or memorandum thereof and properly executed and acknowledged by said husband and wife is recorded in the office of said register of deeds. The instrument which is registered under this section to authorize the conveyance of an interest in real property or the cancellation of the deed of separation or memorandum thereof shall comply with the provisions of G.S. 52-10 or 52-10.1.

All conveyances of any interest in real property by a spouse who had previously executed a valid and lawful deed of separation, or separation agreement, or property settlement, which authorized the parties thereto to convey real property or any interest therein without the consent and joinder of the other, when said deed of separation, separation agreement, or property settlement, or a memorandum of the deed of separation, separation agreement, property settlement, setting forth such authorization, had been previously recorded in the county where the property is located, and when such conveyances were executed before October 1, 1981, shall be valid to pass such title as the conveying spouse may have to his or her grantee, and shall pass such to him free and clear of rights in such property and free and clear of such interest in such property that the other spouse might acquire solely as a result of the marriage, including any rights arising under G.S. 29-30, unless an instrument in writing canceling the deed of separation, separation agreement, or property settlement, or memorandum thereof, properly executed and acknowledged by said husband and wife, is recorded in the office of said register of deeds. The instrument which is registered under this section to authorize the conveyance of an interest in real property or the cancellation of the deed of separation, separation agreement, property settlement, or memorandum thereof shall comply with G.S. 52-10 or 52-10.1. (1959, c. 512; 1973, c. 133; 1977, c. 375, s. 10; 1981, c. 599, ss. 10, 11.)

§ 39-13.5. Creation of tenancy by entirety in partition of real property.

When either a husband or a wife owns an undivided interest in real property as a tenant in common with some person or persons other than his or her spouse and there occurs an actual partition of the property, a tenancy by the entirety may be created in the husband or wife who owned the undivided interest and his or her spouse in the manner hereinafter provided:

(1) In a division by cross-deed or deeds, between or among the tenants in common provided that the intent of the tenant in common to create a tenancy by the entirety with his or her spouse in this exchange of deeds must be clearly stated in the granting clause of the deed or deeds to such tenant and his or her spouse, and further provided that the deed or deeds to such tenant in common and his or her spouse is signed by such tenant in common and is acknowledged before a certifying officer in accordance with G.S. 52-10;

(2) In a judicial proceeding for partition. In such proceeding, both spouses have the right to become parties to the proceeding and to have their pleadings state that the intent of the tenant in common is to create a tenancy by the entirety with his or her spouse. The order of partition shall provide that the real property assigned to such tenant and his or her spouse shall be owned by them as tenants by the entirety. (1969, c. 748, s. 1; 1977, c. 375, s. 11.)

§ 39-13.6. Control of real property held in tenancy by the entirety.

(a) A husband and wife shall have an equal right to the control, use, possession, rents, income, and profits of real property held by them in tenancy by the entirety. Neither spouse may bargain, sell, lease, mortgage, transfer, convey or in any manner encumber any property so held without the written joinder of the other spouse. This section shall not be construed to require the spouse's joinder where a different provision is made under G.S. 39-13, G.S. 39-13.3, G.S. 39-13.4, or G.S. 52-10.

(b) A conveyance of real property, or any interest therein, to a husband and wife vests title in them as tenants by the entirety when the conveyance is to:

(1) A named man "and wife," or

(2) A named woman "and husband," or

(3) Two named persons, whether or not identified in the conveyance as husband and wife, if at the time of conveyance they are legally married;

unless a contrary intention is expressed in the conveyance.

(c) For income tax purposes, each spouse is considered to have received one-half (1/2) the income or loss from property owned by the couple as tenants by the entirety. (1981 (Reg. Sess., 1982), c. 1245, s. 1; 1983, c. 449, ss. 1, 2.)

§ 39-14: Repealed by Session Laws 1943, c. 543.

Article 3.

Fraudulent Conveyances.

§§ 39-15 through 39-23: Repealed by Session Laws 1997-291, s. 1.

Article 3A.

Uniform Fraudulent Transfer Act.

§ 39-23.1. Definitions.

As used in this Article:

(1) "Affiliate" means:

a. A person who directly or indirectly owns, controls, or holds with power to vote, twenty percent (20%) or more of the outstanding voting securities of the debtor, other than a person who holds the securities,

1. As a fiduciary or agent without sole discretionary power to vote the securities; or

2. Solely to secure a debt, if the person has not exercised the power to vote;

b. A corporation twenty percent (20%) or more of whose outstanding voting securities are directly or indirectly owned, controlled, or held with power to vote, by the debtor or a person who directly or indirectly owns, controls, or holds, with power to vote, twenty percent (20%) or more of the outstanding voting securities of the debtor, other than a person who holds the securities,

1. As a fiduciary or agent without sole power to vote the securities; or

2. Solely to secure a debt, if the person has not in fact exercised the power to vote;

c. A person whose business is operated by the debtor under a lease or other agreement, or a person substantially all of whose assets are controlled by the debtor; or

d. A person who operates the debtor's business under a lease or other agreement or controls substantially all of the debtor's assets.

(2) "Asset" means property of a debtor, but the term does not include:

a. Property to the extent it is encumbered by a valid lien;

b. Property to the extent it is generally exempt under nonbankruptcy law; or

c. An interest in property held in tenancy by the entireties to the extent it is not subject to process by a creditor holding a claim against only one tenant.

(3) "Claim" means a right to payment, whether or not the right is reduced to judgment, liquidated, unliquidated, fixed, contingent, matured, unmatured, disputed, undisputed, legal, equitable, secured, or unsecured.

(4) "Creditor" means a person who has a claim.

(5) "Debt" means liability on a claim.

(6) "Debtor" means a person who is liable on a claim.

(7) "Insider" includes:

a. If the debtor is an individual,

1. A relative of the debtor or of a general partner of the debtor;

2. A partnership in which the debtor is a general partner;

3. A general partner in a partnership in which the debtor is a general partner; or

4. A corporation of which the debtor is a director, officer, or person in control;

b. If the debtor is a corporation,

1. A director of the debtor;

2. An officer of the debtor;

3. A person in control of the debtor;

4. A partnership in which the debtor is a general partner;

5. A general partner in a partnership in which the debtor is a general partner; or

6. A relative of a general partner, director, officer, or person in control of the debtor;

c. If the debtor is a partnership,

1. A general partner in the debtor;

2. A relative of a general partner in, a general partner of, or a person in control of the debtor;

3. Another partnership in which the debtor is a general partner;

4. A general partner in a partnership in which the debtor is a general partner; or

5. A person in control of the debtor;

d. An affiliate, or an insider of an affiliate as if the affiliate were the debtor; and

e. A managing agent of the debtor.

(8) "Lien" means a charge against or an interest in property to secure payment of a debt or performance of an obligation and includes a security interest created by agreement, a judicial lien obtained by legal or equitable process or proceedings, a common-law lien, or a statutory lien.

(9) "Person" means an individual, partnership, corporation, association, organization, government or governmental subdivision or agency, business trust, estate, trust, or any other legal or commercial entity.

(10) "Property" means anything that may be the subject of ownership.

(11) "Relative" means an individual related by consanguinity within the third degree as determined in accordance with G.S. 104A-1, a spouse, or an individual related to a spouse within the third degree as so determined, and includes an individual in an adoptive relationship within the third degree.

(12) "Transfer" means every mode, direct or indirect, absolute or conditional, voluntary or involuntary, of disposing of or parting with an asset or an interest in an asset and includes payment of money, release, lease, and creation of a lien or other encumbrance.

(13) "Valid lien" means a lien that is effective against the holder of a judicial lien subsequently obtained by legal or equitable process or proceedings. (1997-291, s. 2.)

§ 39-23.2. Insolvency.

(a) A debtor is insolvent if the sum of the debtor's debts is greater than all of the debtor's assets at a fair valuation.

(b) A debtor who is generally not paying the debtor's debts as they become due is presumed to be insolvent.

(c) A partnership is insolvent under subsection (a) of this section if the sum of the partnership's debts is greater than the aggregate, at a fair valuation, of all of the partnership's assets and the sum of the excess of the value of each general partner's nonpartnership assets over the partner's nonpartnership debts.

(d) Assets under this section do not include property that has been transferred, concealed, or removed with intent to hinder, delay, or defraud creditors or that has been transferred in a manner making transfer voidable under this Article.

(e) Debts under this section do not include an obligation to the extent it is secured by a valid lien on property of the debtor not included as an asset. (1997-291, s. 2.)

§ 39-23.3. Value.

(a) Value is given for a transfer or an obligation if, in exchange for the transfer or obligation, property is transferred or an antecedent debt is secured or satisfied, but value does not include an unperformed promise made otherwise than in the ordinary course of the promisor's business to furnish support to the debtor or another person.

(b) For the purposes of G.S. 39-23.4(a)(2) and G.S. 39-23.5, a person gives a reasonably equivalent value if the person acquires an interest of the debtor in an asset pursuant to a regularly conducted, noncollusive foreclosure sale or execution of a power of sale for the acquisition or disposition of the interest of the debtor upon default under a mortgage, deed of trust, or security agreement.

(c) A transfer is made for present value if the exchange between the debtor and the transferee is intended by them to be contemporaneous and is in fact substantially contemporaneous. (1997-291, s. 2; 1998-217, s. 6.)

§ 39-23.4. Transfers fraudulent as to present and future creditors.

(a) A transfer made or obligation incurred by a debtor is fraudulent as to a creditor, whether the creditor's claim arose before or after the transfer was made or the obligation was incurred, if the debtor made the transfer or incurred the obligation:

(1) With intent to hinder, delay, or defraud any creditor of the debtor; or

(2) Without receiving a reasonably equivalent value in exchange for the transfer or obligation, and the debtor:

a. Was engaged or was about to engage in a business or a transaction for which the remaining assets of the debtor were unreasonably small in relation to the business or transaction; or

b. Intended to incur, or believed that the debtor would incur, debts beyond the debtor's ability to pay as they became due.

(b) In determining intent under subdivision (a)(1) of this section, consideration may be given, among other factors, to whether:

(1) The transfer or obligation was to an insider;

(2) The debtor retained possession or control of the property transferred after the transfer;

(3) The transfer or obligation was disclosed or concealed;

(4) Before the transfer was made or obligation was incurred, the debtor had been sued or threatened with suit;

(5) The transfer was of substantially all the debtor's assets;

(6) The debtor absconded;

(7) The debtor removed or concealed assets;

(8) The value of the consideration received by the debtor was reasonably equivalent to the value of the asset transferred or the amount of the obligation incurred;

(9) The debtor was insolvent or became insolvent shortly after the transfer was made or the obligation was incurred;

(10) The transfer occurred shortly before or shortly after a substantial debt was incurred;

(11) The debtor transferred the essential assets of the business to a lienor who transferred the assets to an insider of the debtor;

(12) The debtor made the transfer or incurred the obligation without receiving a reasonably equivalent value in exchange for the transfer or obligation, and the debtor reasonably should have believed that the debtor would incur debts beyond the debtor's ability to pay as they became due; and

(13) The debtor transferred the assets in the course of legitimate estate or tax planning. (1997-291, s. 2.)

§ 39-23.5. Transfers fraudulent as to present creditors.

(a) A transfer made or obligation incurred by a debtor is fraudulent as to a creditor whose claim arose before the transfer was made or the obligation was incurred if the debtor made the transfer or incurred the obligation without receiving a reasonably equivalent value in exchange for the transfer or obligation, and the debtor was insolvent at that time or the debtor became insolvent as a result of the transfer or obligation.

(b) A transfer made by a debtor is voidable as to a creditor whose claim arose before the transfer was made if the transfer was made to an insider for an antecedent debt, the debtor was insolvent at that time, and the insider had reasonable cause to believe that the debtor was insolvent. (1997-291, s. 2.)

§ 39-23.6. When transfer is made or obligation is incurred.

For the purposes of this Article:

(1) A transfer is made:

a. With respect to an asset that is real property other than a fixture, but including the interest of a seller or purchaser under a contract for the sale of the asset, when the transfer is so far perfected that a good-faith purchaser of the asset from the debtor against whom applicable law permits the transfer to be perfected cannot acquire an interest in the asset that is superior to the interest of the transferee; and

b. With respect to an asset that is not real property or that is a fixture, when the transfer is so far perfected that a creditor on a simple contract cannot acquire a judicial lien otherwise than under this Article that is superior to the interest of the transferee.

(2) If applicable law permits the transfer to be perfected as provided in subdivision (1) of this section and the transfer is not so perfected before the

commencement of an action for relief under this Article, the transfer is deemed made immediately before the commencement of the action.

(3) If applicable law does not permit the transfer to be perfected as provided in subdivision (1) of this section, the transfer is made when it becomes effective between the debtor and the transferee.

(4) A transfer is not made until the debtor has acquired rights in the asset transferred.

(5) An obligation is incurred:

a. If oral, when it becomes effective between the parties; or

b. If evidenced by a writing, when the writing executed by the obligor is delivered to or for the benefit of the obligee. (1997-291, s. 2.)

§ 39-23.7. Remedies of creditors.

(a) In an action for relief against a transfer or obligation under this Article, a creditor, subject to the limitations in G.S. 39-23.8, may obtain:

(1) Avoidance of the transfer or obligation to the extent necessary to satisfy the creditor's claim;

(2) An attachment or other provisional remedy against the asset transferred or other property of the transferee in accordance with the procedure prescribed by Article 35 of Chapter 1 of the General Statutes;

(3) Subject to applicable principles of equity and in accordance with applicable rules of civil procedure,

a. An injunction against further disposition by the debtor or a transferee, or both, of the asset transferred or of other property;

b. Appointment of a receiver to take charge of the asset transferred or of other property of the transferee; or

c. Any other relief the circumstances may require.

(b) If a creditor has obtained a judgment on a claim against the debtor, the creditor, if the court so orders, may levy execution on the asset transferred or its proceeds. (1997-291, s. 2.)

§ 39-23.8. Defenses, liability, and protection of transferee.

(a) A transfer or obligation is not voidable under G.S. 39-23.4(a)(1) against a person who took in good faith and for a reasonably equivalent value or against any subsequent transferee or obligee.

(b) Except as otherwise provided in this section, to the extent a transfer is voidable in an action by a creditor under G.S. 39-23.7(a)(1), the creditor may recover judgment for the value of the asset transferred, as adjusted under subsection (c) of this section, or the amount necessary to satisfy the creditor's claim, whichever is less. The judgment may be entered against:

(1) The first transferee of the asset or the person for whose benefit the transfer was made; or

(2) Any subsequent transferee other than a good-faith transferee who took for value or from any subsequent transferee.

(c) If the judgment under subsection (b) of this section is based upon the value of the asset transferred, the judgment shall be for an amount equal to the value of the asset at the time of the transfer, subject to adjustment as the equities may require.

(d) Notwithstanding voidability of a transfer or an obligation under this Article, a good-faith transferee or obligee is entitled, to the extent of the value given the debtor for the transfer or obligation, to:

(1) A lien on or a right to retain any interest in the asset transferred;

(2) Enforcement of any obligation incurred; or

(3) A reduction in the amount of the liability on the judgment.

(e) A transfer is not voidable under G.S. 39-23.4(a)(2) or G.S. 39-23.5 if the transfer results from:

(1) Termination of a lease upon default by the debtor when the termination is pursuant to the lease and applicable law; or

(2) Enforcement of a security interest in compliance with Article 9 of Chapter 25 of the General Statutes, the Uniform Commercial Code.

(f) A transfer is not voidable under G.S. 39-23.5(b):

(1) To the extent the insider gave new value to or for the benefit of the debtor after the transfer was made unless the new value was secured by a valid lien;

(2) If made in the ordinary course of business or financial affairs of the debtor and the insider; or

(3) If made pursuant to a good-faith effort to rehabilitate the debtor, and the transfer secured present value given for that purpose as well as an antecedent debt of the debtor. (1997-291, s. 2.)

§ 39-23.9. Extinguishment of cause of action.

A cause of action with respect to a fraudulent or voidable transfer or obligation under this Article is extinguished unless action is brought:

(1) Under G.S. 39-23.4(a)(1), within four years after the transfer was made or the obligation was incurred or, if later, within one year after the transfer or obligation was or could reasonably have been discovered by the claimant;

(2) Under G.S. 39-23.4(a)(2) or G.S. 39-23.5(a), within four years after the transfer was made or the obligation was incurred; or

(3) Under G.S. 39-23.5(b), within one year after the transfer was made or the obligation was incurred. (1997-291, s. 2.)

§ 39-23.10. Supplementary provisions.

Unless displaced by the provisions of this Article, the principles of law and equity, including the law merchant and the law relating to principal and agent, estoppel, laches, fraud, misrepresentation, duress, coercion, mistake, insolvency, or other validating or invalidating cause, supplement its provisions. (1997-291, s. 2.)

§ 39-23.11. Uniformity of application and construction.

This act shall be applied and construed to effectuate its general purpose to make uniform the law with respect to the subject of this Article among states enacting it. (1997-291, s. 2.)

§ 39-23.12. Short title.

This Article may be cited as the Uniform Fraudulent Transfer Act. (1997-291, s. 2.)

Article 4.

Voluntary Organizations and Associations.

§§ 39-24, 39-25: Repealed by Session Laws 2006-226, s. 2(a), effective January 1, 2007.

§ 39-26: Recodified as G.S. 59B-15(a) by Session Laws 2006-226, s. 2(b), effective January 1, 2007.

§ 39-27: Recodified as G.S. 59B-15(b) by Session Laws 2006-226, s. 2(b), effective January 1, 2007.

Article 5.

Sale of Building Lots in North Carolina.

§§ 39-28 through 39-32: Repealed by Session Laws 1981, c. 358.

Article 5A.

Control Corners in Real Estate Developments.

§ 39-32.1. Requirement of permanent markers as "control corners."

Whenever any person, firm or corporation shall hereafter divide any parcel of real estate into lots and lay off streets through such real estate development and sell or offer for sale any lot or lots in such real estate development, it shall be the duty of such person, firm or corporation to cause one or more corners of such development to be designated as "control corner" and shall cause two or more street center lines or offset lines within or on the street right-of-way lines to be permanently monumented at intersecting center lines or offset lines, points of curvature or such other control points, which monuments shall also be designated as control corners and to affix or place at such control corner or corners permanent markers which shall be of such material and affixed to the earth in such a manner as to insure as great a degree of permanence as is reasonably practical. (1947, c. 816, s. 1; 1959, c. 1159.)

§ 39-32.2. Control corners fixed at time of recording plat or prior to sale.

Such control corner or corners, as described in G.S. 39-32.1, and such permanent marker or markers, as described in G.S. 39-32.1, must be designated and affixed at the time of recording the plat of said land or prior to the first sale of any lot or lots constituting a part of the real estate development which said person, firm or corporation has caused to be laid off in lots with designated streets. (1947, c. 816, s. 2.)

§ 39-32.3. Recordation of plat showing control corners.

Upon designating a control corner and affixing a permanent marker, said person, firm or corporation shall cause to be filed in the office of the register of deeds of the county in which the real estate development is located a map or plat showing the location of the control corner or corners and permanent marker or markers with adequate and sufficient description to enable a surveyor to locate such control corner or marker. No map or plat of a real estate subdivision or development made after July 1, 1947, shall be certified for recording pursuant to G.S 47-30.2 unless the location of control corners is shown thereon. (1947, c. 816, s. 3; 1997-309, s. 1.)

§ 39-32.4. Description of land by reference to control corner; use of control corner to fix distances and boundaries prima facie evidence of correct method.

Any lot or lots sold or otherwise transferred at the time of or subsequent to the establishment of a control corner may be described in any conveyance so as to include a reference to the location of said lot or lots which are being conveyed with respect to the control corner. Thereafter the use of the control corner in ascertaining distances so as to establish boundary lines of lots within or originally within such real estate development may be admissible as evidence in any court and shall be prima facie evidence of the correct method of determining the boundaries of any lot or lots within any such real estate development. (1947, c. 816, s. 4.)

Article 6.

Power of Appointment.

§ 39-33. Method of release or limitation of power.

A release or limitation of a power of appointment with respect to real or personal property exercisable by deed or will or otherwise may be effected, if such power may be released or limited under the laws of this State, by the execution by the holder of such power of an instrument in writing stating that the power is released or limited to the extent set forth therein, and the delivery of such instrument to any person who might be adversely affected if such power were exercised or to the fiduciary or one of the fiduciaries, if any, having possession or control of the property over which the power is exercisable. (1943, c. 665, s. 1.)

§ 39-34. Method prescribed in § 39-33 not exclusive.

The method of release prescribed in G.S. 39-33 is not exclusive, and this Article shall not invalidate or be construed to invalidate any instrument or contract of release or limitation of a power not executed and delivered in the manner provided in G.S. 39-33 or as invalidating any other act of release or limitation of a power, whether such instrument, contract or act has been heretofore or may be hereafter executed, delivered or done. (1943, c. 665, s. 2.)

§ 39-35. Requisites of release or limitation as against creditors and purchasers for value.

No release or limitation of a power of appointment after March 8, 1943, which is made by the owner of the legal title to real property in this State shall be valid as against creditors and purchasers for a valuable consideration until an instrument in writing setting forth the release or limitation is executed and acknowledged in the manner required for a deed and recorded in the county where the real property is. (1943, c. 665, s. 3.)

§ 39-36. Necessity for actual notice of release or limitation to bind fiduciary.

No fiduciary having possession or control of property over which a power of appointment is exercisable shall be bound or affected by any release or limitation of such power without actual notice thereof. (1943, c. 665, s. 4.)

Article 7.

Uniform Vendor and Purchaser Risk Act.

§ 39-37. Short title.

This Article may be cited as the Uniform Vendor and Purchaser Risk Act. (1959, c. 514.)

§ 39-38. Uniformity of interpretation.

This Article shall be so interpreted and construed as to effectuate its general purpose to make uniform the law of those states which enact it. (1959, c. 514.)

§ 39-39. Risk of loss.

Any contract hereafter made in this State for the purchase and sale of realty shall be interpreted as including an agreement that the parties shall have the following rights and duties, unless the contract expressly provides otherwise:

(1) If, when neither the legal title nor the possession of the subject matter of the contract has been transferred, all or a material part thereof is destroyed without fault of the purchaser, the vendor cannot enforce the contract, and the purchaser is entitled to recover any portion of the price that he has paid;

(2) If, when either the legal title or the possession of the subject matter of the contract has been transferred, all or any part thereof is destroyed without fault of the vendor, the purchaser is not thereby relieved from a duty to pay the price, nor is he entitled to recover any portion thereof that he has paid. (1959, c. 514.)

§ 39-40. Reserved for future codification purposes.

§ 39-41. Reserved for future codification purposes.

§ 39-42. Reserved for future codification purposes.

§ 39-43. Reserved for future codification purposes.

Article 8.

Business Trusts.

§ 39-44. Definition.

The term "business trust" whenever used or referred to in this Article shall mean any unincorporated association, including an Illinois land trust, a Delaware statutory trust, or a Massachusetts business trust, engaged in any business or trade under a written instrument or declaration of trust under which the beneficial interest therein is divided into shares represented by certificates or shares of beneficial interest. (1977, c. 768, s. 1; 2009-174, s. 1.)

§ 39-45. Authority to acquire and hold real estate.

Business trusts are hereby authorized and empowered to acquire real estate and interests therein and to hold the same in their trust names and may sue and be sued in their trust names. (1977, c. 768, s. 1.)

§ 39-46. Title vested; conveyance; probate.

(a) Where real estate has been or may be hereafter conveyed to a business trust in its trust name or in the names of its trustees in their capacity as trustees of such business trust, the said title shall vest in said business trust, and the said real estate and interests therein may be conveyed, encumbered or otherwise disposed of by said business trust in its trust name by an instrument signed by at least one of its trustees, its president, a vice-president or other duly authorized officer, the said conveyance to be proven and probated in the same manner as provided by law for conveyances by corporations. Any conveyance, encumbrance or other disposition thus made by any such business trust shall convey good and sufficient title to said real estate and interests therein in accordance with the provisions of said conveyance; provided, however, that with respect to any such conveyance, encumbrance or other disposition effected after June 28, 1977, there must be recorded in the county where the land lies a memorandum of the written instrument or declaration of trust referred to in G.S. 39-44. As a minimum such memorandum shall set forth the name, date and place of filing, if any, of such written instrument or declaration of trust, and the place where the written instrument or declaration of trust, and all amendments thereto, is kept and may be examined upon reasonable notice, which place need not be a public office. Such memorandum may include designation of trustees and duly authorized officers and the authority granted to them with regard to real estate matters, pursuant to subsection (b) of this section.

(b)   Any business trust may convey or encumber an interest in real property that is transferable by either (i) an instrument duly executed by either an officer of the business trust other than one of its trustees, its president, a vice president, or other authorized agent identified in the recorded memorandum, or (ii) a declaration of trust described in subsection (a) of this section, if the conveyance has attached to it a signed resolution adopted by the board of trustees, as certified by an officer authorized to make such certifications of the business trust, authorizing the officer to execute, sign, seal, and deliver deeds, conveyances, or other instruments. This section is deemed to have been complied with if a resolution required by this subsection is recorded separately in the office of the register of deeds in the county where the land lies. Such a resolution shall be applicable to all instruments executed subsequently to the recording of the resolution and pursuant to its authority.

Notwithstanding the foregoing, this section does not require a signed resolution adopted by the board of directors, as certified by an officer authorized to make such certifications, to be attached to an instrument or separately recorded in the case of an instrument duly executed by one of its trustees, its president, or a vice president of the business trust. All deeds, conveyances, or other instruments so executed shall, if otherwise sufficient, be valid and shall have the effect to pass the title to the real or personal property described in the instrument. Notwithstanding anything to the contrary in the trust agreement, and absent any provision otherwise in the recorded memorandum or declaration of trust required under subsection (a) of this section, when it appears on the face of an instrument registered in the office of the register of deeds that the instrument was signed in the ordinary course of business on behalf of a business trust by at least one of its trustees, its president, a vice president, or an assistant vice president, such an instrument shall be as valid with respect to the rights of innocent third parties for value without notice of a defect or breach of fiduciary duty as if executed pursuant to authorization from the board of trustees, unless the instrument reveals on its face a breach of fiduciary obligation. The provisions of this subsection shall not apply to parties who had actual knowledge of lack of authority or of a breach of fiduciary obligation.

(c) Nothing in this section shall be deemed to exclude the power of any representatives of a business trust to bind the business trust pursuant to express, implied, inherent, or apparent authority, ratification, estoppel, or otherwise.

(d) Nothing in this section shall relieve trustees or officers of a business trust from liability to the business trust or from any other liability that they may have incurred from any violation of their actual authority. (1977, c. 768, s. 1; 2009-174, s. 2.)

§ 39-47. Prior deeds validated.

All deeds, leases, mortgages, deeds of trust or other conveyances heretofore executed in conformity with this Article and which are proper in all other respects are declared to be sufficient to pass title to real estate held by such business trusts in accordance with the provisions of such instruments. (1977, c. 768, s. 1.)

§ 39-48. Reserved for future codification purposes.

§ 39-49. Reserved for future codification purposes.

Article 9.

Disclosure.

§ 39-50. Death, illness, or conviction of certain crimes not a material fact.

In offering real property for sale it shall not be deemed a material fact that the real property was occupied previously by a person who died or had a serious illness while occupying the property or that a person convicted of any crime for which registration is required by Article 27A of Chapter 14 of the General Statutes occupies, occupied, or resides near the property; provided, however, that no seller may knowingly make a false statement regarding any such fact. (1989, c. 592, s. 1; 1998-212, s. 17.16A(a).)

Article 9.

Disclosure.

§§ 39-51 through 39-59: Reserved for future codification purposes.

Article 10.

Real Property Tax Proration.

§ 39-60. Property tax proration on sale of real property.

Unless otherwise provided by contract, property taxes on the real property being sold shall be prorated between the seller and buyer of the real property on a calendar-year basis. (2006-106, s. 7.)

Chapter 39A.

Transfer Fee Covenants Prohibited.

§ 39A-1. Public policy.

(a) The public policy of this State favors the marketability of real property and the transferability of interests in real property free from title defects, unreasonable restraints on alienation, and covenants or servitudes that do not touch and concern the property.

(b) A transfer fee covenant violates this public policy by impairing the marketability of title to the affected real property and constitutes an unreasonable restraint on alienation and transferability of property, regardless of the duration of the covenant or the amount of the transfer fee set forth in the covenant. (2010-32, s. 1.)

§ 39A-2. Definitions.

As used in this Chapter:

(1) "Transfer" means the sale, gift, conveyance, assignment, inheritance, or other transfer of an ownership interest in real property located in this State.

(2) "Transfer fee" means a fee or charge payable upon the transfer of an interest in real property or payable for the right to make or accept such transfer, regardless of whether the fee or charge is a fixed amount or is determined as a percentage of the value of the property, the purchase price, or other consideration given for the transfer. The following shall not be considered a "transfer fee" for the purposes of this Chapter:

a. Any consideration payable by the grantee to the grantor for the interest in real property being transferred, including any subsequent additional consideration for the property payable by the grantee based upon any subsequent appreciation, development, or sale of the property that, once paid, shall not bind successors in title to the property.

b. Any commission payable to a licensed real estate broker for the transfer of real property pursuant to an agreement between the broker and the transferor or transferee, including any subsequent additional commission for the transfer payable by the transferor or the transferee based upon any subsequent additional commission payable by the transferor based upon any subsequent appreciation, development, or sale of the property.

c. Any interest, charges, fees, or other amounts payable by a borrower to a lender pursuant to a loan secured by a mortgage against real property, including any fee payable to the lender for consenting to an assumption of the loan or a transfer of the real property subject to the mortgage, any fees or charges payable to the lender for estoppel letters or certificates, and any other consideration allowed by law and payable to the lender in connection with the loan.

d. Any rent, reimbursement, charge, fee, or other amount payable by a lessee to a lessor under a lease, including any fee payable to the lessor for consenting to an assignment, subletting, encumbrance, or transfer of the lease.

e. Any consideration payable to the holder of an option to purchase an interest in real property or the holder of a right of first refusal or first offer to purchase an interest in real property for waiving, releasing, or not exercising the option or right upon the transfer of the property to another person.

f. Any tax, fee, charge, assessment, fine, or other amount payable to or imposed by a governmental authority.

g. Any fee charged that is a typical real estate closing cost, including closing or escrow fees, settlement fees, attorney fees, or title insurance premiums and fees.

h. Any reasonable fee charged for the preparation of statements of unpaid assessments pursuant to G.S. 47F-3-102(13) or resale certificates or statements of unpaid assessments pursuant to G.S. 47C-3-102(12).

i. Any reasonable fee payable by the original transferee to a unit owners' association as defined in G.S. 47C-1-103(3), or owners' association as defined in G.S. 47F-1-103(3), as long as no portion of the fee is required to be passed through to a third party designated or identifiable by description in the document or another document referenced therein.

j. Any fee payable as part of a conservation or preservation agreement as provided in G.S. 121-38(e).

(3) "Transfer fee covenant" means a declaration or covenant purporting to affect real property that requires or purports to require the payment of a transfer fee to the declarant or other person specified in the declaration or covenant or to

their successors or assigns, upon a subsequent transfer of an interest in the real property. (2010-32, s. 1.)

§ 39A-3. Transfer fee covenants prohibited.

(a) Any transfer fee covenant or any lien that is filed to enforce a transfer fee covenant or purports to secure payment of a transfer fee, shall not run with the title to real property and is not binding on or enforceable at law or in equity against any subsequent owner, purchaser, or mortgagee of any interest in real property as an equitable servitude or otherwise.

(b) A person who records a transfer fee covenant, files a lien that purports to secure payment of a transfer fee, or enters into an agreement imposing a private transfer fee obligation shall be liable for:

(1) Any and all damages resulting from the imposition of the transfer fee obligation on the transfer of an interest in the real property, including the amount of any transfer fee paid by a party to the transfer.

(2) All attorney fees, expenses, and costs incurred by a party to the transfer or mortgagee of the real property to recover the transfer fee paid or in connection with an action to quiet title or register the title or a proceeding subsequent to initial registration. If an agent acts on behalf of a principal to file or secure a private transfer fee obligation, liability shall be assessed to the principal, but not to the agent. (2010-32, s. 1.)

§§ 40-1 through 40-53: Repealed by Session Laws 1981, c. 919, s. 1.

Chapter 40A.

Eminent Domain.

Article 1.

General.

§ 40A-1. Exclusive provisions.

(a) Notwithstanding the provisions of any local act, it is the intent of the General Assembly that, effective August 15, 2006, the uses set out in G.S. 40A-3 are the exclusive uses for which the authority to exercise the power of eminent domain is granted to private condemnors, local public condemnors, and other public condemnors. Effective August 15, 2006, a local act granting the authority to exercise the power of eminent domain to a private condemnor, local public condemnor, or other public condemnor for a use or purpose other than those granted to it in G.S. 40A-3(a), (b), (b1), or (c) is not effective for that use or purpose. Provided that, any eminent domain action commenced before August 15, 2006, for a use or purpose granted in a local act, may be lawfully completed pursuant to the provisions of that local act. The provisions of this subsection shall not repeal any provision of a local act limiting the purposes for which the authority to exercise the power of eminent domain may be used.

(b) It is the intent of the General Assembly that the procedures provided by this Chapter shall be the exclusive condemnation procedures to be used in this State by all private condemnors and all local public condemnors. All other provisions in laws, charters, or local acts authorizing the use of other procedures by municipal or county governments or agencies or political subdivisions thereof, or by corporations, associations or other persons are hereby repealed effective January 1, 1982. Provided, that any condemnation proceeding initiated prior to January 1, 1982, may be lawfully completed pursuant to the provisions previously existing.

(c) This Chapter shall not repeal any provision of a local act limiting the purposes for which property may be condemned. Notwithstanding the language of G.S. 40A-3(b), this Chapter also shall not repeal any provision of a local act creating any substantive or procedural requirement or limitation on the authority of a local public condemnor to exercise the power of eminent domain outside of its boundaries. (1981, c. 919, s. 1; 2006-224, s. 1; 2006-259, s. 47.)

§ 40A-2. Definitions.

As used in this Chapter the following words and phrases have the meanings indicated unless the context clearly requires another meaning:

(1) "Condemnation" means the procedure prescribed by law for exercising the power of eminent domain.

(2) "Condemnor" means those listed in G.S. 40A-3.

(3) "Eminent domain" means the power to divest right, title or interest from the owner of property and vest it in the possessor of the power against the will of the owner upon the payment of just compensation for the right, title or interest divested.

(4) "Judge" means a resident judge of the superior court in the district where the cause is pending, or special judge residing in said district, or a judge of the superior court assigned to hold the courts of said district or an emergency or special judge holding court in the county where the cause is pending.

(5) "Owner" includes the plural when appropriate and means any person having an interest or estate in the property.

(6) "Person" includes the plural when appropriate and means a natural person, and any legal entity capable of owning or having interest in property.

(7) "Property" means any right, title, or interest in land, including leases and options to buy or sell. "Property" also includes rights of access, rights-of-way, easements, water rights, air rights, and any other privilege or appurtenance in or to the possession, use, and enjoyment of land. (1981, c. 919, s. 1.)

§ 40A-3. By whom right may be exercised.

(a) Private Condemnors. - For the public use or benefit, the persons or organizations listed below shall have the power of eminent domain and may acquire by purchase or condemnation property for the stated purposes and other works which are authorized by law.

(1) Corporations, bodies politic or persons have the power of eminent domain for the construction of railroads, power generating facilities, substations, switching stations, microwave towers, roads, alleys, access railroads, turnpikes, street railroads, plank roads, tramroads, canals, telegraphs, telephones, electric power lines, electric lights, public water supplies, public sewerage systems, flumes, bridges, and pipelines or mains originating in North Carolina for the transportation of petroleum products, coal, gas, limestone or minerals. Land condemned for any liquid pipelines shall:

a. Not be less than 50 feet nor more than 100 feet in width; and

b. Comply with the provisions of G.S. 62-190(b).

The width of land condemned for any natural gas pipelines shall not be more than 100 feet.

(2) School committees or boards of trustees or of directors of any corporation holding title to real estate upon which any private educational institution is situated, have the power of eminent domain in order to obtain a pure and adequate water supply for such institution.

(3) Franchised motor vehicle carriers or union bus station companies organized by authority of the Utilities Commission, have the power of eminent domain for the purpose of constructing and operating union bus stations: Provided, that this subdivision shall not apply to any city or town having a population of less than 60,000.

(4) Any railroad company has the power of eminent domain for the purposes of: constructing union depots; maintaining, operating, improving or straightening lines or of altering its location; constructing double tracks; constructing and maintaining new yards and terminal facilities or enlarging its yard or terminal facilities; connecting two of its lines already in operation not more than six miles apart; or constructing an industrial siding.

(5) A condemnation in fee simple by a State-owned railroad company for the purposes specified in subdivision (4) of this subsection and as provided under G.S. 124-12(2).

The width of land condemned for any single or double track railroad purpose shall be not less than 80 feet nor more than 100 feet, except where the road may run through a town, where it may be of less width, or where there may be deep cuts or high embankments, where it may be of greater width.

No rights granted or acquired under this subsection shall in any way destroy or abridge the rights of the State to regulate or control any railroad company or to regulate foreign corporations doing business in this State. Whenever it is necessary for any railroad company doing business in this State to cross the street or streets in a town or city in order to carry out the orders of the Utilities Commission, to construct an industrial siding, the power is hereby conferred upon such railroad company to occupy such street or streets of any such town or city within the State. Provided, license so to do be first obtained from the board of aldermen, board of commissioners, or other governing authorities of such town or city.

No such condemnor shall be allowed to have condemned to its use, without the consent of the owner, his burial ground, usual dwelling house and yard, kitchen and garden, unless condemnation of such property is expressly authorized by statute.

The power of eminent domain shall be exercised by private condemnors under the procedures of Article 2 of this Chapter.

(b)   Local Public Condemnors - Standard Provision. - For the public use or benefit, the governing body of each municipality or county shall possess the power of eminent domain and may acquire by purchase, gift or condemnation any property, either inside or outside its boundaries, for the following purposes.

(1)   Opening, widening, extending, or improving roads, streets, alleys, and sidewalks. The authority contained in this subsection is in addition to the authority to acquire rights-of-way for streets, sidewalks and highways under Article 9 of Chapter 136. The provisions of this subdivision (1) shall not apply to counties.

(2)   Establishing, extending, enlarging, or improving any of the public enterprises listed in G.S. 160A-311 for cities, or G.S. 153A-274 for counties.

(3)   Establishing, enlarging, or improving parks, playgrounds, and other recreational facilities.

(4)   Establishing, extending, enlarging, or improving storm sewer and drainage systems and works, or sewer and septic tank lines and systems.

(5)   Establishing, enlarging, or improving hospital facilities, cemeteries, or library facilities.

(6)   Constructing, enlarging, or improving city halls, fire stations, office buildings, courthouse jails and other buildings for use by any department, board, commission or agency.

(7)   Establishing drainage programs and programs to prevent obstructions to the natural flow of streams, creeks and natural water channels or improving

drainage facilities. The authority contained in this subdivision is in addition to any authority contained in Chapter 156.

(8) Acquiring designated historic properties, designated as such before October 1, 1989, or acquiring a designated landmark designated as such on or after October 1, 1989, for which an application has been made for a certificate of appropriateness for demolition, in pursuance of the purposes of G.S. 160A-399.3, Chapter 160A, Article 19, Part 3B, effective until October 1, 1989, or G.S. 160A-400.14, whichever is appropriate.

(9) Opening, widening, extending, or improving public wharves.

The board of education of any municipality or county or a combined board may exercise the power of eminent domain under this Chapter for purposes authorized by Chapter 115C of the General Statutes.

The power of eminent domain shall be exercised by local public condemnors under the procedures of Article 3 of this Chapter.

(b1) Local Public Condemnors - Modified Provision for Certain Localities. - For the public use or benefit, the governing body of each municipality or county shall possess the power of eminent domain and may acquire by purchase, gift or condemnation any property or interest therein, either inside or outside its boundaries, for the following purposes.

(1) Opening, widening, extending, or improving roads, streets, alleys, and sidewalks. The authority contained in this subsection is in addition to the authority to acquire rights-of-way for streets, sidewalks and highways under Article 9 of Chapter 136. The provisions of this subdivision (1) shall not apply to counties.

(2) Establishing, extending, enlarging, or improving any of the public enterprises listed in G.S. 160A-311 for cities, or G.S. 153A-274 for counties.

(3) Establishing, enlarging, or improving parks, playgrounds, and other recreational facilities.

(4) Establishing, extending, enlarging, or improving storm sewer and drainage systems and works, or sewer and septic tank lines and systems.

(5) Establishing, enlarging, or improving hospital facilities, cemeteries, or library facilities.

(6) Constructing, enlarging, or improving city halls, fire stations, office buildings, courthouse jails and other buildings for use by any department, board, commission or agency.

(7) Establishing drainage programs and programs to prevent obstructions to the natural flow of streams, creeks and natural water channels or improving drainage facilities. The authority contained in this subdivision is in addition to any authority contained in Chapter 156.

(8) Acquiring designated historic properties, designated as such before October 1, 1989, or acquiring a designated landmark designated as such on or after October 1, 1989, for which an application has been made for a certificate of appropriateness for demolition, in pursuance of the purposes of G.S. 160A-399.3, Chapter 160A, Article 19, Part 3, effective until October 1, 1989, or G.S. 160A-400.14, whichever is appropriate.

(9) Opening, widening, extending, or improving public wharves.

(10) Engaging in or participating with other governmental entities in acquiring, constructing, reconstructing, extending, or otherwise building or improving beach erosion control or flood and hurricane protection works, including, but not limited to, the acquisition of any property that may be required as a source for beach renourishment.

(11) Establishing access for the public to public trust beaches and appurtenant parking areas.

The board of education of any municipality or county or a combined board may exercise the power of eminent domain under this Chapter for purposes authorized by Chapter 115C of the General Statutes.

The power of eminent domain shall be exercised by local public condemnors under the procedures of Article 3 of this chapter.

This subsection applies only to Carteret and Dare Counties, the Towns of Atlantic Beach, Carolina Beach, Caswell Beach, Emerald Isle, Holden Beach, Indian Beach, Kill Devil Hills, Kitty Hawk, Kure Beach, Nags Head, North Topsail Beach, Oak Island, Ocean Isle Beach, Pine Knoll Shores, Sunset Beach, Surf

City, Topsail Beach, and Wrightsville Beach, and the Village of Bald Head Island.

(c) Other Public Condemnors. - For the public use or benefit, the following political entities shall possess the power of eminent domain and may acquire property by purchase, gift, or condemnation for the stated purposes.

(1) A sanitary district board established under the provisions of Part 2 of Article 2 of Chapter 130A for the purposes stated in that Part.

(2) The board of commissioners of a mosquito control district established under the provisions of Part 2 of Article 12 of Chapter 130A for the purposes stated in that Part.

(3) A hospital authority established under the provisions of Part B of Article 2 of Chapter 131E for the purposes stated in that Part, provided, however, that the provisions of G.S. 131E-24(c) shall continue to apply.

(4) A watershed improvement district established under the provisions of Article 2 of Chapter 139 for the purposes stated in that Article, provided, however, that the provisions of G.S. 139-38 shall continue to apply.

(5) A housing authority established under the provisions of Article 1 of Chapter 157 for the purposes of that Article, provided, however, that the provisions of G.S. 157-11 shall continue to apply.

(6) A corporation as defined in G.S. 157-50 for the purposes of Article 3 of Chapter 157, provided, however, the provisions of G.S. 157-50 shall continue to apply.

(7) A commission established under the provisions of Article 22 of Chapter 160A for the purposes of that Article.

(8) An authority created under the provisions of Article 1 of Chapter 162A for the purposes of that Article.

(9) A district established under the provisions of Article 4 of Chapter 162A for the purposes of that Article.

(10) A district established under the provisions of Article 5 of Chapter 162A for purposes of that Article.

(11) The board of trustees of a community college established under the provisions of Article 2 of Chapter 115D for the purposes of that Article.

(12) A district established under the provisions of Article 6 of Chapter 162A for the purposes of that Article.

(13) A regional public transportation authority established under Article 26 of Chapter 160A of the General Statutes for the purposes of that Article.

The power of eminent domain shall be exercised by a public condemnor listed in this subsection under the procedures of Article 3 of this Chapter. (1852, c. 92, s. 1; R.C., c. 61, s. 9; 1874-5, c. 83; Code, s. 1698; Rev., s. 2575; 1907, cc. 39, 458, 783; 1911, c. 62, ss. 25, 26, 27; 1917, cc. 51, 132; C.S., s. 1706; 1923, c. 205; Ex. Sess. 1924, c. 118; 1937, c. 108, s. 1; 1939, c. 228, s. 4; 1941, c. 254; 1947, c. 806; 1951, c. 1002, ss. 1, 2; 1953, c. 1211; 1957, c. 65, s. 11; c. 1045, s. 1; 1961, c. 247; 1973, c. 507, s. 5; c. 1262, s. 86; 1977, c. 771, s. 4; 1981, c. 919, s. 1; 1983, c. 378, s. 2; 1983 (Reg. Sess., 1984), c. 1084; 1985, c. 689, s. 10; c. 696, s. 2; 1987, c. 2, s. 1; c. 564, s. 13; c. 783, s. 6; 1989, c. 706, s. 3; c. 740, s. 1.1; 2000-146, s. 8; 2001-36, ss. 1, 3; 2001-478, s. 2; 2001-487, s. 58; 2002-172, s. 4.1; 2003-282, ss. 1, 2; 2004-203, s. 32(a), (b); 2006-224, s. 2; 2006-259, s. 47.)

§ 40A-4. No prior purchase offer necessary.

The power to acquire property by condemnation shall not depend on any prior effort to acquire the same property by gift or purchase, nor shall the power to negotiate for the gift or purchase of property be impaired by initiation of condemnation proceedings. A potential condemnor who seeks to acquire property by gift or purchase shall give the owner written notice of the provisions of G.S. 40A-6. (1981, c. 919, s. 1; 1997-270, s. 4.)

§ 40A-5. Condemnation of property owned by other condemnors.

(a) A condemnor listed in G.S. 40A-3(a), (b) or (c) shall not possess the power of eminent domain with respect to property owned by the State of North Carolina or a State-owned railroad as defined in G.S. 124-11 unless the State consents to the taking. The State's consent shall be given by the Council of State, or by the Secretary of Administration if the Council of State delegates this authority to the Secretary. In a condemnation proceeding against State property consented to by the State, the only issue shall be the compensation to be paid for the property.

(b) Unless otherwise provided by statute a condemnor listed in G.S. 40A-3(a), (b) or (c) may condemn the property of a private condemnor if such property is not in actual public use or not necessary to the operation of the business of the owner. Unless otherwise provided by statute a condemnor listed in G.S. 40A-3(b) or (c) may condemn the property of a condemnor listed in G.S. 40A-3(b) or (c) if the property proposed to be taken is not being used or held for future use for any governmental or proprietary purpose. (1981, c. 919, s. 1; 2000-146, s. 9.)

§ 40A-6. Reimbursement of owner for taxes paid on condemned property.

(a) An owner whose property is totally taken in fee simple by a condemnor exercising the power of eminent domain, under this Chapter or any other statute, shall be entitled to reimbursement from the condemnor of the pro rata portion of real property taxes paid by the owner that are allocable to a period subsequent to vesting of title in the condemnor, or the effective date of possession of the real property, whichever is earlier.

(b) An owner who meets the following conditions is entitled to reimbursement from the condemnor for all deferred taxes paid by the owner pursuant to G.S. 105-277.4(c) as a result of the condemnation:

(1) The owner is a natural person whose property is taken in fee simple by a condemnor exercising the power of eminent domain under this Chapter or any other statute.

(2) The owner also owns agricultural land, horticultural land, or forestland that is contiguous to the condemned property and that is in active production.

The definitions in G.S. 105-277.2 apply in this subsection. (1975, c. 439, s. 1; 1981, c. 919, s. 1; 1997-270, s. 1.)

§ 40A-7. Acquisition of whole parcel or building.

(a) When the proposed project requires condemnation of only a portion of a parcel of land leaving a remainder of such shape, size or condition that it is of little value, a condemnor may acquire the entire parcel by purchase or condemnation. If the remainder is to be condemned the petition filed under the provisions of G.S. 40A-20 or the complaint filed under the provisions of G.S. 40A-41 shall include:

(1) A determination by the condemnor that a partial taking of the land would substantially destroy the economic value or utility of the remainder; or

(2) A determination by the condemnor that an economy in the expenditure of public funds will be promoted by taking the entire parcel; or

(3) A determination by the condemnor that the interest of the public will be best served by acquiring the entire parcel.

(b) Residues acquired under this section may be sold or disposed of in any manner provided for the disposition of property, or may be exchanged for other property needed by the condemnor.

(c) When the proposed project requires condemnation of a portion of a building or other structure, the condemnor may acquire the entire building or structure by purchase or condemnation, together with the right to enter upon the surrounding land for the purpose of removing the building or structure. If the entire building is to be condemned the petition filed under the provisions of G.S. 40A-20, or the complaint filed under the provisions of G.S. 40A-41 shall include a determination by the condemnor either:

(1) That an economy in the expenditure of public funds will be promoted by acquiring the entire building or structure; or

(2) That it is not feasible to cut off a portion of the building or structure without destroying the whole; or

(3) That the convenience, safety, or improvement of the project will be promoted by acquiring the entire building or structure. Nothing in this subsection shall be deemed to compel the condemnor to condemn the underlying fee of the

portion of any building or structure that lies outside the project. (1981, c. 919, s. 1.)

§ 40A-8. Costs.

(a)   In any action under the provisions of Article 2 or Article 3 of this Chapter, the court in its discretion may award to the owner a sum to reimburse the owner for charges he has paid for appraisers, engineers and plats, provided such appraisers or engineers testify as witnesses, and such plats are received into evidence as exhibits by order of the court.

(b)   If a condemnor institutes a proceeding to acquire by condemnation any property and (i) if the final judgment in a resulting action is that the condemnor is not authorized to condemn the property, or (ii) if the condemnor abandons the action, the court with jurisdiction over the action shall after making appropriate findings of fact award each owner of the property sought to be condemned a sum that, in the opinion of the court based upon its findings of fact, will reimburse the owner for: his reasonable costs; disbursements; expenses (including reasonable attorney, appraisal, and engineering fees); and, any loss suffered by the owner because he was unable to transfer title to the property from the date of the filing of the complaint under G.S. 40A-41.

(c)   If an action is brought against a condemnor under the provisions of G.S. 40A-20 or 40A-51 seeking compensation for the taking of any interest in property by the condemnor and judgment is for the owner the court shall award to the owner as a part of the judgment after appropriate finding of fact a sum that, in the opinion of the court based upon its finding of fact, will reimburse the owner as set out in subsection (b). (1981, c. 919, s. 1.)

§ 40A-9. Removal of structures on condemned land; lien.

At the request of the owner the condemnor shall allow the owner of property acquired by condemnation to remove any timber, building, permanent improvement, or fixture wholly or partially located on or affixed to the property unless such removal would be inconsistent with the purpose for which condemnation is made, and shall specify a reasonable time within which it may be removed. If the report of the commissioners deducted the value of any such property to be removed from the award of compensation and allowed the cost of removal as an element of damages and the owner fails to remove it within the time allowed, the condemnor may remove it and the cost of the removal and storage of the property shall be chargeable against the owner and a lien upon any remainder of the property not acquired by the condemnor to be recovered or foreclosed in the manner provided by law for recovery of debt or foreclosure of mortgages. (1981, c. 919, s. 1.)

§ 40A-10. Sale or other disposition of land condemned.

When any property condemned by the condemnor is no longer needed for the purpose for which it was condemned, it may be used for any other public purpose or may be sold or disposed of in the manner prescribed by law for the sale and disposition of surplus property. (1981, c. 919, s. 1.)

§ 40A-11. Right of entry prior to condemnation.

Any condemnor without having filed a petition or complaint, depositing any sum or taking any other action provided for in this Chapter, is authorized to enter upon any lands, but not structures, to make surveys, borings, examinations, and appraisals as may be necessary or expedient in carrying out and performing its rights or duties under this Chapter. The condemnor shall give 30 days' notice in writing to the owner at his last known address and the party in possession of the land of the intended entry authorized by this section.

Entry under this section shall not be deemed a trespass or taking within the meaning of this Chapter, however, the condemnor shall make reimbursement for any damage resulting from such activities, and the owner is entitled to bring an action to recover for the damage. If the owner recovers damages of twenty-five percent (25%) over the amount offered by the condemnor for reimbursement for its activities the court, in its discretion, may award reasonable attorney fees to the owner. (1981, c. 919, s. 1.)

§ 40A-12. Additional rules.

Where the procedure for conducting an action under this Chapter is not expressly provided for in this Chapter or by the statutes governing civil procedure, or where the civil procedure statutes are inapplicable, the judge before whom such proceeding may be pending shall have the power to make all the necessary orders and rules of procedure necessary to carry into effect the object and intent of this Chapter. The practice in each case shall conform as near as may be to the practice in other civil actions. (1981, c. 919, s. 1.)

§ 40A-13. Costs and appeal.

In addition to any reimbursement provided for in G.S. 40A-8 the condemnor shall pay all court costs taxed by the court. Either party shall have a right of appeal to the appellate division for errors of law committed in any proceedings provided for in this Chapter in the same manner as in any other civil actions and it shall not be necessary that an appeal bond be posted. (1981, c. 919, s. 1.)

§§ 40A-14 through 40A-18. Reserved for future codification purposes.

Article 2.

Condemnation Proceedings by Private Condemnors.

§ 40A-19. Proceedings by private condemnors.

Any private condemnor enumerated in G.S. 40A-3(a), possessing by law the right of eminent domain in this State shall have the right to acquire property required for the purposes of its incorporation or for the purposes specified in this Chapter in the manner and by the special proceedings herein prescribed. (1871-2, c. 138, s. 13; Code, ss. 1943, 2009; 1885, c. 168; 1893, c. 63; 1899, c. 64; 1901, cc. 6, 41, s. 2; 1903, c. 159, s. 16; c. 562; Rev., s. 2579; C.S., s. 1715; 1951, c. 59, s. 1; 1981, c. 919, s. 1.)

§ 40A-20. Petition filed; contents.

For the purpose of acquiring property a condemnor listed in G.S. 40A-3(a), or the owner of the property sought to be condemned, may present a petition to the clerk of the superior court of any county in which the real estate described in the petition is situated, praying for the appointment of commissioners of appraisal. The petition shall be signed and verified. If filed by the condemnor, it must contain a description of the property which the condemnor seeks to acquire; and it must state that the condemnor is duly incorporated, and that it is its intention in good faith to conduct and carry on the public business authorized by its charter, stating in detail the nature of its public business, and the specific use of the property; and that the property described in the petition is required for the purpose of conducting the proposed business. The petition, if filed by the condemnor, must also contain a statement as to whether the owner will be permitted to remove all or a specified portion of any buildings, structures, permanent improvements, or fixtures situated on or affixed to the land. The petition, whether filed by the condemnor or the owner, must also state the names and places of residence of all other owners, so far as the same can by reasonable diligence be ascertained, or those who claim to be owners of the property. If any such persons are infants, their ages, as near as may be known, must be stated; and if any such persons are incompetents, inebriates or are unknown, that fact must be stated, together with any other allegations and statements of liens or encumbrances on the property which the condemnor or the owner may see fit to make.

Nothing in this section shall in any manner affect an owner's common-law right to bring an action in tort for damage to his property. (1871-2, c. 138, s. 14; Code, s. 1944; 1893, c. 396; Rev., s. 2580; 1907, c. 783, s. 3; C.S., s. 1716; 1981, c. 919, s. 1.)

§ 40A-21. Notice of proceedings.

Notice of all proceedings brought hereunder shall be filed with the clerk of superior court of each county in which any part of the land is located in the form and manner provided by G.S. 1-116, and the clerk shall index and cross-index this notice as required by G.S. 1-117. In the record of lis pendens and in the judgment docket required by G.S. 7A-109 the clerk shall always index the name of the condemnor as the plaintiff and the name of the property owner as the defendant irrespective of whether the condemning party is the plaintiff or defendant. The filing of such notice shall be constructive notice of the proceeding to any person who subsequently acquires any interest in or lien upon said property, and the condemnor shall take all property condemned under this Article free of the claims of any such person. (1969, c. 864; 1981, c. 919, s. 1.)

§ 40A-22. Service.

A summons as in other cases of special proceedings, together with a copy of the petition, must be served on all persons whose estates or interests are to be affected by the proceedings, at least 10 days prior to the hearing of the same by the court. (1871-2, c. 138, s. 14; Code, s. 1944; Rev., s. 2581; C.S., s. 1717; 1981, c. 919, s. 1.)

§ 40A-23. Service where parties unknown.

If the person on whom service of summons and petition is to be made is unknown, or his residence is unknown and cannot by reasonable diligence be ascertained, then service may be made by publishing a notice, stating the time and place within which such person must appear and plead, the object thereof, with a description of the land to be affected by the proceedings, in accordance with the provisions of G.S. 1A-1, Rule 4(j)(9)c. In such cases the State Treasurer shall be served as custodian of the Escheat Fund and may become a party to the action. (Code, s. 1944, subsec. 5; Rev., s. 2582; C.S., s. 1718; 1971, c. 1093, s. 18; 1981, c. 919, s. 1.)

§ 40A-24. Orders served as in special proceedings in absence of other provisions.

In all cases not herein otherwise provided for, service of orders, notices, and other papers in the special proceedings authorized by this Chapter may be made as in other special proceedings. (Code, s. 1944, subsec. 7; Rev., s. 2583; C.S., s. 1719; 1981, c. 919, s. 1.)

§ 40A-25. Answer to petition; hearing; commissioners appointed.

On presenting such petition to the clerk of superior court, with proof of service of a copy thereof, and of the summons, all or any of the persons whose estates or interests are to be affected by the proceedings may answer such petition and show cause against granting the prayer of the same. The clerk shall hear the proofs and allegations of the parties, and if no sufficient cause is shown against granting the prayer of the petition, shall make an order for the appointment of three commissioners and shall fix the time and place for the first meeting of the commissioners. Each commissioner shall be a resident of the county wherein the property being condemned lies who has no right, title, or interest in or to the property condemned, is not related within the third degree to the owner or to the spouse of the owner, is not an officer, employee or agent of the condemnor, and is disinterested in the rights of the parties in every way. (1871-2, c. 138, s. 15; Code, s. 1945; Rev., s. 2584; C.S., s. 1720; 1981, c. 919, s. 1.)

§ 40A-26. Powers and duties of commissioners.

The commissioners, before entering upon the discharge of their duties, shall take and subscribe an oath that they will fairly and impartially appraise the property in the petition. Any one of them may issue subpoenas, administer oaths to witnesses, and any two of them may adjourn the proceedings before them from time to time, in their discretion. Whenever they meet, except by the appointment of the clerk or pursuant to adjournment, they shall cause 10 days' notice of such meeting to be given to the parties who are affected by their proceedings, or their attorney or agent. They shall view the premises described in the petition, hear the proofs and allegations of the parties, and reduce the testimony, if any is taken by them, to writing. After the testimony is closed in each case, and without any unnecessary delay, and before proceeding to the examination of any other claim, a majority of the commissioners being present and acting, shall ascertain and determine the compensation which ought justly to be made by the condemnor to the owners of the property appraised by them. The commissioners shall determine the compensation to be awarded in accordance with the principles established by Article 4 of this Chapter. They shall report the same to the clerk within 10 days. (1871-2, c. 138, ss. 16-18; Code, s. 1946; 1891, c. 160; Rev., s. 2585; C.S., s. 1721; 1981, c. 919, s. 1.)

§ 40A-27. Form of commissioners' report.

When the commissioners shall have assessed the compensation, they shall forthwith make and subscribe a written report of their proceedings, in substance as follows:

To the Clerk of the Superior Court of ____ :

We, ____, commissioners appointed by the court to assess the damages that have been and will be sustained by____, the owner of certain property lying in the county of____, which ____ the condemnor proposes to condemn for its use, do hereby certify that we met on ____ (or the day to which we were regularly adjourned), and, having first been duly sworn, we visited the premises of the owner, and after taking into full consideration the quality and quantity of the property aforesaid, and all other inconveniences likely to result to the owner, we have estimated and do assess the compensation aforesaid at the sum of $____ .

Given under our hands, the ____ day of____, A.D. ____. (R.C., c. 61, s. 17; 1874-5, c. 83; Code, s. 1700; Rev., s. 2586; C.S., s. 1722; 1981, c. 919, s. 1; 1999-456, s. 59.)

§ 40A-28. Exceptions to report; hearing; when title vests; appeal; restitution.

(a)   Upon the filing of the report, the clerk shall forthwith mail copies to the parties. Within 20 days after the filing of the report any party to the proceedings may file exceptions thereto. The clerk, after notice to the parties, shall hear any exceptions so filed and may thereafter direct a new appraisal, modify or confirm the report, or make such other orders as the clerk may deem right and proper.

(b)   If no exceptions are filed to the report, and if the clerk's final judgment rendered upon the petition and proceedings shall be in favor of the condemnor, and upon the deposit by the condemnor of the sum adjudged, together with all costs allowed, into the office of the clerk of superior court, then, in that event, all owners who have been made parties to the proceedings shall be divested of the property or interest therein to the extent set forth in the proceedings. A copy of the judgment, certified under the seal of the court, shall be registered in the county or counties where the land is situated, and the original judgment, or a certified copy thereof, or a certified copy of the registered judgment, may be given in evidence in all actions and proceedings as deeds for property are now allowed in evidence.

(c) Any party to the proceedings may file exceptions to the clerk's final determination on any exceptions to the report and may appeal to the judge of superior court having jurisdiction. Notice of appeal shall be filed within 10 days of the clerk's final determination. Upon appeal the clerk shall transfer the proceedings to the civil issue docket of the superior court. A judge in session shall hear and determine all matters in controversy and, subject to G.S. 40A-29 regarding trial by jury, shall determine any issues of compensation to be awarded in accordance with the provisions of Article 4 of this Chapter.

(d) Notwithstanding the filing of exceptions by any party to any orders or final determination of the clerk or the filing of a notice of appeal to the superior court, the condemnor may, at the time of the filing of the report of commissioners, deposit with the clerk of superior court in the proceedings the sum appraised by the commissioners and, in that event, the condemnor may enter, take possession of, and hold said property in the manner and to the extent sought to be acquired by the proceedings until final judgment is rendered on any appeal.

(e) If, on appeal, the judge shall refuse to condemn the property, then the money deposited with the clerk of court in the proceedings, or so much thereof as shall be adjudged, shall be refunded to the condemnor and the condemnor shall have no right to the property and shall surrender possession of the same, on demand, to the owner. The judge shall have full power and authority to make such orders, judgments and decrees as may be necessary to carry into effect the final judgment rendered in such proceedings, including compensation in accordance with the provisions of G.S. 40A-8.

(f) If the amount adjudged to be paid the owner of any property condemned under this Article shall not be paid within 60 days after final judgment in the proceedings, the right under the judgment to take the property shall ipso facto cease and determine, but the claimant under the judgment shall still remain liable for all amounts adjudged against said claimant except the compensation awarded for the taking of the property.

(g) The provisions of this section shall not preclude any injunctive relief otherwise available to the owner or the condemnor. (Code, s. 1946; 1893, c.

148; Rev., s. 2587; 1915, c. 207; C.S., s. 1723; 1951, c. 59, s. 2; 1955, c. 29, s. 1; 1969, c. 44, s. 47; 1971, c. 528, s. 37; 1981, c. 919, s. 1.)

§ 40A-29. Provision for jury trial on appeal.

In any proceedings under this Article by a condemnor to acquire property, any party to the proceedings shall be entitled on appeal to superior court to have the amount of compensation determined by a jury unless trial by jury has been waived by all parties. A jury shall determine the compensation to be awarded in accordance with the provisions of Article 4 of this Chapter. (1893, c. 148; Rev., s. 2588; C.S., s. 1724; 1957, c. 582; 1971, c. 528, s. 38; 1981, c. 919, s. 1.)

§ 40A-30. Title of infants, incompetents, inebriates, and trustees without power of sale, acquired.

In case any property required by a condemnor shall be vested in any trustee not authorized to sell, release and convey the same, or in any infant, incompetent, or inebriate, the superior court shall have power, by a special proceeding, on petition, to authorize and empower such trustee or the general guardian or committee of such infant, incompetent or inebriate, to sell and convey the same to such condemnor, on such terms as may be just. In case any infant, incompetent or inebriate has no general guardian or committee, the court may appoint a special guardian or committee for the purpose of making a sale, release or conveyance, and may require security from the general or special guardian or committee as the court may deem proper. Before any conveyance or release authorized by this section shall be executed, the terms on which it is to be executed shall be reported to the court on oath. If the court is satisfied that the terms are just to the owner of the property, the court shall confirm the report and direct the proper conveyance or release to be executed, which shall have the same effect as if executed by an owner of the property having legal power to sell and convey the same. (1871-2, c. 138, s. 28; Code, s. 1956; Rev., s. 2590; C.S., s. 1726; 1981, c. 919, s. 1.)

§ 40A-31. Rights of claimants of fund determined.

If there are adverse and conflicting claimants to the money, or any part of it, to be paid as compensation for the property taken, the clerk or the judge on appeal may direct the money to be paid into the court by the condemnor, and may determine who is entitled to the same and direct to whom the same shall be paid, and may order a reference to ascertain the facts on which such determination and order are to be made. (1871-2, c. 138, s. 19; Code, s. 1947; Rev., s. 2591; C.S., s. 1727; 1981, c. 919, s. 1.)

§ 40A-32. Attorney for unknown parties appointed; pleadings amended; new commissioners appointed.

(a)   The clerk or the judge on appeal shall appoint some competent attorney to appear for and protect the rights of any party in interest who is unknown or whose residence is unknown, and who has not appeared in the proceedings by an attorney or agent, and shall make an allowance to said attorney for his services which shall be taxed in the bill of costs. In such cases the State Treasurer as custodian of the Escheat Fund shall be notified of the appointment of such an attorney.

(b)   The clerk or the judge on appeal shall have power at any time to amend any defect or informality in any of the special proceedings authorized by this Chapter as may be necessary, or to cause new parties to be added, and to direct such further notices to be given to any party in interest as it deems proper; and also to appoint other commissioners in place of any who shall die, refuse or neglect to serve or be incapable of serving. (1871-2, c. 138, s. 20; Code, s. 1948; Rev., s. 2592; C.S., s. 1728; 1981, c. 919, s. 1.)

§ 40A-33. Change of ownership pending proceedings.

When any proceedings under this Article shall have been commenced, no change of ownership by voluntary conveyance or transfer of the property shall in any manner affect such proceedings, but the same may be carried on and perfected as if no such conveyance or transfer had been made or attempted to be made. (1871-2, c. 138, s. 22; Code, s. 1950; Rev., s. 2594; C.S., s. 1730; 1981, c. 919, s. 1.)

§ 40A-34. Defective title; how cured.

If at any time after an attempt to acquire title under this Article has commenced it shall be found that the title thereby attempted to be acquired is defective, the condemnor may commence new proceedings to acquire or perfect such title in the same manner as if no previous attempt had been commenced. At any stage in the new proceedings the court may authorize the condemnor, if in possession, to continue in possession, and if not in possession, to take possession and use the property during the pendency and until the final conclusion of the new proceedings. If the condemnor pays into court a sum determined by the court to be adequate compensation for the property, the court, in its discretion, may stay all actions or proceedings against the condemnor for its possession. In every such case the party interested in the property may conduct the proceedings to a conclusion if the condemnor delays or omits to prosecute the same. (1871-2, c. 138, s. 23; Code, s. 1951; Rev., s. 2595; C.S., s. 1731; 1981, c. 919, s. 1.)

§§ 40A-35 through 40A-39. Reserved for future codification purposes.

Article 3.

Condemnation by Public Condemnors.

§ 40A-40. Notice of action.

(a)　　Not less than 30 days prior to the filing of a complaint under the provisions of G.S. 40A-41, a public condemnor listed in G.S. 40A-3(b) or (c) shall provide notice to each owner (whose name and address can be ascertained by reasonable diligence) of its intent to institute an action to condemn property. (The notice shall be sent to each owner by certified mail, return receipt requested. The providing of notice shall be complete upon deposit of the notice enclosed in a postpaid, properly addressed wrapper in a post office or official depository under the exclusive care and custody of the United States Postal Service. Notice by publication is not required. Notice to an owner whose name and/or address cannot be ascertained by reasonable diligence is not required in any manner.)

The notice shall contain a general description of the property to be taken and of the amount estimated by the condemnor to be just compensation for the property to be condemned. The notice shall also state the purpose for which the property is being condemned and the date condemnor intends to file the complaint.

(b) In the case of a condemnation action to be commenced pursuant to G.S. 40A-42(a), the notice required by subsection (a) of this section shall substantially comply with the following requirements:

(1) The notice shall be printed in at least 12 point bold legible type.

(2) The words "Notice of condemnation" or similar words shall conspicuously appear on the notice.

(3) The notice shall include the information required by subsection (a) of this section.

(4) The notice shall contain a plain language summary of the owner's rights, including:

a. The right to commence an action for injunctive relief.

b. The right to answer the complaint after it has been filed.

(5) The notice shall include a statement advising the owner to consult with an attorney regarding the owner's rights.

An owner is entitled to no relief because of any defect or inaccuracy in the notice unless the owner was actually prejudiced by the defect or inaccuracy, and the owner is otherwise entitled to relief under Rules 55(d) or 60(b) of the North Carolina Rules of Civil Procedure or other applicable law. (1981, c. 919, s. 1; 1981 (Reg. Sess., 1982), c. 1243, s. 3; 1999-410, s. 1.)

§ 40A-41. Institution of action and deposit.

A public condemnor listed in G.S. 40A-3(b) or (c) shall institute a civil action to condemn property by filing in the superior court of any county in which the land is located a complaint containing a declaration of taking declaring that property therein is thereby taken for the use of the condemnor.

The complaint shall contain or have attached thereto the following:

(1)   A statement of the authority under which and the public use for which the property is taken;

(2)   A description of the entire tract or tracts of land affected by the taking sufficient for the identification thereof;

(3)   A statement of the property taken and a description of the area taken sufficient for the identification thereof;

(4)   The names and addresses of those persons who the condemnor is informed and believes may be or, claim to be, owners of the property so far as the same can by reasonable diligence be ascertained, and if any such persons are infants, incompetents, inebriates or under any other disability, or their whereabouts or names unknown, it must be so stated;

(5)   A statement of the sum of money estimated by the condemnor to be just compensation for the taking; and

(6)   A statement as to whether the owner will be permitted to remove all or a specified portion of any timber, buildings, structures, permanent improvements, or fixtures situated on or affixed to the property.

(7)   A statement as to such liens or other encumbrances as the condemnor is informed and believes are encumbrances upon the property and can by reasonable diligence be ascertained.

(8)   A prayer that there be a determination of just compensation in accordance with the provisions of this Article.

The filing of the complaint shall be accompanied by the deposit to the use of the owner of the sum of money estimated by the condemnor to be just compensation for the taking. Upon the filing of the complaint and the deposit of said sum, summons shall be issued to each owner of the property. The summons, together with a copy of the complaint and notice of the deposit shall be served upon the person named therein in the manner provided for the service of process under the provisions of G.S. 1A-1, Rule 4. The condemnor may amend the complaint and may increase the amount of its deposit with the court at any time while the proceeding is pending, and the owner shall have the same rights of withdrawal of this additional amount as set forth in G.S. 40A-44 of this Chapter. (1935, c. 470, ss. 4, 5; 1947, c. 781; 1971, c. 382, s. 1; 1981, c. 919, s. 1.)

§ 40A-42. Vesting of title and right of possession; injunction not precluded.

(a) (1) Standard Provision. - When a local public condemnor is acquiring property by condemnation for a purpose set out in G.S. 40A-3(b)(1), (4) or (7), or when a city is acquiring property for a purpose set out in G.S. 160A-311(1), (2), (3), (4), (6), or (7), or when a county is acquiring property for a purpose set out in G.S. 153A-274(1), (2) or (3), or when a local board of education or any combination of local boards of education is acquiring property for any purpose set forth in G.S. 115C-517, or when a condemnor is acquiring property by condemnation as authorized by G.S. 40A-3(c)(1), (8), (9), (10), (12), or (13) title to the property and the right to immediate possession shall vest pursuant to this subsection. Unless an action for injunctive relief has been initiated, title to the property specified in the complaint, together with the right to immediate possession thereof, shall vest in the condemnor upon the filing of the complaint and the making of the deposit in accordance with G.S. 40A-41.

(2) Modified Provision for Certain Localities. - When a local public condemnor is acquiring property by condemnation for a purpose set out in G.S. 40A-3(b1)(1), (4), (7), (10), or (11), or when a city is acquiring property for a purpose set out in G.S. 160A-311(1), (2), (3), (4), (6), or (7), or when a county is acquiring property for a purpose set out in G.S. 153A-274(1), (2) or (3), or when a local board of education or any combination of local boards of education is acquiring property for any purpose set forth in G.S. 115C-517, or when a condemnor is acquiring property by condemnation as authorized by G.S. 40A-3(c)(8), (9), (10), (12), or (13) title to the property and the right to immediate possession shall vest pursuant to this subsection. Unless an action for injunctive relief has been initiated, title to the property specified in the complaint, together with the right to immediate possession thereof, shall vest in the condemnor upon the filing of the complaint and the making of the deposit in accordance with G.S. 40A-41.

This subdivision applies only to Carteret and Dare Counties, the Towns of Atlantic Beach, Carolina Beach, Caswell Beach, Emerald Isle, Holden Beach, Indian Beach, Kill Devil Hills, Kitty Hawk, Kure Beach, Nags Head, North Topsail Beach, Oak Island, Ocean Isle Beach, Pine Knoll Shores, Sunset Beach, Surf City, Topsail Beach, and Wrightsville Beach, and the Village of Bald Head Island.

(b) When a local public condemnor is acquiring property by condemnation for purposes other than for the purposes listed in subsection (a) above, title to the property taken and the right to possession shall vest in the condemnor pursuant to this subsection. Unless an action for injunctive relief has been initiated, title to the property specified in the complaint, together with the right to immediate possession thereof, shall vest in the condemnor:

(1) Upon the filing of an answer by the owner who requests only that there be a determination of just compensation and who does not challenge the authority of the condemnor to condemn the property; or

(2) Upon the failure of the owner to file an answer within the 120-day time period established by G.S. 40A-46; or

(3) Upon the disbursement of the deposit in accordance with the provisions of G.S. 40A-44.

(c) If the property is owned by a private condemnor, the vesting of title in the condemnor and the right to immediate possession of the property shall not become effective until the superior court has rendered final judgment (after any appeals) that the property is not in actual public use or is not necessary to the operation of the business of the owner, as set forth in G.S. 40A-5(b).

(d) If the answer raises any issues other than the issue of compensation, the issues so raised shall be determined under the provisions of G.S. 40A-47.

(e) The judge shall enter such orders in the cause as may be required to place the condemnor in possession.

(f) The provisions of this section shall not preclude or otherwise affect any remedy of injunction available to the owner or the condemnor. (1981, c. 919, s. 1; 1989 (Reg. Sess., 1990), c. 871, s. 1; 1998-212, s. 9.10; 2001-36, ss. 2, 3; 2001-239, s. 1; 2001-478, s. 2; 2003-282, s. 2; 2004-203, s. 33; 2009-85, s. 1.)

§ 40A-43. Memorandum of action.

The condemnor, at the time of the filing of the complaint containing the declaration of taking and deposit of estimated compensation, shall record a memorandum of action with the register of deeds in all counties in which the land involved is located and said memorandum shall be recorded among the land records of said county. Upon the amending of any complaint affecting the property taken, the condemnor shall record a supplemental memorandum of action. The memorandum of action shall contain:

(1) The names of those persons who the condemnor is informed and believes to be or claim to be owners of the property and who are parties to said action;

(2) A description of the entire tract or tracts affected by said taking sufficient for the identification thereof;

(3) A statement of the property taken for public use;

(4) The date of institution of said action, the county in which said action is pending, and such other reference thereto as may be necessary for the identification of said action. (1981, c. 919, s. 1.)

§ 40A-44. Disbursement of deposit.

Where there is no dispute as to title the person named in the complaint may apply to the court for disbursement of the money deposited in the court, or any part thereof, as full compensation, or as a credit against just compensation without prejudice to further proceedings in the cause to determine just compensation. Upon such application, the judge shall order that the money deposited be paid forthwith to the person entitled thereto in accordance with the application. Subject to the provisions of G.S. 40A-68 the judge shall have power to make such orders with respect to encumbrances, liens, rents, taxes, assessments, insurance and other charges, if any, as shall be just and equitable.

No notice to the condemnor of the hearing upon the application for disbursement of deposit shall be necessary. (1981, c. 919, s. 1.)

§ 40A-45. Answer, reply and plat.

(a) Any person whose property has been taken by the condemnor by the filing of a complaint containing a declaration of taking, may within the time set forth in G.S. 40A-46 file an answer to the complaint. No answer shall be filed to the declaration of taking and notice of deposit. Said answer shall contain the following:

(1) Such admissions or denials of the allegations of the complaint as are appropriate;

(2) The names and addresses of the persons filing said answer, together with a statement as to their interest in the property taken;

(3) Such affirmative defenses or matters as are pertinent to the action; and

(4) A request that there be a determination of just compensation.

(b) A copy of the answer shall be served on the condemnor provided that failure to serve the answer shall not deprive the answer of its validity. The affirmative allegations of said answer shall be deemed denied. The condemnor may, however, file a reply within 30 days from receipt of a copy of this answer.

(c) The condemnor, within 90 days from the receipt of the answer shall file in the cause a plat of the property taken and such additional area as may be necessary to properly determine the compensation, and a copy thereof shall be mailed to the parties or their attorney; provided, however, the condemnor shall not be required to file a map or plat in less than six months from the date of the filing of the complaint. (1981, c. 919, s. 1.)

§ 40A-46. Time for filing answer; failure to answer.

Any person named in and served with a complaint containing a declaration of taking shall have 120 days from the date of service thereof to file answer.

Failure to answer within said time shall constitute an admission that the amount deposited is just compensation and shall be a waiver of any further proceeding to determine just compensation; in such event the judge shall enter final judgment in the amount deposited and order disbursement of the money deposited to the owner. Provided, however, at any time prior to the entry of the final judgment the judge may, for good cause shown and after notice to the condemnor extend the time for filing answer for 30 days. (1981, c. 919, s. 1.)

§ 40A-47. Determination of issues other than damages.

The judge, upon motion and 10 days' notice by either the condemnor or the owner, shall, either in or out of session, hear and determine any and all issues raised by the pleadings other than the issue of compensation, including, but not limited to, the condemnor's authority to take, questions of necessary and proper parties, title to the land, interest taken, and area taken. (1981, c. 919, s. 1.)

§ 40A-48. Appointment of commissioners.

(a) A request to the clerk for the appointment of commissioners to determine compensation for the taking may be made in the answer of the owner, or may be made by motion of either the owner or the condemnor within 60 days after the filing of the answer. After the determination of other issues as provided by G.S. 40A-47, the clerk shall appoint three competent, disinterested persons residing in the county to serve as commissioners. The commissioners shall be sworn and shall go upon the land to appraise the compensation for the property taken and report their findings to the court within a time certain. Each commissioner shall be a person who has no right, title, or interest in or to the property being condemned, is not related within the third degree to the owner or to the spouse of the owner, is not an officer, employee, or agent of the condemnor, and is disinterested in the rights of the parties in every way.

(b) The commissioners shall have the power to inspect the property, hold hearings, swear witnesses, and take evidence as they may, in their discretion, deem necessary, and shall file with the court a report of their determination of the damages sustained.

(c) The report of commissioners shall be in writing and in a form substantially as follows:

TO THE SUPERIOR COURT OF _____ COUNTY

We, _____ and _____ Commissioners appointed by the Court to assess the compensation to be awarded to_____, the owner of property interest in certain land lying in _____ County, North Carolina, which has been taken by the _____ (condemnor), for public purposes, do hereby certify that we convened, and, having first been duly sworn, visited the premises, and took such evidence as was presented to us, and after taking into full consideration the quality and quantity of the land and all other facts which reasonably affect its fair market value at the time of the taking, we have determined the fair market value of the property taken to be the sum of $____ and the compensation for the damage to the remainder of the land of the owner by reason of the taking to be the sum of $_____ (if applicable). GIVEN under our hands, this the ____ day of_____, _____

_____ (SEAL)

_____ (SEAL)

_____ (SEAL)

(d) A copy of the report shall at the time of filing be mailed certified or registered mail by the clerk to each of the parties or to their counsel of record. Within 30 days after the mailing of the report, either the condemnor or the owner, may except thereto and demand a trial de novo by a jury as to the issue of compensation. Upon the receipt of such demand the action shall be placed on the civil issue docket of the superior court for trial de novo by a jury as to the issue of compensation, provided, that upon agreement of both parties trial by jury may be waived and the issue determined by the judge. The report of commissioners shall not be competent as evidence upon the trial of the issue of compensation in the superior court, nor shall evidence of the deposit by the condemnor into the court be competent upon the trial of the issue of compensation. If no exception to the report of commissioners is filed within the time prescribed, final judgment shall be entered by the judge upon a determination and finding by him that the report of commissioners plus interest computed in accordance with G.S. 40A-53 of this Chapter, awards to the property owners just compensation. In the event that the judge is of the opinion and, in his discretion, determines that the award does not provide just compensation, he shall set aside the award and order the case placed on the civil issue docket for determination of the issue of compensation by a jury. (1981, c. 919, s. 1; 1999-456, s. 59.)

§ 40A-49. No request for commissioners.

After the determination of other issues as provided by G.S. 40A-47, if no request has been made for the appointment of commissioners within the time permitted by G.S. 40A-48(a), the cause shall be transferred to the civil issue docket for trial as to the issue of just compensation. (1981, c. 919, s. 1.)

§ 40A-50. Parties, orders; continuances.

The judge shall appoint an attorney to appear for and protect the rights of any party or parties in interest who are unknown, or whose residence is unknown and who has not appeared in the proceeding by an attorney or agent. The State Treasurer as custodian of the Escheat Fund shall be notified of the appointment of such an attorney. The judge shall appoint guardians ad litem for such parties as are infants, incompetents, or other parties who may be under a disability, and without general guardian, and the judge shall have the authority to make such additional parties as are necessary to the complete determination of the proceeding.

Upon his own motion, or upon motion of any of the parties the judge may, in his discretion, continue the cause until the project is completed or until such earlier time as, in the opinion of the judge, the effect of condemnation upon said property may be determined. The motion may be heard at a hearing pursuant to G.S. 40A-47 or upon the coming on of the cause for trial, and shall be granted upon a proper showing that the effect of condemnation upon the subject property cannot presently be determined. (1981, c. 919, s. 1.)

§ 40A-51. Remedy where no declaration of taking filed; recording memorandum of action.

(a) If property has been taken by an act or omission of a condemnor listed in G.S. 40A-3(b) or (c) and no complaint containing a declaration of taking has been filed the owner of the property, may initiate an action to seek compensation for the taking. The action may be initiated within 24 months of the date of the taking of the affected property or the completion of the project involving the taking, whichever shall occur later. The complaint shall be filed in the superior court and shall contain the following: the names and places of residence of all persons who are, or claim to be, owners of the property, so far as the same can by reasonable diligence be ascertained; if any persons are under a legal disability, it must be so stated; a statement as to any encumbrances on the property; the particular facts which constitute the taking together with the dates that they allegedly occurred, and; a description of the property taken. Upon the filing of said complaint summons shall issue and together with a copy of the complaint be served on the condemnor. The allegations of said complaint shall be deemed denied; however, the condemnor within 60 days of service summons and complaint may file answer thereto. If the taking is admitted by the condemnor, it shall, at the time of filing the answer, deposit with the court the estimated amount of compensation for the taking. Notice of the deposit shall be given to the owner. The owner may apply for disbursement of the deposit and disbursement shall be made in accordance with the applicable provisions of G.S. 40A-44. If a taking is admitted, the condemnor shall, within 90 days of the filing of the answer to the complaint, file a map or plat of the property taken. The procedure hereinbefore set out in this Article and in Article 4 shall be followed for the purpose of determining all matters raised by the pleadings and the determination of just compensation.

(b) The owner at the time of filing of the complaint shall record a memorandum of action with the register of deeds in all counties in which the property involved is located. The memorandum is to be recorded among the land records of the county. The memorandum of action shall contain:

(1) The names of those persons who the owner is informed and believes to be or claim to be owners of the property;

(2) A description of the entire tract or tracts affected by the alleged taking sufficient for the identification thereof;

(3) A statement of the property allegedly taken; and

(4) The date on which owner alleges the taking occurred, the date on which said action was instituted, the county in which it was instituted, and such other reference thereto as may be necessary for the identification of said action.

(c) Nothing in this section shall in any manner affect an owner's common-law right to bring an action in tort for damage to his property. (1981, c. 919, s. 1.)

§ 40A-52. Measure of compensation.

The commissioners, jury or judge shall determine the issue of compensation in accordance with the provisions of Article 4 of this Chapter. (1981, c. 919, s. 1.)

§ 40A-53. Interest as a part of just compensation.

To the amount awarded as compensation by the commissioners or a jury or judge, the judge shall add interest at the rate of six percent (6%) per annum on said amount from the date of taking to the date of judgment. Interest shall not be allowed from the date of deposit on so much thereof as shall have been paid into court as provided in this Article. (1981, c. 919, s. 1.)

§ 40A-54. Final judgments.

Final judgments entered in actions instituted under the provisions of this Article shall contain a description of the land affected, together with a description of the property acquired by the condemnor and a copy of said judgment shall be certified to the register of deeds in each county in which the land or any part thereof lies and be recorded among the land records of said county. (1981, c. 919, s. 1.)

§ 40A-55. Payment of compensation.

If there are adverse and conflicting claimants to the deposit made into the court by the condemnor or the additional amount determined as just compensation, on which the judgment is entered in said action, the judge may direct the full amount determined to be paid into said court by the condemnor and may retain said cause for determination of who is entitled to said moneys. The judge may by further order in the cause direct to whom the same shall be paid and may in its discretion order a reference to ascertain the facts on which such determination and order are to be made. (1981, c. 919, s. 1.)

§ 40A-56. Refund of deposit.

In the event the amount of the final judgment is less than the amount deposited by the condemnor pursuant to the provisions of this Article, the condemnor shall be entitled to recover the excess of the amount of the deposit over the amount of the final judgment and court costs incident thereto. In the event there are not sufficient funds on deposit to cover said excess, the condemnor shall be entitled to a judgment for said sum against the person or persons having received said deposit. (1981, c. 919, s. 1.)

§§ 40A-57 through 40A-61. Reserved for future codification purposes.

Article 4.

Just Compensation.

§ 40A-62. Application.

The principles set down in this Article shall govern the determination of compensation to be awarded to the owner by the condemnor for the taking of his property. (1981, c. 919, s. 1.)

§ 40A-63. In general.

The determination of the amount of compensation shall reflect the value of the property immediately prior to the filing of the petition under G.S. 40A-20 or the complaint under G.S. 40A-41 and except as provided in the following sections shall not reflect an increase or decrease due to the condemnation. The day of the filing of a petition or complaint shall be the date of valuation of the interest taken. (1981, c. 919, s. 1.)

§ 40A-64. Compensation for taking.

(a) Except as provided in subsection (b), the measure of compensation for a taking of property is its fair market value.

(b) If there is a taking of less than the entire tract, the measure of compensation is the greater of either (i) the amount by which the fair market value of the entire tract immediately before the taking exceeds the fair market value of the remainder immediately after the taking; or (ii) the fair market value of the property taken.

(c) If the owner is to be allowed to remove any timber, building or other permanent improvement, or fixtures from the property, the value thereof shall not be included in the compensation award, but the cost of removal shall be considered as an element to be compensated. (1981, c. 919, s. 1; 2001-487, s. 17.)

§ 40A-65. Effect of condemnation procedure on value.

(a) The value of the property taken, or of the entire tract if there is a partial taking, does not include an increase or decrease in value before the date of valuation that is caused by (i) the proposed improvement or project for which the property is taken; (ii) the reasonable likelihood that the property would be acquired for that improvement or project; or (iii) the condemnation proceeding in which the property is taken.

(b) If before completion the project is expanded or changed to require the taking of additional property, the fair market value of the additional property does not include a decrease in value before the date of valuation caused by any of the factors described in subsection (a), but does include an increase in value before the date on which it became reasonably likely that the expansion or change of the project would occur, if the increase is caused by any of the factors described in subsection (a).

(c) Notwithstanding subsections (a) and (b), a decrease in value before the date of valuation which is caused by physical deterioration of the property within the reasonable control of the property owner, and by his unjustified neglect, may be considered in determining value. (1981, c. 919, s. 1.)

§ 40A-66. Compensation to reflect project as planned.

(a) If there is a taking of less than the entire tract, the value of the remainder on the valuation date shall reflect increases or decreases in value caused by the proposed project including any work to be performed under an agreement between the parties.

(b) The value of the remainder, as of the date of valuation, shall reflect the time the damage or benefit caused by the proposed improvement or project will be actually realized. (1981, c. 919, s. 1.)

§ 40A-67. Entire tract.

For the purpose of determining compensation under this Article, all contiguous tracts of land that are in the same ownership and are being used as an integrated economic unit shall be treated as if the combined tracts constitute a single tract. (1981, c. 919, s. 1.)

§ 40A-68. Acquisition of property subject to lien.

Notwithstanding the provisions of an agreement, if any, relating to a lien encumbering the property:

(1) If there is a partial taking, the lienholder may share in the amount of compensation awarded only to the extent determined by the commissioners or by the jury or by the judge to be necessary to prevent an impairment of his

security, and the lien shall continue upon the part of the property not taken as security for the unpaid portion of the indebtedness until it is paid; and

(2) Neither the condemnor nor owner is liable to the lienholder for any penalty for prepayment of the debt secured by the lien, and the amount awarded by the judgment to the lienholder shall not include any penalty therefor. (1981, c. 919, s. 1.)

§ 40A-69. Property subject to life tenancy.

If the property taken is subject to a life tenancy, the commissioners, the jury, or the judge may include in the judgment a requirement that:

(1) The award be apportioned and distributed on the basis of the respective values of the interests of the life tenant and remainderman;

(2) The compensation be used to purchase comparable property to be held subject to the life tenancy;

(3) The compensation be held in trust and administered subject to the terms of the instrument that created the life tenancy; or

(4) Any other equitable arrangement be carried out. (1981, c. 919, s. 1.)

Article 5.

Return of Condemned Property.

§ 40A-70. Return of condemned property.

Whenever a public condemnor listed in G.S. 40A-3(b) or (c) acquires real property by condemnation and thereafter determines that the property is not needed for the purpose for which it was condemned, and the public condemnor still owns the property, the public condemnor may reconvey the property to the original owner upon payment to the public condemnor of the full price paid to the owner when the property was taken by eminent domain, the cost of any improvements, together with interest at the legal rate to the date when the decision was made to offer the return of the property. Unless the public condemnor acquired the entire lot, block, or tract of land belonging to the original owner, the original owner must own the remainder of the original lot, block, or tract of land from which the property was acquired to purchase the property pursuant to this section. The public condemnor shall specify a date by which the property must be reconveyed and the payment made, which may not be less than 30 days after written notification to the original owner that the public condemnor has decided to offer the return of the property. (1991 (Reg. Sess., 1992), c. 980, s. 1.)

§ 40A-71. Reserved for future codification purposes.

§ 40A-72. Reserved for future codification purposes.

§ 40A-73. Reserved for future codification purposes.

§ 40A-74. Reserved for future codification purposes.

§ 40A-75. Reserved for future codification purposes.

§ 40A-76. Reserved for future codification purposes.

§ 40A-77. Reserved for future codification purposes.

§ 40A-78. Reserved for future codification purposes.

§ 40A-79. Reserved for future codification purposes.

Article 6.

Condemnation of Property Encumbered by a Conservation Easement.

§ 40A-80. Applicability of Article; definition.

(a)   Applicability. -

(1)   The provisions of this Article shall apply only to a condemnation action initiated by a public condemnor, which for purposes of this Article shall be any entity exercising the power of eminent domain under any authority except G.S. 40A-3(a).

(2)   Except with respect to G.S. 40A-84, the provisions of this Article shall not apply to those circumstances in which: (i) the terms of the conservation easement provide an express exception for uses, purposes, and rights that may be subject to condemnation in the future, or circumstances in which the condemnation action to be taken would not extinguish, restrict, or impair the property rights of the holder of the conservation easement. "Property rights" as used herein shall include the purposes for which the easement was created; and (ii) a local public condemnor or other public condemnor under G.S. 40A-3 is constructing, enlarging, or improving electric distribution systems; gas production, storage, transmission, and distribution systems; water supply and distribution systems; wastewater collection, treatment, and disposal systems of all types; storm sewer and drainage systems; or trails associated with greenways. In condemnation actions exempt pursuant to this subdivision, a condemnor shall make reasonable efforts, after completion of the project for which the condemnation was undertaken, to return the property to the condition that the property existed in prior to condemnation to the extent practicable.

(b)   Definition. - As used in this Article, the term "conservation easement" means a conservation or historic preservation easement that meets all of the following criteria, as each of the criteria are defined under 26 U.S.C. § 170(h): (i) a qualified real property interest, (ii) held by a qualified organization, and (iii) exclusively for conservation purposes. (2009-439, s. 1.)

§ 40A-81. Additional information required in petition or complaint filed.

Any public entity that acts to exercise the power of eminent domain on property encumbered by a conservation easement shall initiate the action as required by this Chapter or Chapter 136 of the General Statutes as applicable. The complaint filed as required by those Chapters also shall include a statement that alleges that there is no prudent and feasible alternative to condemnation of the property encumbered by the conservation easement. (2009-439, s. 1.)

§ 40A-82. Demonstration of no prudent and feasible alternative required in certain actions; judicial determination.

(a) If a holder of a conservation easement contests an action to condemn property encumbered by a conservation easement on the basis that the condemnor failed to sufficiently consider alternatives to the action or that a prudent and feasible alternative exists to the action, the holder of the conservation easement may file an answer to the complaint within 30 days from the date of service of the complaint as to that issue. If the holder of the conservation easement does not assert that the condemnor failed to sufficiently consider alternatives to the action or that a prudent and feasible alternative exists to the action, the holder of the conservation easement may file an answer within 120 days from the date of service of the complaint.

(b) If the holder of a conservation easement contests an action pursuant to subsection (a) of this section, the judge shall hear and determine whether or not a prudent and feasible alternative exists to condemnation of the property. The burden of persuasion on this issue is on the condemnor if the holder of the conservation easement, after discovery, has identified at least one alternative. If no alternative identified by the holder of the conservation easement is adjudged prudent and feasible, then the condemnation action shall proceed under the provisions of Article 3 of this Chapter, or Article 9 of Chapter 136 of the General Statutes, as applicable. If the judge determines that a prudent and feasible alternative does exist to condemnation of the property, the court shall dismiss the action and award the holder of the conservation easement costs, disbursements, and expenses in accordance with G.S. 40A-8(b) or G.S. 136-119, as applicable, except that attorneys' fees may not be awarded. The procedure for this hearing shall be as set forth in G.S. 40A-47 or G.S. 136-108, as applicable.

(c) A determination as to whether a prudent or feasible alternative exists to condemnation of the property as set forth in subsection (b) of this section shall not be required for actions meeting all of the following criteria:

(1) The Department of Transportation or the North Carolina Turnpike Authority is the condemnor.

(2) Prior to filing the condemnation action, a review of the project for which the property is being condemned was conducted that considered the alternatives to the condemnation of the property encumbered by the conservation easement and mitigation measures to minimize the impact. The condemnor shall, in the complaint filed with the court, identify the alternatives and mitigation measures considered with regard to condemnation of the property encumbered by the conservation easement.

(3) The review was conducted pursuant to any of the following:

a. The State Environmental Policy Act (SEPA), G.S. 113A-1, et seq.

b. The National Environmental Policy Act (NEPA), 42 U.S.C. § 4321, et seq.

c. 49 U.S.C. § 303. (2009-439, s. 1.)

§ 40A-83. Vesting of title and right of possession.

Notwithstanding the provisions of G.S. 40A-42 or G.S. 136-104, title and right to immediate possession of property subject to this Article shall not vest in a condemnor any earlier than any of the following:

(1) The failure of the easement holder to file an answer within the 30-day time period established by G.S. 40A-82(a).

(2) Determination by the court that no prudent or feasible alternative exists to condemnation of the property pursuant to G.S. 40A-82(b).

(3) Filing of the complaint and deposit in actions meeting all of the requirements of G.S. 40A-82(c). (2009-439, s. 1.)

§ 40A-84. Compensation for condemnation.

In any action to condemn property encumbered by a conservation easement, the court shall determine just compensation pursuant to Article 4 of this Chapter or in accordance with Chapter 136 of the General Statutes, as applicable, by first determining the value of the property taken as a whole, unencumbered by the conservation easement, as well as any other, separately owned interest in the property. The court shall allocate the just compensation award between or among any holders of the conservation easement and any owners of the property as provided by the easement agreement or, if the agreement fails to address the issue, as the judge finds equitable based upon evidence to include the opinion of a real estate valuation expert with experience in the valuation of conservation easements. Any party may demand trial by jury on the issue of total just compensation for the taking. (2009-439, s. 1.)

§ 40A-85. Appeal.

The parties shall have a right of appeal as provided in G.S. 40A-13. (2009-439, s. 1.)

Chapter 41.

Estates

Article 1.

Survivorship Rights and Future Interests.

§ 41-1. Fee tail converted into fee simple.

Every person seized of an estate in tail shall be deemed to be seized of the same in fee simple. (1784, c. 204, s. 5; R.C., c. 43, s. 1; Code, s. 1325; Rev., s. 1578; C.S., s. 1734; 1995, c. 190, s. 1; c. 525, s. 1.)

§ 41-2. Survivorship in joint tenancy defined; proviso as to partnership; unequal ownership interests.

(a) Except as otherwise provided herein, in all estates, real or personal, held in joint tenancy, the part or share of any tenant dying shall not descend or go to the surviving tenant, but shall descend or be vested in the heirs, executors, or administrators, respectively, of the tenant so dying, in the same manner as estates held by tenancy in common: Provided, that estates held in joint tenancy for the purpose of carrying on and promoting trade and commerce, or any useful work or manufacture, established and pursued with a view of profit to the parties therein concerned, are vested in the surviving partner, in order to enable the surviving partner to settle and adjust the partnership business, or pay off the debts which may have been contracted in pursuit of the joint business; but as soon as the same is effected, the survivor shall account with, and pay, and deliver to the heirs, executors and administrators respectively of such deceased partner all such part, share, and sums of money as the deceased partner may be entitled to by virtue of the original agreement, if any, or according to the deceased partner's share or part in the joint concern, in the same manner as partnership stock is usually settled between joint merchants and the representatives of their deceased partners. Nothing in this section prevents the creation of a joint tenancy with right of survivorship in real or personal property if the instrument creating the joint tenancy expressly provides for a right of survivorship, and no other document shall be necessary to establish said right of survivorship. Upon conveyance to a third party by less than all of three or more joint tenants holding property in joint tenancy with right of survivorship, a tenancy in common is created among the third party and the remaining joint tenants, who remain joint tenants with right of survivorship as between themselves. Upon conveyance to a third party by one of two joint tenants holding property in joint tenancy with right of survivorship, a tenancy in common is created between the third party and the remaining joint tenant. A conveyance of any interest in real property by a party to one or more other parties, whether or not jointly with the grantor-party, as joint tenants with right of survivorship, creates in the parties that interest, if the instrument of conveyance expressly provides for a joint tenancy with right of survivorship.

(a1) Upon conveyance to the trustee of a deed of trust by any or all of the joint tenants holding property in joint tenancy with right of survivorship to secure a loan, the joint tenancy with right of survivorship shall be deemed not to be severed, and upon satisfaction of the deed of trust, legal title to the property subject to the joint tenancy shall revert to the grantors as joint tenants with right of survivorship in the respective shares as owned by the respective grantors at the time of the execution of the deed of trust, unless a contrary intent is expressed in the deed of trust or other instrument recorded subsequent to the deed of trust.

(b) The interests of the grantees holding property in joint tenancy with right of survivorship shall be deemed to be equal unless otherwise specified in the conveyance. Any joint tenancy interest held by a husband and wife, unless otherwise specified, shall be deemed to be held as a single tenancy by the entirety, which shall be treated as a single party when determining interests in the joint tenancy with right of survivorship. Joint tenancy interests among two or more joint tenants holding property in joint tenancy with right of survivorship are subject to the provisions of G.S. 28A-24-3 upon the death of one or more of the joint tenants.

This subsection shall apply to any conveyance of an interest in property created at any time that explicitly sought to create unequal ownership interests in a joint tenancy with right of survivorship. Distributions made prior to the enactment of this subsection that were made in equal amounts from a joint tenancy with the right of survivorship that sought to create unequal ownership shares shall remain valid and shall not be subject to modification on the basis of this subsection. (1784, c. 204, s. 6; R.C., c. 43, s. 2; Code, s. 1326; Rev., s. 1579; C.S., s. 1735; 1945, c. 635; 1989 (Reg. Sess., 1990), c. 891, s. 1; 1991, c. 606, s. 1; 2009-268, s. 1; 2010-96, s. 9; 2012-69, s. 2; 2013-204, s. 1.11.)

§ 41-2.1. Right of survivorship in bank deposits created by written agreement.

(a) A deposit account may be established with a banking institution in the names of two or more persons, payable to either or the survivor or survivors, with incidents as provided by subsection (b) of this section, when both or all parties have signed a written agreement, either on the signature card or by separate instrument, expressly providing for the right of survivorship.

(b) A deposit account established under subsection (a) of this section shall have the following incidents:

(1) Either party to the agreement may add to or draw upon any part or all of the deposit account, and any withdrawal by or upon the order of either party shall be a complete discharge of the banking institution with respect to the sum withdrawn.

(2) During the lifetime of both or all the parties, the deposit account shall be subject to their respective debts to the extent that each has contributed to the unwithdrawn account. In the event their respective contributions are not determined, the unwithdrawn fund shall be deemed owned by both or all equally.

(3) Upon the death of either or any party to the agreement, the survivor, or survivors, become the sole owner, or owners, of the entire unwithdrawn deposit, subject to the following claims listed below in subdivisions a. through e. upon that portion of the unwithdrawn deposit which would belong to the deceased had the unwithdrawn deposit been divided equally between both or among all the joint tenants at the time of the death of the deceased:

a. The allowance of the year's allowance to the surviving spouse of the deceased;

b. The funeral expenses of the deceased;

c. The cost of administering the estate of the deceased;

d. The claims of the creditors of the deceased; and

e. Governmental rights.

(4) Upon the death of one of the joint tenants provided herein the banking institution in which said joint deposit is held shall pay to the legal representative of the deceased, or to the clerk of the superior court if the amount is less than two thousand dollars ($2,000), the portion of the unwithdrawn deposit made subject to the claims and expenses as provided in subdivision (3) above, and may pay the remainder to the surviving joint tenant or joint tenants. Said legal representative shall hold the portion of said unwithdrawn deposit paid to him and not use the same for the payment of the claims and expenses as provided in subdivision (3) above unless and until all other personal assets of the estate

have been exhausted, and shall then use so much thereof as may be necessary to pay said claims and expenses. Any part of said unwithdrawn deposit not used for the payment of said claims and expenses shall, upon the settlement of the estate, be paid to the surviving joint tenant or tenants.

(c)   This section shall be subject to the provisions of law applicable to transfers in fraud of creditors.

(d)   This section shall not be deemed exclusive; deposit accounts not conforming to this section, and other property jointly owned, shall be governed by other applicable provisions of the law.

(e)   As used in this section:

(1)   "Banking institution" includes commercial banks, industrial banks, building and loan associations, savings and loan associations, and credit unions.

(2)   "Deposit account" includes both time and demand deposits in commercial banks and industrial banks, installment shares, optional shares and fully paid share certificates in building and loan associations and savings and loan associations, and deposits and shares in credit unions.

(3)   "Unwithdrawn deposit" shall be the amount in the deposit account held by the banking institution at the time of the death of the joint tenant; provided, however, that the banking institution shall not be held responsible for any amount properly paid out of said account prior to notice of such death.

(f)   This section does not repeal or modify any provisions of the law relating to estate or inheritance taxes.

(g)   A deposit account under subsection (a) of this section may be established by a written agreement in substantially the following form:

"We, the undersigned, hereby agree that all sums deposited at any time, including sums deposited prior to this date, in the _____ (name of institution) in the joint account of the undersigned, shall be held by us as co-owners with the right of survivorship, regardless of whose funds are deposited in said account and regardless of who deposits the funds in said account. Either or any of us shall have the right to draw upon said account, without limit, and in case of the death of either or any of us the survivor or survivors shall be the sole owner or owners of the entire account. This agreement is governed by the provisions of § 41-2.1 of the General Statutes of North Carolina.

Witness our hands and seals, this _____ day of _____, _____.

_____ (Seal)

_____ (Seal)

_____ (Seal)

_____ (Seal)"

(1959, c. 404; 1963, c. 779; 1969, c. 863; 1973, c. 840; 1975, c. 19, s. 14; 1977, c. 671, ss. 1, 2; 1998-69, s. 11; 1999-337, s. 9; 1999-456, s. 59.)

§ 41-2.2. Joint ownership of securities.

(a) In addition to other forms of ownership, securities may be owned by any parties as joint tenants with rights of survivorship, and not as tenants in common, in the manner provided in this section.

(b) (1) A joint tenancy in securities as provided by this section shall exist when such securities indicate that they are owned with the right of survivorship, or otherwise clearly indicate an intention that upon the death of either party the interest of the decedent shall pass to the surviving party.

(2) Such a joint tenancy may also exist when a broker or custodian holds the securities for the joint tenants and by book entry or otherwise indicates (i) that the securities are owned with the right of survivorship, or (ii) otherwise clearly indicates that upon the death of either party, the interest of the decedent shall pass to the surviving party. Money in the hands of such broker or custodian derived from the sale of, or held for the purpose of, such securities shall be treated in the same manner as such securities.

(c) Upon the death of a joint tenant his interest shall pass to the surviving joint tenant. The interest of the deceased joint tenant, even though it has passed to the surviving joint tenant, remains liable for the debts of the decedent in the same manner as the personal property included in his estate, and recovery thereof shall be made from the surviving joint tenant when the decedent's estate is insufficient to satisfy such debts.

(d)   This section does not repeal or modify any provisions of the law relating to estate or inheritance taxes.

(e)   As used in this section, "securities" has the same meaning as in G.S. 41-40(9) and includes "security account" as that term is defined in G.S. 41-40(10). (1967, c. 864, s. 1; 1969, c. 1115, s. 2; 1989 (Reg. Sess., 1990), c. 891, s. 2; 1998-69, s. 12; 1999-337, s. 10; 2005-411, s. 3.)

§§ 41-2.3 through 41-2.4. Reserved for future codification purposes.

§ 41-2.5. Tenancy by the entirety in mobile homes.

(a)   When a husband and wife become co-owners of a mobile home, in the absence of anything to the contrary appearing in the instrument of title, they become tenants by the entirety with all the incidents of an estate by the entirety in real property, including the right of survivorship in the case of death of either.

(b)   For the purpose of this section it shall be immaterial whether the property at any particular time shall be classified for any purpose as either real or personal. The provisions of subsection (a) shall not limit or prohibit any other type of ownership otherwise authorized by law.

(c)   For purposes of this section "mobile home" means a portable manufactured housing unit designed for transportation on its own chassis and placement on a temporary or semipermanent foundation having a measurement of over 32 feet in length and over eight feet in width. As used in this Article, "mobile home" also means a double-wide mobile home which is two or more portable manufactured housing units designed for transportation on their own chassis, which connect on site for placement on a temporary or semipermanent foundation having a measurement of over 32 feet in length and over eight feet in width.

(d)   This section does not repeal or modify any provisions of the law relating to estate or inheritance taxes. (1981, c. 507, s. 1; 1999-337, s. 11.)

§ 41-3. Survivorship among trustees.

In all cases where only a naked trust not coupled with a beneficial interest has been created or exists, or shall be created, and the conveyance is to two or more trustees, the right to perform the trust and make estates under the same shall be exercised by any one of such trustees, in the event of the death of his cotrustee or cotrustees or the refusal or inability of the cotrustee or cotrustees to perform the trust; and in cases of trusts herein named the trustees shall hold as joint tenants, and in all respects as joint tenants held before the year 1784. (1885, c. 327, s. 1; Rev., s. 1580; C.S., s. 1736.)

§ 41-4. Limitations on failure of issue.

Every contingent limitation in any deed or will, made to depend upon the dying of any person without heir or heirs of the body, or without issue or issues of the body, or without children, or offspring, or descendant, or other relative, shall be held and interpreted a limitation to take effect when such person dies not having such heir, or issue, or child, or offspring, or descendant, or other relative (as the case may be) living at the time of his death, or born to him within 10 lunar months thereafter, unless the intention of such limitation be otherwise, and expressly and plainly declared in the face of the deed or will creating it: Provided, that the rule of construction contained in this section shall not extend to any deed or will made and executed before the fifteenth of January, 1828. (1827, c. 7; R.C., c. 43, s. 3; Code, s. 1327; Rev., s. 1581; C.S., s. 1737.)

§ 41-5. Unborn infant may take by deed or writing.

An infant unborn, but in esse, shall be deemed a person capable of taking by deed or other writing any estate whatever in the same manner as if he were born. (R.C., c. 43, s. 4; Code, s. 1328; Rev., s. 1582; C.S., s. 1738.)

§ 41-6. "Heirs" construed to be "children" in certain limitations.

A limitation by deed, will, or other writing, to the heirs of a living person, shall be construed to be to the children of such person, unless a contrary intention appear by the deed or will. (R.C., c. 43, s. 5; Code, s. 1329; Rev., s. 1583; C.S., s. 1739.)

§ 41-6.1. Meaning of "next of kin."

A limitation by deed, will, or other writing, to the "next of kin" of any person shall be construed to be to those persons who would take under the law of intestate succession, unless a contrary intention appears by the instrument. (1967, c. 948.)

§ 41-6.2. Doctrine of worthier title abolished.

(a)   The law of this State does not include: (i) the common-law rule of worthier title that a grantor or testator cannot convey or devise an interest to the grantor's or testator's own heirs, or (ii) a presumption or rule of interpretation that a grantor or testator does not intend, by a grant or devise to the grantor's or testator's own heirs or next of kin, to transfer an interest to them. The meaning of a grant or devise of a legal or equitable interest to a grantor's or testator's own heirs or next of kin, however designated, shall be determined by the general rules applicable to the interpretation of grants or wills.

(b)   Subdivision (a)(i) of this section shall apply to all revocable trusts in existence as of February 26, 1979 and to all instruments, including revocable trusts, becoming effective after February 26, 1979, and subdivision (a)(ii) of this section shall apply to all instruments in existence as of February 26, 1979 and to all instruments becoming effective after February 26, 1979. If the application of this section to any instrument is held invalid, its application to other instruments to which it may validly be applied shall not be affected thereby. (1979, c. 88, s. 1; 2011-284, s. 49.)

§ 41-6.3. Rule in Shelley's case abolished.

(a) The rule of property known as the rule in Shelley's case is abolished.

(b) This section shall become effective October 1, 1987, and applies to transfers of property that take effect on or after that date. (1987, c. 706, s. 1.)

§ 41-6.4. Rule in Dumpor's Case abolished.

(a) The rule of property known as the Rule in Dumpor's Case is abolished.

(b) This section shall become effective October 1, 2012, and applies to transfers of property that take effect on or after that date. (2012-163, s. 1.)

§ 41-7. Possession transferred to use in certain conveyances.

By deed of bargain and sale, or by deeds of lease and release, or by covenant to stand seized to use, or deed operating by way of covenant to stand seized to use, or otherwise, by any manner or means whatsoever it be, the possession of the bargainor, releasor, or covenanter shall be deemed to be transferred to the bargainee, releasee, or person entitled to the use, for the estate or interest which such person shall have in the use, as perfectly as if the bargainee, releasee or person entitled to the use had been enfeoffed at common law with livery of seizin of the land intended to be conveyed by such deed or covenant. (27 Hen. VIII, c. 10; R.C., c. 43, s. 6; Code, s. 1330; Rev., s. 1584; C.S., s. 1740.)

§ 41-8. Collateral warranties abolished; warranties by life tenants deemed covenants.

All collateral warranties are abolished; and all warranties made by any tenant for life of lands, tenements or hereditaments, the same descending or coming to any person in reversion or remainder, shall be void; and all such warranties, as aforesaid, shall be deemed covenants only, and bind the covenanter in like manner as other obligations. (4 Anne, c. 16, s. 21; 1852, c. 16; R.C., c. 43, s. 10; Code, s. 1334; Rev., s. 1587; C.S., s. 1741.)

§ 41-9: Repealed by Session Laws 1979, c. 180, s. 2.

§ 41-10. Titles quieted.

An action may be brought by any person against another who claims an estate or interest in real property adverse to him for the purpose of determining such adverse claims; and by any man or woman against his or her wife or husband or alleged wife or husband who have not lived together as man and wife within the two years preceding, and who at the death of such plaintiff might have or claim to have an interest in his or her estate, and a decree for the plaintiff shall debar all claims of the defendant in the property of the plaintiff then owned or afterwards acquired: Provided, that no such relief shall be granted against such husband or wife or alleged wife or husband, except in case the summons in said action is personally served on such defendant.

If the defendant in such action disclaim in his answer any interest or estate in the property, or suffer judgment to be taken against him without answer, the plaintiff cannot recover costs. In any case in which judgment has been or shall be docketed, whether such judgment is in favor of or against the person bringing such action, or is claimed by him, or affects real estate claimed by him, or whether such judgment is in favor of or against the person against whom such action may be brought, or is claimed by him, or affects real estate claimed by him, the lien of said judgment shall be such claim of an estate or interest in real estate as is contemplated by this section. (1893, c. 6; 1903, c. 763; Rev., s. 1589; 1907, c. 888; C.S., s. 1743.)

§ 41-10.1. Trying title to land where State claims interest.

Whenever the State of North Carolina or any agency or department thereof asserts a claim of title to land which has not been taken by condemnation and any individual, firm or corporation likewise asserts a claim of title to the said land, such individual, firm or corporation may bring an action in the superior court of the county in which the land lies against the State or such agency or department thereof for the purpose of determining such adverse claims.

Provided, however, that this section shall not apply to lands which have been condemned or taken for use as roads or for public buildings. (1957, c. 514.)

§ 41-11. Sale, lease or mortgage in case of remainders.

In all cases where there is a vested interest in real estate, and a contingent remainder over to persons who are not in being, or when the contingency has not yet happened which will determine who the remaindermen are, there may be a sale, lease or mortgage of the property by a special proceeding in the superior court, which proceeding shall be conducted in the manner pointed out in this section. Said proceeding may be commenced by summons by any person having a vested interest in the land, and all persons in esse who are interested in said land shall be made parties defendant and served with summons in the way and manner now provided by law for the service of summons in other special proceedings, as provided by Rule 4 of the Rules of Civil Procedure, and service of summons upon nonresidents, or persons whose names and residences are unknown, shall be by publication as now required by law or such service in lieu of publication as now provided by law. In cases where the remainder will or may go to minors, or persons under other disabilities, or to persons not in being, or whose names and residences are not known, or who may in any contingency become interested in said land, but because of such contingency cannot be ascertained, the clerk of the superior court shall, after due inquiry of persons who are in no way interested in or connected with such proceeding, designate and appoint some discreet person as guardian ad litem, to represent such remainderman, upon whom summons shall be served as provided by law for other guardians ad litem, and it shall be the duty of such guardian ad litem to defend such actions, and when counsel is needed to represent him, to make this known to the clerk, who shall by an order give instructions as to the employment of counsel and the payment of fees.

The court shall, if the interest of all parties require or would be materially enhanced by it, order a sale of such property or any part thereof for reinvestment, either in purchasing or in improving real estate, less expense allowed by the court for the proceeding and sale, and such newly acquired or improved real estate shall be held upon the same contingencies and in like manner as was the property ordered to be sold. The court may authorize the loaning of such money subject to its approval until such time when it can be reinvested in real estate. And after the sale of such property in all proceedings hereunder, where there is a life estate, in lieu of said interest or investment of proceeds to which the life tenant would be entitled to, or to the use of, the court may in its discretion order the value of said life tenant's share during the probable life of such life tenant, to be ascertained as now provided by law, and paid out of the proceeds of such sale absolutely, and the remainder of such proceeds be reinvested as herein provided. Any person or persons owning a life estate in lands which are unproductive and from which the income is insufficient to pay the taxes on and reasonable upkeep of said lands shall be entitled to maintain an action, without the joinder of any of the remaindermen or reversioners as parties plaintiff, for the sale of said property for the purpose of obtaining funds for improving other nonproductive and unimproved real estate so as to make the same profit-bearing, all to be done under order of the court, or reinvestment of the funds under the provisions of this section, but in every such action when the rights of minors or other persons not sui juris are involved, a competent and disinterested attorney shall be appointed by the court to file answer and represent their interests. The provisions of the preceding sentence, being remedial, shall apply to cases where any title in such lands shall have been acquired before, as well as after, its passage - March 7, 1927.

The clerk of the superior court is authorized to make all orders for the sale, lease or mortgage of property under this section, and for the reinvestment or securing and handling of the proceeds of such sales, but no sale under this section shall be held or mortgage given until the same has been approved by the resident judge of the district, or the judge holding the courts of the district at the time said order of sale is made. The approval by the resident judge of the district may be made by him either during a session of court or at chambers. All orders of approval under said statute by judges resident in the district heretofore made either during a session of court or at chambers are hereby ratified and validated.

The court may authorize the temporary reinvestment, pending final investment in real estate, of funds derived from such sale in any direct obligation of the United States of America or any indirect obligation guaranteed both as to principal and interest or bonds of the State of North Carolina issued since the year 1972; but in the event of such reinvestment, the commissioners, trustees or other officers appointed by the court to hold such funds shall hold the bonds in their possession and shall pay to the life tenant and owner of the vested interest in the lands sold only the interest accruing on the bonds, and the principal of the bonds shall be held subject to final reinvestment and to such expense only as is provided in this section. Temporary reinvestments, as aforesaid, in any direct obligation of the United States of America or any indirect obligation guaranteed both as to principal and interest or State bonds heretofore made with the approval of the court of all or a part of the funds derived from such sales are ratified and declared valid.

The court shall, if the interest of the parties require it and would be materially enhanced by it, order such property mortgaged for such term and on such condition as to the court seems proper and to the best interest of the interested parties. The proceeds derived from the mortgage shall be used for the purpose of adding improvements to the property or to remove existing liens on the property as the court may direct, but for no other purpose. The mortgagees shall not be held responsible for determining the validity of the liens, debts and expenses where the court directs such liens, debts and expenses to be paid. In all cases of mortgages under this section the court shall authorize and direct the guardian representing the interest of minors and the guardian ad litem representing the interest of those persons unknown or not in being to join in the mortgage for the purpose of conveying the interest of such person or persons. In all cases of mortgages under this section the owner of the vested interest or his or her legal representative shall within six months from the date of the mortgage file with the court an itemized statement showing how the money derived from the said mortgage has been expended, and shall exhibit to the court receipts for said money. Said report shall be audited in the same manner as provided for the auditing of guardian's accounts. The owner of the vested interest or his or her legal representative shall collect the rents and income from the property mortgaged and apply the proceeds first to taxes and discharge of interest on the mortgage and the annual curtailment as provided thereby, or if said person uses or occupies said premises he or she shall pay the said taxes, interest and curtailments and said party shall enter into a bond to be approved by the court for the faithful performance of the duties hereby imposed, and such person shall annually file with the court a report and receipts showing that taxes, interest and the curtailment as provided by the mortgage have been paid.

The mortgagee shall not be held responsible for the application of the funds secured or derived from the mortgage. The word "mortgage" whenever used herein shall be construed to include deeds in trust. (1903, c. 99; 1905, c. 548; Rev., s. 1590; 1907, cc. 956, 980; 1919, c. 17; C.S., s. 1744; Ex. Sess. 1921, c. 88; 1923, c. 69; 1925, c. 281; 1927, cc. 124, 186; 1933, c. 123; 1935, c. 299; 1941, c. 328; 1943, cc. 198, 729; 1947, c. 377; 1951, c. 96; 1967, c. 954, s. 3; 1971, c. 528, s. 39.)

§ 41-11.1. Sale, lease or mortgage of property held by a "class," where membership may be increased by persons not in esse.

(a) Wherever there is a gift, devise, transfer or conveyance of a vested estate or interest in real or personal property, or both, to persons described as a class, and at the effective date thereof, one or more members of the class are in esse, and there is a possibility in law that the membership of the class may later be increased by one or more members not then in esse, a special proceeding may be instituted in the superior court for the sale, lease or mortgage of such real or personal property, or both, as provided in this section.

(b) All petitions filed under this section wherein an order is sought for the sale, lease or mortgage of real property, or of both real and personal property, shall be filed in the office of the clerk of the superior court of the county in which all or any part of the real property is situated. If the order sought is for sale, lease or mortgage of personal property, the petition may be filed in the office of the clerk of the superior court of the county in which any or all of such personal estate is situated.

(c) All members of the class in esse shall be parties to the proceeding, and where any of such members are under legal disability, their duly appointed general guardians or their guardians ad litem shall be made parties. The clerk of the superior court shall appoint a guardian ad litem to represent the interests of the possible members of the class not in esse, and such guardian ad litem shall be a party to the proceeding.

(d) Upon a finding by the clerk of the superior court that the interests of all members of the class, both those in esse and those not in esse, would be materially promoted by a sale, lease or mortgage of any such property, he shall enter an order that the sale, lease or mortgage be made, and shall appoint a trustee to make such sale, lease or mortgage, in such manner and on such terms as the clerk may find to be most advantageous to the interests of the members of the class, both those in esse and those not in esse; but no sale, lease or mortgage shall be made, or shall be valid, until approved and confirmed by the resident judge of the district, or the judge holding the courts of the district. As a condition precedent to receiving the proceeds of the sale, lease or mortgage, the trustee shall be bonded in the same manner as a guardian for minors.

(e) In the event of a sale of any such property, the proceeds of sale shall be owned in the identical manner as the property was owned immediately prior to the sale; provided,

(1) The trustee appointed by the clerk as provided above may hold, manage, invest and reinvest said proceeds for the benefit of all members of the class, both those in esse and those not in esse, until the occurrence of the event which will finally determine the identity of all members of the class; all such investments and reinvestments shall be made in accordance with the laws of North Carolina relating to the investment of funds held by guardians or minors; and all the provisions of G.S. 36-4, relating to the reduction in bonds of guardians or trustees upon investment in certain registered securities and the deposit of the securities with the clerk of the superior court, shall be applicable to the trustee appointed hereunder;

(2) The clerk by appropriate order, in lieu of holding, managing, investing and reinvesting the proceeds of sale, may pay or authorize the trustee to pay the entire amount of such proceeds to the living members of the class as they may be then constituted or to their duly appointed guardians, or to pay the ratable portion or portions of such proceeds to one or more of such living members or to their guardians; provided that, where the class would be closed by the death of the mother or mothers of the members of the class, said mother or mothers are living and have attained the age of 55, and upon the further condition that there be first filed with the clerk a bond conditioned upon the payment of the lawful share of any member of the class not then in esse, but who may thereafter come into being or otherwise become a member of the class, to such member or his guardian whenever he becomes a living member of the class. Such bond shall be payable to the State to the use of the additional members of the class and shall be either a cash bond or a premium bond executed by a surety company authorized to transact business in North Carolina. The penalty of such bond shall not be less than one and one fourth the amount of the proceeds of sale. Any bond filed hereunder shall be acknowledged before and approved by the clerk of the superior court.

(f) In the event the proceeds of sale shall be paid over to a trustee and invested by him as authorized above, the entire income actually received by the trustee from such investment shall be paid by said trustee periodically, and not less often than annually, in equal shares to the living members of the class as they shall be constituted at the time of each such payment, or to the duly appointed guardians of any such living members under legal disability.

(g) In the event the court orders a lease of the property, the proceeds from the lease shall be first used to defray the expenses, if any, of the upkeep and maintenance of the property, and the discharge of taxes, liens, charges and encumbrances thereon, and any remaining proceeds shall be paid over by the trustee in their entirety, not less often than annually, in equal shares to the living members of the class as they shall be constituted at the time of each such payment or to the duly appointed guardians of any such members under legal disability.

(h) Payments of income to the living members of the class as aforesaid shall constitute a full and final acquittance and disposition of the income so paid, it being the intent of this section that only the living members of the class (as they may be constituted at the time of each respective income payment) shall be entitled to the income which is the subject of the respective payment, and that possible members of the class not in esse shall not share in, or become entitled to the benefit of any income payment made prior to the time that such members are born and become living members of the class.

(i) In the event that there has been a sale of any of the property, and the proceeds of sale are being held, managed, invested and reinvested by a trustee as provided above, any member of the class who is of legal age and who is not otherwise under legal disability may sell, assign and transfer his entire right, title and interest (both as to principal and income) in the funds or investments so held by the trustee. Upon receiving written notice of such sale, assignment or transfer, the trustee shall recognize the purchaser, assignee and transferee as the lawful successor in all respects whatsoever to the right, title and interest (both as to principal and income) of the seller, assignor and transferor; but no such sale, transfer or assignment shall divest the trustee of his legal title in, or possession of, said funds or investments or (except as provided above) affect his administration of the trusts for which he was appointed.

(j) The court shall order a mortgage of the property only for one or more of the following purposes:

(1) To provide funds for the costs and expenses of court incurred in carrying out any of the provisions of this section;

(2) To provide funds for the necessary upkeep and maintenance of the property;

(3) To make reasonable improvements to the property;

(4) To pay off taxes, other existing liens, charges and encumbrances on the property.

(k) The mortgagee shall not be held responsible for the application of the funds secured or derived from the mortgage. As used in this section, references to mortgages shall also apply to deeds of trust executed for loan security purposes.

(l) Every trustee appointed pursuant to the provisions of this section shall file with the clerk of the superior court an inventory and annual accounts in the same manner as is now provided by law with respect to guardians.

(m) The superior court shall allow commissions to the trustee for his time and trouble in the effectuation of a sale, lease or mortgage, and in the investment and management of the proceeds, in the same manner and under the same rules and restrictions as allowances are made to executors, administrators, and collectors.

(n) Provided, however, this section shall not be applicable where the instrument creating the gift, devise, transfer or conveyance specifically directs, by means of the creation of a trust or otherwise, the manner in which the property shall be used or disposed of, or contains specific limitations, conditions or restrictions as to the use, form, investment, leasing, mortgage, or other disposition of the property.

(o) And provided further, this section shall not alter or affect in any way laws or legal principles heretofore, now, or hereafter existing relating to the determination of the nature, extent or vesting of estates or property interests, and of the persons entitled thereto. But where, under the laws and legal principles existing without regard to this section, a gift, devise, transfer or conveyance has the legal effect of being made to all members of a class, some of whom are in esse and some of whom are in posse, the procedures authorized hereby may be utilized for the purpose of promoting the best interests of all members of the class, and this section shall be liberally construed to effectuate this intent. The remedies and procedures herein specified shall not be exclusive, but shall be cumulative, in addition to, and without prejudice to, all other remedies and procedures, if any, which now exist or hereafter may exist either by virtue of statute, or by virtue of the inherent powers of any court of competent jurisdiction, or otherwise.

(p) The provisions of this section shall apply to gifts, devises, transfers, and conveyances made both before and after April 5, 1949. (1949, c. 811, s. 1; 1971, c. 641, s. 1; 1997-456, s. 27; 2011-284, s. 50(a)-(d).)

§ 41-12. Sales or mortgages of contingent remainders validated.

In all cases where property has been conveyed by deed, or devised by will, upon contingent remainder, executory devise, or other limitations, where a judgment of a superior court has been rendered authorizing the sale or mortgaging, including execution of deeds of trust, of such property discharged of such contingent remainder, executory devise, or other limitations in actions or special proceedings where all persons in being who would have taken such property if the contingency had then happened were parties, such judgment shall be valid and binding upon the parties thereto and upon all other persons not then in being or whose estates had not been vested: Provided, that nothing herein contained shall be construed to impair or destroy any vested right or estate. (1905, c. 93; Rev., s. 1591; C.S., s. 1745; 1923, c. 64; 1935, c. 36.)

§ 41-13. Freeholders in petition for special taxes defined.

In all cases where a petition by a specific number of freeholders is required as a condition precedent to ordering an election to provide for the assessment or levy of taxes upon realty, all residents of legal age owning realty for life or longer term, irrespective of sex, shall be deemed freeholders within the meaning of such requirement. (1915, c. 22; C.S., s. 1746.)

§ 41-14. Reserved for future codification purposes.

Article 2.

Uniform Statutory Rule Against Perpetuities.

§ 41-15. Statutory rule against perpetuities.

(a) Except as otherwise provided in G.S. 41-23, a nonvested property interest is invalid unless:

(1) When the interest is created, it is certain to vest or terminate no later than 21 years after the death of an individual then alive; or

(2) The interest either vests or terminates within 90 years after its creation.

(b) A general power of appointment not presently exercisable because of a condition precedent is invalid unless:

(1) When the power is created, the condition precedent is certain to be satisfied or become impossible to satisfy no later than 21 years after the death of an individual then alive; or

(2) The condition precedent either is satisfied or becomes impossible to satisfy within 90 years after its creation.

(c) A nongeneral power of appointment or a general testamentary power of appointment is invalid unless:

(1) When the power is created, it is certain to be irrevocably exercised or otherwise to terminate no later than 21 years after the death of an individual then alive; or

(2) The power is irrevocably exercised or otherwise terminates within 90 years after its creation.

(d) In determining whether a nonvested property interest or a power of appointment is valid under subdivision (a)(1), (b)(1), or (c)(1) of this section, the possibility that a child will be born to an individual after the individual's death is disregarded.

(e) If, in measuring a period from the creation of a property arrangement, language in a governing instrument:

(1) Seeks to disallow the vesting or termination of any interest beyond,

(2) Seeks to postpone the vesting or termination of any interest until, or

(3) Seeks to operate in effect in any similar fashion upon,

the later of (i) the expiration of a period of time not exceeding 21 years after the death of the survivor of specified lives in being at the creation of the property arrangement or (ii) the expiration of a period of time that exceeds or might exceed 21 years after the death of the survivor of lives in being at the creation of the property arrangement, that language is inoperative to the extent it produces a period of time that exceeds 21 years after the death of the survivor of the specified lives. (1995, c. 190, s. 1; 2007-390, s. 2.)

§ 41-16. When nonvested property interest or power of appointment created.

(a) Except as provided in subsections (b) and (c) of this section and in G.S. 41-19(a), the time for creation of a nonvested property interest or a power of appointment is determined under general principles of property law.

(b) For purposes of this Article, if there is a person who alone can exercise a power created by a governing instrument to become the unqualified beneficial owner of (i) a nonvested property interest or (ii) a property interest subject to a power of appointment described in G.S. 41-15(b) or (c), the nonvested property interest or power of appointment is created when the power to become the unqualified beneficial owner terminates.

(c) For purposes of this Article, a nonvested property interest or a power of appointment arising from a transfer of property to a previously funded trust or other existing property arrangement is created when the nonvested property interest or power of appointment in the original contribution was created. (1995, c. 190, s. 1.)

§ 41-17. Reformation.

Upon the petition of an interested person, a court shall reform a disposition in the manner that most closely approximates the transferor's manifested plan of distribution and is within the 90 years allowed by G.S. 41-15(a)(2), 41-15(b)(2), or 41-15(c)(2) if:

(1) A nonvested property interest or a power of appointment becomes invalid under G.S. 41-15;

(2) A class gift is not invalid under G.S. 41-15, but might become invalid under G.S. 41-15, and the time has arrived when the share of any class is to take effect in possession or enjoyment; or

(3) A nonvested property interest that is not validated by G.S. 41-15(a)(1) can vest but not within 90 years after its creation. (1995, c. 190, s. 1.)

§ 41-18. Exclusions from statutory rule against perpetuities.

G.S. 41-15 does not apply to:

(1) A nonvested property interest or a power of appointment arising out of a nondonative transfer, except a nonvested property interest or a power of appointment arising out of:

a. A premarital or postmarital agreement;

b. A separation or divorce settlement;

c. A spouse's election;

d. A similar arrangement arising out of a prospective, existing, or previous marital relationship between the parties;

e. A contract to make or not to revoke a will or trust;

f. A contract to exercise or not to exercise a power of appointment;

g. A transfer in satisfaction of a duty of support; or

h. A reciprocal transfer;

(2) A fiduciary's power relating to the administration or management of assets, including the power of a fiduciary to sell, lease, or mortgage property, and the power of a fiduciary to determine principal and income;

(3) A power to appoint a fiduciary;

(4) A discretionary power of a trustee to distribute principal before termination of a trust to a beneficiary having an indefeasibly vested interest in the income and principal;

(5) A nonvested property interest held by a charity, government, or governmental agency or subdivision, if the nonvested property interest is preceded by an interest held by another charity, government, or governmental agency or subdivision;

(6) A nonvested property interest in or a power of appointment with respect to a trust or other property arrangement forming part of a pension, profit-sharing, stock bonus, health, disability, death benefit, income deferral, or other current or deferred benefit plan for one or more employees, independent contractors, or their beneficiaries or spouses, to which contributions are made for the purpose of distributing to or for the benefit of the participants or their beneficiaries or spouses the property, income, or principal in the trust or other property arrangement, except a nonvested property interest or a power of appointment that is created by an election of a participant or a beneficiary or spouse;

(7) A property interest, power of appointment, or arrangement that was not subject to the common-law rule against perpetuities or is excluded by another statute of this State;

(8) A property interest or arrangement subjected to a time limit under Article 14 of Chapter 36A, "Honorary Trusts; Trusts for Pets; Trusts for Cemetery Lots"; or

(9) A property interest or arrangement subjected to a time limit under Article 3 of this Chapter, "Time Limits on Options in Gross and Certain Other Interests in Land". (1995, c. 190, ss. 1-3.)

§ 41-19. Prospective application.

(a) Except as extended by subsection (b) of this section, this Article applies to a nonvested property interest or a power of appointment that is created on or after October 1, 1995. For purposes of this section, a nonvested property interest or a power of appointment created by the exercise of a power of appointment is created when the power is irrevocably exercised or when a revocable exercise becomes irrevocable.

(b)   If a nonvested property interest or a power of appointment was created prior to October 1, 1995, and is determined in a judicial proceeding, commenced on or after October 1, 1995, to violate this State's rule against perpetuities as that rule existed before October 1, 1995, a court upon the petition of an interested person may reform the disposition in the manner that most closely approximates the transferor's manifested plan of distribution and is within the limits of the rule against perpetuities applicable when the nonvested property interest or power of appointment was created. (1995, c. 190, s. 1; 1997, c. 456, s. 8.)

§ 41-20. Short title.

This Article may be cited as the Uniform Statutory Rule Against Perpetuities. (1995, c. 190, s. 1.)

§ 41-21. Uniformity of application and construction.

This Article shall be applied and construed to effectuate its general purpose to make uniform the law with respect to the subject of this Article among states enacting it. (1995, c. 190, s. 1.)

§ 41-22. Supersession.

This Article supersedes the rule of the common law known as the rule against perpetuities. (1995, c. 190, s. 1.)

§ 41-23. Perpetuities and suspension of power of alienation for trusts.

(a) A trust is void if it suspends the power of alienation of trust property, as that term is defined in G.S. 36C-1-103, for longer than the permissible period. The permissible period is no later than 21 years after the death of an individual then alive or lives then in being plus a period of 21 years.

(b) If the settlor of a revocable trust, as those terms are defined in G.S. 36C-1-103, has an unlimited power to revoke or amend the trust, the permissible period under subsection (a) of this section is computed from the termination of that power.

(c) If a trust is created by exercise of a power of appointment, the permissible period under subsection (a) of this section is computed from the time the power is exercised if the power is a general power even if the power is only exercisable as a testamentary power. In the case of other powers, the permissible period is computed from the time the power is created, but facts at the time the power is exercised shall be considered in determining whether the power of alienation is suspended beyond a life or lives in being at the time of the creation of the power plus 21 years.

(d) The power of alienation is suspended only when there are no persons in being who, alone or in combination with others, can convey an absolute fee in possession of land, or full ownership of personal property.

(e) Notwithstanding subsection (a) of this section, there is no suspension of the power of alienability by a trust or by equitable interests under a trust if the trustee has the power to sell, either expressed or implied, or if there exists an unlimited power to terminate the trust in one or more persons in being.

(f) This section does not apply to a transfer in trust (i) for charitable purposes, as defined in G.S. 36C-4-405; (ii) to a literary or charitable organization; (iii) to a veterans' memorial organization; (iv) to a cemetery corporation, society, or association; or (v) as part of a pension, retirement, insurance, savings, stock bonus, profit sharing, death, disability, or similar plan established by an employer for the benefit of some or all of its employees for the purpose of accumulating and distributing to such employees the earnings or the principal, or both earnings and principal, of the trust.

(g) This section does not apply to a future interest other than a future interest in trust and, other than as set forth in this section, this section does not modify the common law of the State regarding the power of alienation in this State.

(h) The provisions of G.S. 41-15 and the common law rule against perpetuities do not apply to trusts created or administered in this State. (2007-390, s. 1.)

§ 41-24. Reserved for future codification purposes.

§ 41-25. Reserved for future codification purposes.

§ 41-26. Reserved for future codification purposes.

§ 41-27. Reserved for future codification purposes.

Article 3.

Time Limits on Options in Gross and Certain Other Interests in Land.

§ 41-28. Definitions.

As used in this Article:

(1) "Nonvested easement in gross" means a nonvested easement which is not created to benefit or which does not benefit the possessor of any tract of land in his or her use of it as the possessor.

(2) "Option in gross with respect to an interest in land" means an option in which the holder of the option does not own any leasehold or other interest in the land which is the subject of the option.

(3) "Preemptive right in the nature of a right of first refusal in gross with respect to an interest in land" means a preemptive right in which the holder of

the preemptive right does not own any leasehold or other interest in the land which is the subject of the preemptive right. (1995, c. 525, s. 1.)

§ 41-29. Options in gross, etc.

An option in gross with respect to an interest in land or a preemptive right in the nature of a right of first refusal in gross with respect to an interest in land becomes invalid if it is not actually exercised within 30 years after its creation. For purposes of this section, the term "interest in land" does not include arrangements relating solely to an interest in oil, gas, or minerals. (1995, c. 525, s. 1.)

§ 41-30. Leases to commence in the future.

A lease to commence at a time certain or upon the occurrence or nonoccurrence of a future event becomes invalid if its term does not actually commence in possession within 30 years after its execution. For purposes of this section, the term "lease" does not include an oil, gas, or mineral lease. (1995, c. 525, s. 1.)

§ 41-31. Nonvested easements.

A nonvested easement in gross becomes invalid if it does not actually vest within 30 years after its creation. (1995, c. 525, s. 1.)

§ 41-32. Possibilities of reverter, etc.

(a) Except as otherwise provided in this section:

(1) A possibility of reverter preceded by a fee simple determinable;

(2) A right of entry preceded by a fee simple subject to a condition subsequent; or

(3) An executory interest preceded by either a fee simple determinable or a fee simple subject to an executory limitation;

becomes invalid, and the preceding fee simple becomes a fee simple absolute, if the right to vest in possession of the possibility of reverter, right of entry, or executory interest depends on an event or events affecting the use of land and if the possibility of reverter, right of entry, or executory interest does not actually vest in possession within 60 years after its creation.

(b) This section does not apply to a possibility of reverter, right of entry, or executory interest held by a charity, a government or governmental agency or subdivision excluded from the Uniform Statutory Rule Against Perpetuities by G.S. 41-18(5) or to an arrangement relating solely to an interest in oil, gas, or minerals. (1995, c. 525, s. 1.)

§ 41-33. Prospective application.

This Article applies only to a property interest or arrangement that is created on or after October 1, 1995. (1995, c. 525, s. 1.)

§ 41-34. Reserved for future codification purposes.

§ 41-35. Reserved for future codification purposes.

§ 41-36. Reserved for future codification purposes.

§ 41-37. Reserved for future codification purposes.

§ 41-38. Reserved for future codification purposes.

§ 41-39. Reserved for future codification purposes.

Article 4.

The Uniform Transfer on Death (TOD) Security Registration Act.

§ 41-40. Definitions.

In this Article, unless the context otherwise requires:

(1)   "Beneficiary form" means a registration of a security that indicates the present owner of the security and the intention of the owner regarding the person who will become the owner of the security upon the death of the owner.

(2)   "Devisee" means any person designated in a will to receive a disposition of real or personal property.

(3)   "Heirs" means those persons, including the surviving spouse, who are entitled under Chapter 29 of the General Statutes or the statutes of intestate succession of other states to take the property of a decedent by intestate succession.

(4)   "Person" means an individual, a corporation, an organization, or other legal entity.

(5)   "Personal representative" includes executor, administrator, collector, successor personal representative, special administrator, and persons who perform substantially the same function under the law governing their status.

(6)   "Property" includes both real and personal property or any interest in real or personal property and means anything that may be the subject of ownership.

(7) "Register", including its derivatives, means to issue a certificate showing the ownership of a certificated security or, in the case of an uncertificated security, to initiate or transfer an account showing ownership of securities.

(8) "Registering entity" means a person who originates or transfers a security title by registration and includes a broker maintaining security accounts for customers and a transfer agent or other person acting for or as an issuer of securities.

(9) "Security" means a share, participation, or other interest in property, a business, or an obligation of an enterprise or other issuer, and includes a certificated security, an uncertificated security, a security account, and a security entitlement as defined in G.S. 25-8-102.

(10) "Security account" means (i) a reinvestment account associated with a security, a securities account with a broker, a cash balance in a brokerage account, cash, interest, earnings, or dividends earned or declared on a security in an account, a reinvestment account, or a brokerage account, whether or not credited to the account before the owner's death, or (ii) a cash balance or other property held for or due to the owner of a security as a replacement for or product of an account security, whether or not credited to the account before the owner's death.

(11) "State" includes any state of the United States, the District of Columbia, the Commonwealth of Puerto Rico, and any territory or possession subject to the legislative authority of the United States. (2005-411, s. 1.)

§ 41-41. Registration in beneficiary form; sole or joint tenancy ownership.

Only individuals whose registration of a security shows sole ownership by one individual or multiple ownership by two or more individuals with right of survivorship, rather than as tenants in common, may obtain registration in beneficiary form. Multiple owners of a security registered in beneficiary form hold as joint tenants with right of survivorship, as tenants by the entireties, or as owners of community property held in survivorship form, and not as tenants in common. (2005-411, s. 1.)

§ 41-42. Registration in beneficiary form; applicable law.

A security may be registered in beneficiary form if the form is authorized by this or a similar statute of the state of organization of the issuer or registering entity, the location of the registering entity's principal office, the office of its transfer agent or its office making the registration, or by this or a similar statute of the law of the state listed as the owner's address at the time of registration. A registration governed by the law of a jurisdiction in which this or similar legislation is not in force or was not in force when a registration in beneficiary form was made is nevertheless presumed to be valid and authorized as a matter of contract law. (2005-411, s. 1.)

§ 41-43. Origination of registration in beneficiary form.

A security, whether evidenced by certificate or account, is registered in beneficiary form when the registration includes a designation of a beneficiary to take the ownership at the death of the owner or the deaths of all multiple owners. (2005-411, s. 1.)

§ 41-44. Form of registration in beneficiary form.

Registration in beneficiary form may be shown by the words "transfer on death" or the abbreviation "TOD", or by the words "pay on death" or the abbreviation "POD", after the name of the registered owner or owners and before the name of a beneficiary. (2005-411, s. 1.)

§ 41-45. Effect of registration in beneficiary form.

The designation of a TOD beneficiary on a registration in beneficiary form has no effect on ownership of the security until the owner's death. A registration of a security in beneficiary form may be cancelled or changed at any time by the sole owner or all then-surviving owners, without the consent of the beneficiary. (2005-411, s. 1.)

§ 41-46. Ownership on death of owner.

On death of a sole owner or the last to die of all multiple owners, ownership of securities registered in beneficiary form passes to the beneficiary or beneficiaries who survive all owners. On proof of death of all owners and compliance with any applicable requirements of the registering entity, a security registered in beneficiary form may be reregistered in the name of the beneficiary or beneficiaries who survive the death of all owners. Until division of the security after the death of all owners, multiple beneficiaries surviving the death of all owners hold their interests as tenants in common. If no beneficiary survives the death of all owners, the security belongs to the estate of the deceased sole owner or the estate of the last to die of all multiple owners. (2005-411, s. 1.)

§ 41-47. Protection of registering entity.

(a) A registering entity is not required to offer or to accept a request for security registration in beneficiary form. If a registration in beneficiary form is offered by a registering entity, the owner requesting registration in beneficiary form assents to the protections given to the registering entity by this Article.

(b) By accepting a request for registration of a security in beneficiary form, the registering entity agrees that the registration will be implemented on death of the deceased owner as provided in this Article.

(c) A registering entity is discharged from all claims to a security by the estate, creditors, heirs, or devisees of a deceased owner if it registers a transfer of a security in accordance with G.S. 41-46 and does so in good faith reliance (i) on the registration, (ii) on this Article, and (iii) on information provided to it by affidavit of the personal representative of the deceased owner, or by the surviving beneficiary or by the surviving beneficiary's representatives, or other information available to the registering entity. The protections of this Article do not extend to a reregistration or payment made after a registering entity has received written notice, addressed to the registering entity, from any claimant to any interest in the security objecting to implementation of a registration in beneficiary form. No other notice or other information available to the registering entity affects its right to protection under this Article.

(d) The protection provided by this Article to the registering entity of a security does not affect the rights of beneficiaries in disputes between themselves and other claimants to ownership of the security transferred or its value or proceeds. (2005-411, s. 1; 2006-226, s. 11.)

§ 41-48. Nontestamentary transfer on death.

(a) A transfer on death resulting from a registration in beneficiary form is effective by reason of the contract regarding the registration between the owner and the registering entity and this Article and is not testamentary.

(b) The interest of a deceased owner when there are one or more surviving owners remains liable for the debts of the decedent in the same manner as the personal property included in the decedent's estate, and recovery of that interest shall be made from the surviving owner or owners when the decedent's estate is insufficient to satisfy the debts. The interest of a deceased sole owner, or the last to die of several owners, remains liable for the debts of the decedent in the same manner as the personal property included in the decedent's estate, and recovery of that interest shall be made from the TOD beneficiary when the decedent's estate is insufficient to satisfy the debts.

(c) This Article does not repeal or modify any provision of law relating to estate taxes. (2005-411, s. 1.)

§ 41-49. Terms, conditions, and forms for registration.

(a) A registering entity offering to accept registrations in beneficiary form may establish the terms and conditions under which it will receive requests (i) for registrations in beneficiary form, and (ii) for implementation of registrations in beneficiary form, including requests for cancellation of previously registered TOD beneficiary designations and requests for reregistration to effect a change of beneficiary. The terms and conditions established may provide for proving death, avoiding or resolving any problems concerning fractional shares, and designating primary or contingent beneficiaries. Forms of identifying beneficiaries who are to take on one or more contingencies, and rules for providing proofs and assurances needed to satisfy reasonable concerns by registering entities regarding conditions and identities relevant to accurate implementation of registrations in beneficiary form, may be contained in a registering entity's terms and conditions.

(b) The following are illustrations of registrations in beneficiary form that a registering entity may authorize:

(1) Sole owner-sole beneficiary: "John S. Brown TOD (or POD) John S. Brown, Jr."

(2) Multiple owners-sole beneficiary: "John S. Brown, Mary B. Brown JT TEN WROS TOD John S. Brown, Jr."

(3) Multiple owners-primary and secondary (substituted) beneficiaries: "John S. Brown, Mary B. Brown JT TEN WROS TOD John S. Brown, Jr. SUB BENE Peter O. Brown". (2005-411, s. 1.)

§ 41-50. Short title; rules of construction.

(a) This Article shall be known as and may be cited as the "Uniform TOD Security Registration Act".

(b) This Article shall be applied and construed to effectuate its general purposes and to make uniform the laws with respect to the subject of this Article among states enacting it.

(c) This Article does not repeal G.S. 41-2.2. G.S. 41-2.2 applies in determining whether a right of survivorship exists among multiple owners of a security. (2005-411, s. 1.)

§ 41-51. Application of Article.

This Article applies to registrations of securities in beneficiary form made before, on, or after October 1, 2005, by decedents dying on or after October 1, 2005. (2005-411, s. 1.)

Chapter 41A.

State Fair Housing Act.

§ 41A-1. Title.

This Chapter shall be known and may be cited as the State Fair Housing Act. (1983, c. 522, s. 1.)

§ 41A-2. Purpose.

The purpose of this Chapter is to provide fair housing throughout the State of North Carolina. (1983, c. 522, s. 1.)

§ 41A-3. Definitions.

For the purposes of this Chapter, the following definitions apply:

(1) The "Commission" means the North Carolina Human Relations Commission;

(1a) "Covered multifamily dwellings" means:

a. A building, including all units and common use areas, in which there are four or more units if the building has one or more elevators; or

b. Ground floor units and ground floor common use areas in a building with four or more units.

(1b) "Familial status" means one or more persons who have not attained the age of 18 years being domiciled with:

a. A parent or another person having legal custody of the person or persons; or

b. The designee of the parent or other person having custody, provided the designee has the written permission of the parent or other person.

The protections against discrimination on the basis of familial status shall apply to any person who is pregnant or is in the process of securing legal custody of any person who has not attained the age of 18 years.

(2) "Family" includes a single individual;

(3) "Financial institution" means any banking corporation or trust company, savings and loan association, credit union, insurance company, or related corporation, partnership, foundation, or other institution engaged primarily in lending or investing funds;

(3a) "Handicapping condition" means (i) a physical or mental impairment which substantially limits one or more of a person's major life activities, (ii) a record of having such an impairment, or (iii) being regarded as having such an impairment. Handicapping condition does not include current, illegal use of or addiction to a controlled substance as defined in 21 U.S.C. § 802, the Controlled Substances Act. The protections against discrimination on the basis of handicapping condition shall apply to a buyer or renter of a dwelling, a person residing in or intending to reside in the dwelling after it is sold, rented, or made available, or any person associated with the buyer or renter.

(4) "Housing accommodation" means any improved or unimproved real property, or part thereof, which is used or occupied, or is intended, arranged, or designed to be used or occupied, as the home or residence of one or more individuals;

(5) "Person" means any individual, association, corporation, political subdivision, partnership, labor union, legal representative, mutual company, joint stock company, trust, trustee in bankruptcy, unincorporated organization, or other legal or commercial entity, the State, or governmental entity or agency;

(6) "Real estate broker or salesman" means a person, whether licensed or not, who, for or with the expectation of receiving a consideration, lists, sells, purchases, exchanges, rents, or leases real property, or who negotiates or attempts to negotiate any of these activities, or who holds himself out as engaged in these activities, or who negotiates or attempts to negotiate a loan secured or to be secured by mortgage or other encumbrance upon real property, or who is engaged in the business of listing real property in a publication; or a person employed by or acting on behalf of any of these persons;

(7) "Real estate transaction" means the sale, exchange, rental, or lease of real property;

(8) "Real property" means a building, structure, real estate, land, tenement, leasehold, interest in real estate cooperatives, condominium, and hereditament, corporeal and incorporeal, or any interest therein. (1983, c. 522, s. 1; 1989, c. 507, s. 1; 1989 (Reg. Sess., 1990), c. 979, s. 1(1).)

§ 41A-4. Unlawful discriminatory housing practices.

(a) It is an unlawful discriminatory housing practice for any person in a real estate transaction, because of race, color, religion, sex, national origin, handicapping condition, or familial status to:

(1) Refuse to engage in a real estate transaction;

(2) Discriminate against a person in the terms, conditions, or privileges of a real estate transaction or in the furnishing of facilities or services in connection therewith;

(2a), (2c) Repealed by Session Laws 2009-388, s. 1, effective October 1, 2009.

(3) Refuse to receive or fail to transmit a bona fide offer to engage in a real estate transaction;

(4) Refuse to negotiate for a real estate transaction;

(5) Represent to a person that real property is not available for inspection, sale, rental, or lease when in fact it is so available, or fail to bring a property listing to his attention, or refuse to permit him to inspect real property;

(6) Make, print, circulate, post, or mail or cause to be so published a statement, advertisement, or sign, or use a form or application for a real estate transaction, or make a record or inquiry in connection with a prospective real estate transaction, which indicates directly or indirectly, an intent to make a limitation, specification, or discrimination with respect thereto;

(7) Offer, solicit, accept, use, or retain a listing of real property with the understanding that any person may be discriminated against in a real estate transaction or in the furnishing of facilities or services in connection therewith; or

(8) Otherwise make unavailable or deny housing.

(b) Repealed by Session Laws 1989, c. 507, s. 2.

(b1) It is an unlawful discriminatory housing practice for any person or other entity whose business includes engaging in residential real estate related transactions to discriminate against any person in making available such a transaction, or in the terms and conditions of such a transaction, because of race, color, religion, sex, national origin, handicapping condition, or familial status. As used in this subsection, "residential real estate related transaction" means:

(1) The making or purchasing of loans or providing financial assistance (i) for purchasing, constructing, improving, repairing, or maintaining a dwelling, or (ii) where the security is residential real estate; or

(2) The selling, brokering, or appraising of residential real estate.

The provisions of this subsection shall not prohibit any financial institution from using a loan application which inquires into a person's financial and dependent obligations or from basing its actions on the income or financial abilities of any person.

(c) It is an unlawful discriminatory housing practice for a person to induce or attempt to induce another to enter into a real estate transaction from which such person may profit:

(1) By representing that a change has occurred, or may or will occur in the composition of the residents of the block, neighborhood, or area in which the real property is located with respect to race, color, religion, sex, national origin, handicapping condition, or familial status of the owners or occupants; or

(2) By representing that a change has resulted, or may or will result in the lowering of property values, an increase in criminal or antisocial behavior, or a decline in the quality of schools in the block, neighborhood, or area in which the real property is located.

(d)   It is an unlawful discriminatory housing practice to deny any person who is otherwise qualified by State law access to or membership or participation in any real estate brokers' organization, multiple listing service, or other service, organization, or facility relating to the business of engaging in real estate transactions, or to discriminate in the terms or conditions of such access, membership, or participation because of race, color, religion, sex, national origin, handicapping condition, or familial status.

(e)   It is an unlawful discriminatory housing practice to coerce, intimidate, threaten, or interfere with any person in the exercise or enjoyment of, on account of having exercised or enjoyed, or on account of having aided or encouraged any other person in the exercise or enjoyment of any right granted or protected by this Chapter.

(f)   It is an unlawful discriminatory housing practice to:

(1)   Refuse to permit, at the expense of a handicapped person, reasonable modifications of existing premises occupied or to be occupied by the person if the modifications are necessary to the handicapped person's full enjoyment of the premises; except that, in the case of a rental unit, the landlord may, where it is reasonable to do so, condition permission for modifications on agreement by the renter to restore the interior of the premises to the condition that existed before the modifications, reasonable wear and tear excepted.

(2)   Refuse to make reasonable accommodations in rules, policies, practices, or services, when these accommodations may be necessary to a handicapped person's equal use and enjoyment of a dwelling.

(3)   Fail to design and construct covered multifamily dwellings available for first occupancy after March 13, 1991, so that:

a.   The dwellings have at least one building entrance on an accessible route, unless it is impractical to do so because of terrain or unusual site characteristics; or

b.   With respect to dwellings with a building entrance on an accessible route:

1.   The public and common use portions are readily accessible to and usable by handicapped persons;

2. There is an accessible route into and through all dwellings and units;

3. All doors designed to allow passage into, within, and through these dwellings and individual units are wide enough for wheelchairs;

4. Light switches, electrical switches, electrical outlets, thermostats, and other environmental controls are in accessible locations;

5. Bathroom walls are reinforced to allow later installation of grab bars; and

6. Kitchens and bathrooms have space for an individual in a wheelchair to maneuver.

(g) It is an unlawful discriminatory housing practice to discriminate in land-use decisions or in the permitting of development based on race, color, religion, sex, national origin, handicapping condition, familial status, or, except as otherwise provided by law, the fact that a development or proposed development contains affordable housing units for families or individuals with incomes below eighty percent (80%) of area median income. It is not a violation of this Chapter if land-use decisions or permitting of development is based on considerations of limiting high concentrations of affordable housing. (1983, c. 522, s. 1; 1989, c. 507, s. 2; 1989 (Reg. Sess., 1990), c. 979, s. 3; 2009-388, s. 1; 2009-533, s. 1.)

§ 41A-5. Proof of violation.

(a) It is a violation of this Chapter if:

(1) A person by his act or failure to act intends to discriminate against a person. A person intends to discriminate if, in committing an unlawful discriminatory housing practice described in G.S. 41A-4 he was motivated in full, or in any part at all, by race, color, religion, sex, national origin, handicapping condition, or familial status. An intent to discriminate may be established by direct or circumstantial evidence.

(2) A person's act or failure to act has the effect, regardless of intent, of discriminating, as set forth in G.S. 41A-4, against a person of a particular race, color, religion, sex, national origin, handicapping condition, or familial status. However, it is not a violation of this Chapter if a person whose action or inaction

has an unintended discriminatory effect, proves that his action or inaction was motivated and justified by business necessity.

(3)   A person's act or failure to act violates G.S. 41A-4(f).

(4)   A local government's act or failure to act in land-use decisions or in the permitting of development is intended to discriminate against affordable housing. A local government intends to discriminate if, in committing an unlawful discriminatory housing practice described in G.S. 41A-4(g), the local government was motivated in full, or in any part at all, by the fact that a development or proposed development contains affordable housing units for families or individuals with incomes below eighty percent (80%) of area median income. It is not a violation of this Chapter if land-use decisions or permitting of development is based on considerations of limiting high concentrations of affordable housing. An intent to discriminate may be established by direct or circumstantial evidence.

(5)   A local government's act or failure to act has the effect, regardless of intent, of discriminating against affordable housing in land-use decisions or in the permitting of development, as set forth in G.S. 41A-4(g). It is not a violation of this Chapter if land-use decisions or permitting of development is based on considerations of limiting high concentrations of affordable housing. It is not a violation of this Chapter if a local government whose action or inaction has an unintended discriminatory effect proves that the action or inaction was motivated and justified by a legitimate, bona fide governmental interest.

(b)   It shall be no defense to a violation of this Chapter that the violation was requested, sought, or otherwise procured by another person. (1983, c. 522, s. 1; 1987, c. 603, s. 1; 1989, c. 507, s. 3; 2009-388, s. 2; 2009-533, s. 2.)

§ 41A-6. Exemptions.

(a)   The provisions of G.S. 41A-4, except for subdivision (a)(6), do not apply to the following:

(1)   The rental of a housing accommodation in a building which contains housing accommodations for not more than four families living independently of each other, if the lessor or a member of his family resides in one of the housing accommodations;

(2) The rental of a room or rooms in a private house, not a boarding house, if the lessor or a member of his family resides in the house;

(3) Religious institutions or organizations or charitable or educational organizations operated, supervised, or controlled by religious institutions or organizations which give preference to members of the same religion in a real estate transaction, as long as membership in such religion is not restricted by race, color, sex, national origin, handicapping condition, or familial status;

(4) Private clubs, not in fact open to the public, which incident to their primary purpose or purposes provide lodging, which they own or operate for other than a commercial purpose, to their members or give preference to their members;

(5) With respect to discrimination based on sex, the rental or leasing of housing accommodations in single-sex dormitory property; and

(6) Repealed by Session Laws 1989 (Reg. Sess., 1990), c. 979, s. 4.

(7) The sale, rental, exchange, or lease of commercial real estate. For the purposes of this Chapter, commercial real estate means real property which is not intended for residential use.

(b) No provision of this Chapter requires that a dwelling be made available to a person whose tenancy would constitute a direct threat to the health or safety of other persons or whose tenancy would result in substantial physical damage to the property of others.

(c) No provision of this Chapter limits the applicability of any reasonable local or State restrictions regarding the maximum number of occupants permitted to occupy a dwelling unit.

(d) Nothing in this Chapter shall be deemed to nullify any provisions of the North Carolina Building Code applicable to the construction of residential housing for the handicapped.

(e) No provision of this Chapter regarding familial status applies with respect to housing for older persons. "Housing for older persons" means housing:

(1) Provided under any State or federal program specifically designed and operated to assist elderly persons as defined in the program;

(2) Intended for and solely occupied by person 62 years or older. Housing satisfies the requirements of this subdivision even though there are persons residing in such housing on September 13, 1988, who are under 62 years of age, provided that all new occupants after September 13, 1988, are 62 years or older; or

(3) Intended for and operated for occupancy by at least one person 55 years of age or older per unit as shown by such factors as (i) the existence of significant facilities and services specifically designed to meet the physical and social needs of older persons or, if this is not practicable, that the housing provides important housing opportunities for older persons, (ii) at least eighty percent (80%) of the units are occupied by at least one person 55 years of age or older per unit; and (iii) the publication of and adherence to policies and procedures which demonstrate an intent by the owner or manager to provide housing for persons 55 years or older. Housing satisfies the requirements of this subdivision even though on September 13, 1988, under eighty percent (80%) of the units in the housing facility are occupied by at least one person 55 years or older per unit, provided that eighty percent (80%) of the units that are occupied by new tenants after September 13, 1988, are occupied by at least one person 55 years or older per unit until such time as eighty percent (80%) of all the units in the housing facility are occupied by at least one person 55 years or older. Housing facilities newly constructed for first occupancy after March 12, 1989, shall satisfy the requirements of this subdivision if (i) when twenty-five percent (25%) of the units are occupied, eighty percent (80%) of the occupied units are occupied by at least one person 55 years or older, and thereafter (ii) eighty percent (80%) of all newly occupied units are occupied by at least one person 55 years or older until such time as eighty percent (80%) of all the units in the housing facility are occupied by at least one person 55 years of age or older.

Housing satisfies the requirements of subdivisions (2) and (3) of this subsection even though there are units occupied by employees of the housing facility who are under the minimum age or family members of the employees residing in the same unit who are under the minimum age, provided the employees perform substantial duties directly related to the management of the housing. (1983, c. 522, s. 1; 1985, c. 371, ss. 1, 2; 1989, c. 507, s. 4, c. 721, s. 1; 1989 (Reg. Sess., 1990), c. 979, s. 4.)

§ 41A-7. Enforcement.

(a)   Any person who claims to have been injured by an unlawful discriminatory housing practice or who reasonably believes that he will be irrevocably injured by an unlawful discriminatory housing practice may file a complaint with the North Carolina Human Relations Commission. A fair housing enforcement organization, as defined in regulations adopted under 42 U.S.C. § 3602 (1968), may file a complaint with the Commission on behalf of a person who claims to have been injured by or reasonably believes he will be irrevocably injured by an unlawful discriminatory housing practice. Complaints shall be in writing, shall state the facts upon which the allegation of an unlawful discriminatory housing practice is based, and shall contain such other information and be in such form as the Commission requires. Commission employees shall assist complainants in reducing complaints to writing and shall assist in setting forth the information in the complaint as may be required by the Commission. Within 10 days after receipt of the complaint, the Director of the Commission shall serve on the respondent a copy of the complaint and a notice advising the respondent of his procedural rights and obligations under this Chapter. Within 10 days after receipt of the complaint, the Director of the Commission shall serve on the complainant a notice acknowledging the filing of the complaint and informing the complainant of his time limits and choice of forums under this Chapter.

No complaint may be filed with the Commission under this section during any period in which the Commission is not certified by the Secretary of the United States Department of Housing and Urban Development in accordance with 42 U.S.C. § 3610(f) to have jurisdiction over the subject matter of the complaint. Provided, however, that during any such period in which the Commission is not certified, any person who claims to have been injured by an unlawful discriminatory practice or who reasonably believes that he will be irrevocably injured by an unlawful discriminatory housing practice may bring a civil action directly in superior court in accordance with the provisions of subsection (j) of this section, except that any such civil action shall be commenced within one year after the occurrence or termination of the alleged unlawful discriminatory housing practice.

(b)   A complaint under subsection (a) shall be filed within one year after the alleged unlawful discriminatory housing practice occurred. A respondent may file an answer to the complaint against him within 10 days after receiving a copy of the complaint. With the leave of the Commission, which shall be granted whenever it would be reasonable and fair to do so, the complaint and the answer may be amended at any time. Complaints and answers shall be verified. The Commission shall make final administrative disposition of a complaint within one year of the date the complaint is filed, unless it is impracticable to do so. If the Commission is unable to do so, it shall notify the complainant and respondent, in writing, of the reasons for not doing so.

(c) Whenever another agency of the State or any other unit of government of the State has jurisdiction over the subject matter of any complaint filed under this section, and such agency or unit of government has legal authority equivalent to or greater than the authority under this Chapter to investigate or act upon the complaint, the Commission shall be divested of jurisdiction over such complaint. The Commission shall, within 30 days, notify the agency or unit of government of the apparent unlawful discriminatory housing practice, and request that the complaint be investigated in accordance with such authority.

(d) Complaints may be resolved at any time by informal conference, conciliation, or persuasion. Nothing said or done in the course of such informal procedure may be made public by the Commission or used as evidence in a subsequent proceeding under this Chapter without the written consent of the person concerned.

(e) Within 30 days after the filing of the complaint, the Commission shall commence an investigation of the complaint to ascertain the facts relating to the alleged unlawful discriminatory housing practice. If the complaint is not resolved before the investigation is complete, upon completion of the investigation, the Commission shall determine whether or not there are reasonable grounds to believe that an unlawful discriminatory housing practice has occurred. The Commission shall make a determination within 90 days after the filing of the complaint. If the Commission is unable to complete the investigation and issue a determination within 90 days after the filing of the complaint, the Commission shall notify the complainant and respondent in writing of the reasons for not doing so. If the Commission concludes at any time following the filing of a complaint under this section that prompt judicial action is necessary to carry out the purposes of this Chapter, the Commission may commence a civil action for, and the court may grant, appropriate temporary or preliminary relief pending final disposition of the complaint. Any temporary restraining order or other order granting preliminary or temporary relief shall be issued in accordance with G.S. 1A-1, et seq., Rules of Civil Procedure. The commencement of a civil action under this subsection does not affect the continuation of the Commission's investigation or the initiation of a separate civil action pursuant to other subsections of this section.

(f) If the Commission finds no reasonable ground to believe that an unlawful discriminatory housing practice has occurred or is about to occur it shall dismiss the complaint and issue to the complainant a right-to-sue letter which will enable him to bring a civil action in superior court in accordance with the provisions of subsection (j) of this section.

(g) If the Commission finds reasonable grounds to believe that an unlawful discriminatory housing practice has occurred or is about to occur it shall proceed to try to eliminate or correct the discriminatory housing practice by informal conference, conciliation, or persuasion. Each conciliation agreement arising out of conciliation efforts by the Commission, whether reached before or after the Commission makes a determination of the complaint pursuant to subsection (e), shall be:

(1) An agreement between the respondent and the complainant and shall be subject to the approval of the Commission. The Commission may also be a party to such conciliation agreements; and

(2) Made public unless the complainant and respondent otherwise agree, and the Commission determines that disclosure is not required to further the purposes of this Chapter.

(h) If the Commission is unable to resolve the alleged unlawful discriminatory housing practice it shall notify the parties in writing that conciliation efforts have failed.

(i) A complainant may make a written request to the Commission for a right-to-sue letter:

(1) Within 10 days following the receipt of a notice of conciliation failure; or

(2) After 130 days following the filing of a complaint, if the Commission has not issued a notice of conciliation failure.

Upon receipt of a timely request, the Commission shall issue to the complainant a right-to-sue letter which will enable him to bring a civil action in superior court in accordance with the provisions of subsection (j) of this section.

(j) A civil action brought by a complainant pursuant to subsections (f) or (i) of this section shall be commenced within one year after the right-to-sue letter is issued. The court may grant relief, as it deems appropriate, including any permanent or temporary injunction, temporary restraining order, or other order, and may award to the plaintiff, actual and punitive damages, and may award court costs, and reasonable attorney's fees to the prevailing party. Provided, however, that a prevailing respondent may be awarded court costs and reasonable attorney's fees only upon a showing that the case is frivolous, unreasonable, or without foundation.

(k) After the Commission has issued a notice of conciliation failure pursuant to subsection (h) of this section, if the complainant does not request a right-to-sue letter pursuant to subsection (i) of this section, the complainant, the respondent, or the Commission may elect to have the claims and issues asserted in the reasonable grounds determination decided in a civil action commenced and maintained by the Commission.

(1) An election for a civil action under this subsection shall be made no later than 20 days after an electing complainant or respondent receives the notice of conciliation failure, or if the Commission makes the election, not more than 20 days after the notice of conciliation failure is issued. A complainant or respondent who makes an election for a civil action pursuant to this subsection shall give notice to the Commission. If the Commission makes an election, it shall notify all complainants and respondents of the election.

(2) If an election is made under this subsection, no later than 60 days after the election is made the Commission shall commence a civil action in superior court in its own name on behalf of the complainant. In such an action, the Commission shall be represented by an attorney employed by the Commission, and G.S. 114-2 shall not apply.

In a civil action brought under this subsection, the court may grant relief as it deems appropriate, including any permanent or temporary injunction, temporary restraining order, or other equitable relief and may award to any person aggrieved by an unlawful discriminatory housing practice compensatory and punitive damages. Parties to a civil action brought pursuant to this Chapter shall have the right to a jury trial as provided for by the North Carolina Rules of Civil Procedure.

(l) After the Commission has issued a notice of conciliation failure pursuant to subsection (h) of this section, if the complainant does not request a right-to-sue letter pursuant to subsection (i) of this section, and if an election for a civil action is not made pursuant to subsection (k) of this section, the Commission shall apply to the Director of the Office of Administrative Hearings for the designation of an administrative law judge to preside at a hearing of the case. Upon receipt of the application, the Director of the Office of Administrative Hearings shall, without undue delay, assign an administrative law judge to hear the case.

(1) All hearings shall be conducted pursuant to the provisions of Article 3A of Chapter 150B of the General Statutes, except that the case in support of the complaint shall be presented at the hearing by the Commission's attorney or agent, and G.S. 114-2 shall not apply. The parties to the complaint shall otherwise be given an opportunity to participate in the hearing as provided in G.S. 150B-40(a).

(2) The administrative law judge assigned to hear a case pursuant to this subsection shall sit in place of the Commission and shall have the authority of a presiding officer in a contested case under Article 3A of Chapter 150B of the General Statutes. The administrative law judge shall make a proposal for decision, which shall contain proposed findings of fact, proposed conclusions of law, and proposed relief, if appropriate. The Commission may make its final decision only after carefully reviewing and considering the administrative law judge's proposal for decision, and after a copy of that proposal for decision is served on the parties and an opportunity is given each party to file exceptions and proposed findings of fact and to present oral and written arguments to the Commission.

(3) The Commission's final decision may be made by a panel consisting of three Commission members appointed by the chairperson of the Commission. If the Commission, in its final decision, finds that a respondent has violated or is about to violate this Chapter, it may order such relief as may be appropriate, including payment to the complainant by the respondent of compensatory damages and injunctive or other equitable relief. The Commission's order may also assess a civil penalty against the respondent:

a. In an amount not exceeding ten thousand dollars ($10,000) if the respondent has not been adjudged to have committed any prior unlawful discriminatory housing practices;

b. In an amount not exceeding twenty-five thousand dollars ($25,000) if the respondent has been adjudged to have committed one other unlawful discriminatory housing practice during the five-year period ending on the date of the filing of the complaint; or

  c. In an amount not exceeding fifty thousand dollars ($50,000) if the respondent has been adjudged to have committed two or more unlawful discriminatory housing practices during the seven-year period ending on the date of the filing of the complaint.

If the acts constituting the unlawful discriminatory housing practice that is the object of the complaint are committed by the same natural person who has been previously adjudged to have committed acts constituting an unlawful discriminatory housing practice, then the civil penalties set forth in sub-subdivisions b and c of this subsection may be imposed without regard to the period of time within which any subsequent discriminatory housing practice occurred.

  The clear proceeds of civil penalties assessed pursuant to this subdivision shall be remitted to the Civil Penalty and Forfeiture Fund in accordance with G.S. 115C-457.2.

(m) Any person aggrieved by the final agency decision following a hearing may petition for judicial review in accordance with the provisions of G.S. 150B-43 through G.S. 150B-52. The court in a review proceeding may:

(1) Affirm, modify, or reverse the Commission's decision in accordance with G.S. 150B-51;

(2) Remand the case to the Commission for further proceedings;

(3) Grant to any party such temporary relief, restraining order, or other order as it deems appropriate; or

(4) Issue an order to enforce the Commission's order to the extent that the order is affirmed or modified.

(n) If, within 30 days after service on the parties of the Commission's decision and order following a hearing, no party has petitioned for judicial review, the Commission or the person entitled to relief may file with the clerk of superior court in the county where the unlawful discriminatory housing practice occurred, or in the county where the real property is located, a certified copy of the Commission's final order. Upon such a filing, the clerk of the court shall enter an order enforcing the Commission's final order. (1983, c. 522, s. 1; 1985, c. 371, ss. 3-5; 1987, c. 603, ss. 2-4; 1989, c. 721, s. 2; 1989 (Reg. Sess., 1990), c. 979, ss. 1(2), 5, 6; 1998-215, s. 1; 2003-136, s. 1.)

§ 41A-8. Investigation; subpoenas.

(a) In conducting an investigation, the Commission shall have access at all reasonable times to premises, records, documents, individuals, and other evidence or possible sources of evidence and may examine, record, and copy such materials and take and record the testimony or statements of such persons as are reasonably necessary for the furtherance of the investigation: Provided, however, that the Commission first complies with the provisions of the Fourth Amendment to the United States Constitution relating to unreasonable searches and seizures.

(b) The Commission may issue subpoenas to compel access to or the production of such materials, or the appearance of such persons, and may issue interrogatories to a respondent, to the same extent and subject to the same limitations as would apply if the subpoenas or interrogatories were issued or served in aid of a civil action in the general court of justice.

(c) Upon written application to the Commission, a respondent shall be entitled to the issuance of a reasonable number of subpoenas subject to the same limitations as subpoenas issued by the Commission. Subpoenas issued at the request of a respondent shall show on their face the name and address of such respondent and shall state that they were issued at his request.

(d) In case of contumacy or refusal to obey a subpoena, the Commission or the respondent may petition for its enforcement in the superior court for the district in which the person to whom the subpoena was addressed resides, was served, or transacts business. (1983, c. 522, s. 1; 1989 (Reg. Sess., 1990), c. 979, s. 1(3).)

§ 41A-9: Repealed by Session Laws 1989, c. 721, s. 3.

§ 41A-10. Venue.

All civil actions shall be commenced in the county where the alleged unlawful discriminatory housing practice occurred, or in the county where the real property is located. (1983, c. 522, s. 1.)

Chapter 42.

Landlord and Tenant.

Article 1.

General Provisions.

§ 42-1. Lessor and lessee not partners.

No lessor of property, merely by reason that he is to receive as rent or compensation for its use a share of the proceeds or net profits of the business in which it is employed, or any other uncertain consideration, shall be held a partner of the lessee. (1868-9, c. 156, s. 3; Code, s. 1744; Rev., s. 1982; C.S., s. 2341.)

§ 42-2. Attornment unnecessary on conveyance of reversions, etc.

Every conveyance of any rent, reversion, or remainder in lands, tenements or hereditaments, otherwise sufficient, shall be deemed complete without attornment by the holders of particular estates in said lands: Provided, no holder of a particular estate shall be prejudiced by any act done by him as holding under his grantor, without notice of such conveyance. (4 Anne, c. 16, s. 9; 1868-9, c. 156, s. 17; Code, s. 1764; Rev., s. 947; C.S., s. 2342.)

§ 42-3. Term forfeited for nonpayment of rent.

In all verbal or written leases of real property of any kind in which is fixed a definite time for the payment of the rent reserved therein, there shall be implied a forfeiture of the term upon failure to pay the rent within 10 days after a demand is made by the lessor or his agent on said lessee for all past-due rent, and the lessor may forthwith enter and dispossess the tenant without having declared such forfeiture or reserved the right of reentry in the lease. (1919, c. 34; C.S., s. 2343; 2001-502, s. 2; 2004-143, s. 1.)

§ 42-4. Recovery for use and occupation.

When any person occupies land of another by the permission of such other, without any express agreement for rent, or upon a parol lease which is void, the landlord may recover a reasonable compensation for such occupation, and if by such parol lease a certain rent was reserved, such reservation may be received as evidence of the value of the occupation. (1868-9, c. 156, s. 5; Code, s. 1746; Rev., s. 1986; C.S., s. 2344.)

§ 42-5. Rent apportioned, where lease terminated by death.

If a lease of land, in which rent is reserved, payable at the end of the year or other certain period of time, is determined by the death of any person during one of the periods in which the rent was growing due, the lessor or his personal representative may recover a part of the rent which becomes due after the death, proportionate to the part of the period elapsed before the death, subject to all just allowances; and if any security was given for such rent it shall be apportioned in like manner. (1868-9, c. 156, s. 6; Code, s. 1747; Rev., s. 1987; C.S., s. 2345.)

§ 42-6. Rents, annuities, etc., apportioned, where right to payment terminated by death.

In all cases where rents, rent charges, annuities, pensions, dividends, or any other payments of any description, are made payable at fixed periods to successive owners under any instrument, or by any will, and where the right of any owner to receive payment is terminable by a death or other uncertain event, and where such right so terminates during a period in which a payment is growing due, the payment becoming due next after such terminating event shall be apportioned among the successive owners according to the parts of such periods elapsing before and after the terminating event. (1868-9, c. 156, s. 7; Code, s. 1748; Rev., s. 1988; C.S., s. 2346.)

§ 42-7. In lieu of emblements, farm lessee holds out year, with rents apportioned.

When any lease for years of any land let for farming on which a rent is reserved determines during a current year of the tenancy, by the happening of any uncertain event determining the estate of the lessor, or by a sale of said land under any mortgage or deed of trust, the tenant in lieu of emblements shall continue his occupation to the end of such current year, and shall then give up such possession to the succeeding owner of the land, and shall pay to such succeeding owner a part of the rent accrued since the last payment became due, proportionate to the part of the period of payment elapsing after the termination of the estate of the lessor to the giving up such possession; and the tenant in such case shall be entitled to a reasonable compensation for the tillage and seed of any crop not gathered at the expiration of such current year from the person succeeding to the possession. (1868-9, c. 156, s. 8; Code, s. 1749; Rev., s. 1990; C.S., s. 2347; 1931, c. 173, s. 1.)

§ 42-8. Grantees of reversion and assigns of lease have reciprocal rights under covenants.

The grantee in every conveyance of reversion in lands, tenements or hereditaments has the like advantages and remedies by action or entry against the holders of particular estates in such real property, and their assigns, for nonpayment of rent, and for the nonperformance of other conditions and agreements contained in the instruments by the tenants of such particular estates, as the grantor or lessor or his heirs might have; and the holders of such particular estates, and their assigns, have the like advantages and remedies against the grantee of the reversion, or any part thereof, for any conditions and agreements contained in such instruments, as they might have had against the grantor or his lessors or his heirs. (32 Hen. VIII, c. 34; 1868-9, c. 156, s. 18; Code, s. 1765; Rev., s. 1989; C.S., s. 2348.)

§ 42-9. Agreement to rebuild, how construed in case of fire.

An agreement in a lease to repair a demised house shall not be construed to bind the contracting party to rebuild or repair in case the house shall be destroyed or damaged to more than one half of its value, by accidental fire not occurring from the want of ordinary diligence on his part. (1868-9, c. 156, s. 11; Code, s. 1752; Rev., s. 1985; C.S., s. 2349.)

§ 42-10. Tenant not liable for accidental damage.

A tenant for life, or years, or for a less term, shall not be liable for damage occurring on the demised premises accidentally, and notwithstanding reasonable diligence on his part, unless he so contract. (1868-9, c. 156, s. 10; Code, s. 1751; Rev., s. 1991; C.S., s. 2350.)

§ 42-11. Willful destruction by tenant misdemeanor.

If any tenant shall, during his term or after its expiration, willfully and unlawfully demolish, destroy, deface, injure or damage any tenement house, uninhabited house or other outhouse, belonging to his landlord or upon his premises by removing parts thereof or by burning, or in any other manner, or shall unlawfully and willfully burn, destroy, pull down, injure or remove any fence, wall or other inclosure or any part thereof, built or standing upon the premises of such landlord, or shall willfully and unlawfully cut down or destroy any timber, fruit, shade or ornamental tree belonging to said landlord, he shall be guilty of a Class 1 misdemeanor. (1883, c. 224; Code, s. 1761; Rev., s. 3686; C.S., s. 2351; 1993, c. 539, s. 402; 1994, Ex. Sess., c. 24, s. 14(c).)

§ 42-12. Lessee may surrender, where building destroyed or damaged.

If a demised house, or other building, is destroyed during the term, or so much damaged that it cannot be made reasonably fit for the purpose for which it was hired, except at an expense exceeding one year's rent of the premises, and the damage or destruction occur without negligence on the part of the lessee or his agents or servants, and there is no agreement in the lease respecting repairs, or providing for such a case, and the use of the house damaged or destroyed was the main inducement to the hiring, the lessee may surrender his estate in the demised premises by a writing to that effect delivered or tendered to the landlord within 10 days from the damage or destruction, and by paying or tendering at the same time all rent in arrear, and a part of the rent growing due at the time of the damage or destruction, proportionate to the time between the last period of payment and the occurrence of the damage or destruction, and the lessee shall be thenceforth discharged from all rent accruing afterwards; but not from any other agreement in the lease. This section shall not apply if a contrary intention appear from the lease. (1868-9, c. 156, s. 12; Code, s. 1753; Rev., s. 1992; C.S., s. 2352.)

§ 42-13. Wrongful surrender to other than landlord misdemeanor.

Any tenant or lessee of lands who shall willfully, wrongfully and with intent to defraud the landlord or lessor, give up the possession of the rented or leased premises to any person other than his landlord or lessor, shall be guilty of a Class 1 misdemeanor. (1883, c. 138; Code, s. 1760; Rev., s. 3682; C.S., s. 2353; 1993, c. 539, s. 403; 1994, Ex. Sess., c. 24, s. 14(c).)

§ 42-14. Notice to quit in certain tenancies.

A tenancy from year to year may be terminated by a notice to quit given one month or more before the end of the current year of the tenancy; a tenancy from month to month by a like notice of seven days; a tenancy from week to week, of two days. Provided, however, where the tenancy involves only the rental of a space for a manufactured home as defined in G.S. 143-143.9(6), a notice to quit must be given at least 60 days before the end of the current rental period, regardless of the term of the tenancy. (1868-9, c. 156, s. 9; Code, s. 1750; 1891, c. 227; Rev., s. 1984; C.S., s. 2354; 1985, c. 541; 2005-291, s. 1.)

§ 42-14.1. Rent control.

No county or city as defined by G.S. 160A-1 may enact, maintain, or enforce any ordinance or resolution which regulates the amount of rent to be charged for privately owned, single-family or multiple unit residential or commercial rental property. This section shall not be construed as prohibiting any county or city, or any authority created by a county or city for that purpose, from:

(1) Regulating in any way property belonging to that city, county, or authority;

(2) Entering into agreements with private persons which regulate the amount of rent charged for subsidized rental properties; or

(3) Enacting ordinances or resolutions restricting rent for properties assisted with Community Development Block Grant Funds. (1987, c. 458, s. 1.)

§ 42-14.2. Death, illness, or conviction of certain crimes not a material fact.

In offering real property for rent or lease it shall not be deemed a material fact that the real property was occupied previously by a person who died or had a serious illness while occupying the property or that a person convicted of any crime for which registration is required by Article 27A of Chapter 14 of the General Statutes occupies, occupied, or resides near the property; provided, however, that no landlord or lessor may knowingly make a false statement regarding any such fact. (1989, c. 592, s. 2; 1998-212, s. 17.16A(b).)

§ 42-14.3. Notice of conversion of manufactured home communities.

(a) In the event that an owner of a manufactured home community (defined as a parcel of land, whether undivided or subdivided, that has been designed to accommodate at least five manufactured homes) intends to convert the manufactured home community, or any part thereof, to another use that will require movement of the manufactured homes, the owner of the manufactured home community shall give each owner of a manufactured home and the North Carolina Housing Finance Agency notice of the intended conversion at least 180 days before the owner of a manufactured home is required to vacate and move the manufactured home, regardless of the term of the tenancy. Failure to give notice to each manufactured home owner as required by this section is a defense in an action for possession. The respective rights and obligations of the community owner and the owner of the manufactured home under their lease shall continue in effect during the notice period.

(b) Notwithstanding subsection (a) of this section, if a manufactured home community is being closed pursuant to a valid order of any unit of State or local government, the owner of the community shall be required to give notice of the closure of the community to each resident of the community and the North Carolina Housing Finance Agency within three business days of the date on which the order is issued. (2003-400, s. 5; 2008-107, s. 28.27(c).)

§ 42-14.4. Notice to State Bar of attorney default on lease.

(a) If a landlord has actual knowledge that a tenant is an attorney, the landlord shall deliver notice to the North Carolina State Bar (hereinafter "State Bar") at least 15 days prior to the destruction or discard of any "potentially confidential materials" remaining in the premises after the landlord obtains possession of the premises, whether by summary ejectment under Article 3 of this Chapter or by any other means, including the tenant vacating the premises. For purposes of this section, the term "potentially confidential materials" means client files, trust or operating account records, or other materials relating to client matters. For purposes of this section, the term "landlord" means any owner and any rental management company, rental agency, or any other person having the actual or apparent authority of an agent to perform the duties imposed by this Article. The landlord's notice to the State Bar shall contain the name of the attorney who is presumed to be the tenant, the location of the potentially confidential materials, and a phone number, address, or other means to contact the landlord. During the 15-day period after notice, a landlord may move for storage purposes, but shall not throw away, dispose of, or sell, potentially confidential materials remaining in the premises.

(b) The State Bar or its designee may take possession of the materials, at its sole expense, within the 15-day period provided for in subsection (a) of this section without the necessity of a court order. Upon the request of the State Bar, the landlord shall cooperate with and allow the State Bar to take possession of the potentially confidential materials, and the landlord shall not be liable in any way to the tenant for his or her cooperation. However, if the tenant elects to take possession of the potentially confidential materials prior to the State Bar obtaining possession of them, and there is no court order to the contrary having been previously delivered to the landlord, the landlord may deliver possession of the potentially confidential materials to the tenant and shall promptly notify the State Bar of his or her actions. If neither the State Bar nor its designee takes possession of the potentially confidential materials within the 15-day period provided for in subsection (a) of this section, the landlord may destroy or discard the materials in accordance with the lease agreement with the defaulting tenant.

(c) A landlord that attempts in good faith to comply with the requirements of this section shall not be liable for losses to any person arising directly or indirectly out of the disposal of any potentially confidential materials. Failure to comply with this section shall not constitute an unfair trade practice under G.S. 75-1.1. (2012-76, s. 1.)

Article 2.

Agricultural Tenancies.

§ 42-15. Landlord's lien on crops for rents, advances, etc.; enforcement.

When lands are rented or leased by agreement, written or oral, for agricultural purposes, or are cultivated by a cropper, unless otherwise agreed between the parties to the lease or agreement, any and all crops raised on said lands shall be deemed and held to be vested in possession of the lessor or his assigns at all times, until the rents for said lands are paid and until all the stipulations contained in the lease or agreement are performed, or damages in lieu thereof paid to the lessor or his assigns, and until said party or his assigns is paid for all advancements made and expenses incurred in making and saving said crops.

This lien shall be preferred to all other liens, and the lessor or his assigns is entitled, against the lessee or cropper, or the assigns of either, who removes the crop or any part thereof from the lands without the consent of the lessor or his assigns, or against any other person who may get possession of said crop or any part thereof, to the remedies given in an action upon a claim for the delivery of personal property.

Provided, that when advances have been made by the federal government or any of its agencies, to any tenant or tenants on lands under the control of any guardian, executor and/or administrator for the purpose of enabling said tenant or tenants to plant, cultivate and harvest crops grown on said land, the said guardian, executor, and/or administrator may waive the above lien in favor of the federal government, or any of its agencies, making said advances. (1876-7, c. 283; Code, s. 1754; Rev., s. 1993; 1917, c. 134; C.S., s. 2355; 1933, c. 219; 1985, c. 689, s. 11.)

§ 42-15.1. Landlord's lien on crop insurance for rents, advances, etc.; enforcement.

Where lands are rented or leased by agreement, written or oral, for agricultural purposes, or are cultivated by a cropper, unless otherwise agreed between the parties to the lease or agreement, the landlord or his assigns shall have a lien on all the insurance procured by the tenant or cropper on the crops raised on the lands leased or rented to the extent of any rents due or advances made to the tenant or cropper.

The lien provided herein shall be preferred to all other liens on said insurance, and the landlord or his assigns shall be entitled to all the remedies at law for the enforcement of the lien. (1959, c. 1291; 1985, c. 689, s. 12.)

§ 42-16. Rights of tenants.

When the lessor or his assigns gets the actual possession of the crop or any part thereof otherwise than by the mode prescribed in G.S. 42-15, and refuses or neglects, upon a notice, written or oral, of five days, given by the lessee or cropper or the assigns of either, to make a fair division of said crop, or to pay over to such lessee or cropper or the assigns of either, such part thereof as he may be entitled to under the lease or agreement, then and in that case the lessee or cropper or the assigns of either is entitled to the remedies against the lessor or his assigns given in an action upon a claim for the delivery of personal property to recover such part of the crop as he, in law and according to the lease or agreement, may be entitled to. The amount or quantity of such crop claimed by said lessee or cropper or the assigns of either, together with a statement of the grounds upon which it is claimed, shall be fully set forth in an affidavit at the beginning of the action. (1876-7, c. 283, s. 2; Code, s. 1755; Rev., s. 1994; C.S., s. 2356.)

§ 42-17. Action to settle dispute between parties.

When any controversy arises between the parties, and neither party avails himself of the provisions of this Chapter, it is competent for either party to proceed at once to have the matter determined in the appropriate trial division of the General Court of Justice. (1876-7, c. 283, s. 3; Code, s. 1756; Rev., s. 1995; C.S., s. 2357; 1971, c. 533, s. 1.)

§ 42-18. Tenant's undertaking on continuance or appeal.

In case there is a continuance or an appeal from the magistrate's decision to the district court, the lessee or cropper, or the assigns of either, shall be allowed to retain possession of said property upon his giving an undertaking to the lessor or his assigns, or the adverse party, in a sum double the amount of the claim, if such claim does not amount to more than the value of such property, otherwise to double the value of such property, with good and sufficient surety, to be approved by the magistrate or the clerk of the superior court, conditioned for the faithful payment to the adverse party of such damages as he shall recover in said action. (1876-7, c. 283, s. 3; Code, s. 1756; Rev., s. 1995; C.S., s. 2358; 1971, c. 533, s. 2.)

§ 42-19. Crops delivered to landlord on his undertaking.

In case the lessee or cropper, or the assigns of either, at the time of the appeal or continuance mentioned in G.S. 42-18, fails to give the undertaking therein required, then the sheriff or other lawful officer shall deliver the property into the actual possession of the lessor or his assigns, upon the lessor or his assigns giving to the adverse party an undertaking in double the amount of said property, to be justified as required in G.S. 42-18, conditioned for the forthcoming of such property, or the value thereof, in case judgment is pronounced against him. (1876-7, c. 283, s. 4; Code, s. 1757; Rev., s. 1996; C.S., s. 2359; 1973, c. 108, s. 17.)

§ 42-20. Crops sold, if neither party gives undertaking.

If neither party gives the undertaking described in G.S. 42-18 and 42-19, it is the duty of the clerk of the superior court to issue an order to the sheriff, or other lawful officer, directing him to take into his possession all of said property, or so much thereof as may be necessary to satisfy the claimant's demand and costs, and to sell the same under the rules and regulations prescribed by law for the sale of personal property under execution, and to hold the proceeds thereof subject to the decision of the court upon the issue or issues pending between the parties. (1876-7, c. 283, s. 5; Code, s. 1758; Rev., s. 1997; C.S., s. 2360; 1971, c. 533, s. 3.)

§ 42-21. Tenant's crop not subject to execution against landlord.

Whenever servants and laborers in agriculture shall by their contracts, oral or written, be entitled, for wages, to a part of the crops cultivated by them, such part shall not be subject to sale under executions against their employers, or the owners of the land cultivated. (Code, s. 1796; Rev., s. 1998; C.S., s. 2361.)

§ 42-22. Unlawful seizure by landlord or removal by tenant misdemeanor.

If any landlord shall unlawfully, willfully, knowingly and without process of law, and unjustly seize the crop of his tenant when there is nothing due him, he shall be guilty of a Class 1 misdemeanor. If any lessee or cropper, or the assigns of either, or any other person, shall remove a crop, or any part thereof, from land without the consent of the lessor or his assigns, and without giving him or his agent five days' notice of such intended removal, and before satisfying all the liens held by the lessor or his assigns, on said crop, he shall be guilty of a Class 1 misdemeanor. (1876-7, c. 283, s. 6; 1883, c. 83; Code, s. 1759; Rev., ss. 3664, 3665; C.S., s. 2362; 1993, c. 539, s. 404; 1994, Ex. Sess., c. 24, s. 14(c).)

§ 42-22.1. Failure of tenant to account for sales under tobacco marketing cards.

Any tenant or share cropper having possession of a tobacco marketing card issued by any agency of the State or federal government who sells tobacco authorized to be sold thereby and fails to account to his landlord, to the extent of the net proceeds of such sale or sales, for all liens, rents, advances, or other claims held by his landlord against the tobacco or the proceeds of the sale of such tobacco, shall be guilty of a Class 1 misdemeanor. (1949, c. 193; 1993, c. 539, s. 405; 1994, Ex. Sess., c. 24, s. 14(c).)

§ 42-23. Terms of agricultural tenancies in certain counties.

All agricultural leases and contracts hereafter made between landlord and tenant for a period of one year or from year to year, whether such tenant pay a specified rental or share in the crops grown, such year shall be from December first to December first, and such period of time shall constitute a year for agricultural tenancies in lieu of the law and custom heretofore prevailing, namely from January first to January first. In all cases of such tenancies a notice to quit of one month as provided in G.S. 42-14 shall be applicable. If on account of illness or any other good cause, the tenant is unable to harvest all the crops grown on lands leased by him for any year prior to the termination of his lease contract on December first, he shall have a right to return to the premises vacated by him at any time prior to December thirty-first of said year, for the purpose only of harvesting and dividing the remaining crops so ungathered. But he shall have no right to use the houses or outbuildings or that part of the lands from which the crops have been harvested prior to the termination of the tenant year, as defined in this section.

This section shall only apply to the counties of Alamance, Anson, Ashe, Bladen, Brunswick, Columbus, Craven, Cumberland, Duplin, Edgecombe, Gaston, Greene, Hoke, Jones, Lenoir, Lincoln, Montgomery, Onslow, Pender, Person, Pitt, Robeson, Sampson, Wayne and Yadkin. (Pub. Loc. 1929, c. 40; Pub. Loc. 1935, c. 288; Pub. Loc. 1937, cc. 96, 600; Pub. Loc. 1941, c. 41; 1943, c. 68; 1945, c. 700; 1949, c. 136; 1953, c. 499, s. 1; 1955, c. 136; 1959, c. 1076; 1981, c. 97, s. 1.)

§ 42-24. Turpentine and lightwood leases.

This Chapter shall apply to all leases or contracts to lease turpentine trees, or use lightwood for purposes of making tar, and the parties thereto shall be fully subject to the provisions and penalties of this Chapter. (1876-7, c. 283, s. 7; Code, s. 1762; 1893, c. 517; Rev., s. 1999; C.S., s. 2363.)

§ 42-25. Mining and timberland leases.

If in a lease of land for mining, or of timbered land for the purpose of manufacturing the timber into goods, rent is reserved, and if it is agreed in the lease that the minerals, timber or goods, or any portion thereof, shall not be removed until the payment of the rent, in such case the lessor shall have the rights and be entitled to the remedy given by this Chapter. (1868-9, c. 156, s. 16; Code, s. 1763; Rev., s. 2000; C.S., s. 2364.)

§§ 42-25.1 through 42-25.5: Reserved for future codification purposes.

Article 2A.

Ejectment of Residential Tenants.

§ 42-25.6. Manner of ejectment of residential tenants.

It is the public policy of the State of North Carolina, in order to maintain the public peace, that a residential tenant shall be evicted, dispossessed or otherwise constructively or actually removed from his dwelling unit only in accordance with the procedure prescribed in Article 3 or Article 7 of this Chapter. (1981, c. 566, s. 1; 1995, c. 419, s. 1.1.)

§ 42-25.7. Distress and distraint not permitted.

It is the public policy of the State of North Carolina that distress and distraint are prohibited and that landlords of residential rental property shall have rights concerning the personal property of their residential tenants only in accordance with G.S. 42-25.9(d), 42-25.9(g), 42-25.9(h), 42-36.2, or 28A-25-7. (1981, c. 566, s. 1; 1995, c. 460, s. 8; 2012-17, s. 8.)

§ 42-25.8. Contrary lease provisions.

Any lease or contract provision contrary to this Article shall be void as against public policy. (1981, c. 566, s. 1.)

§ 42-25.9. Remedies.

(a) If any lessor, landlord, or agent removes or attempts to remove a tenant from a dwelling unit in any manner contrary to this Article, the tenant shall be entitled to recover possession or to terminate his lease and the lessor, landlord or agent shall be liable to the tenant for damages caused by the tenant's removal or attempted removal. Damages in any action brought by a tenant under this Article shall be limited to actual damages as in an action for trespass or conversion and shall not include punitive damages, treble damages or damages for emotional distress.

(b) If any lessor, landlord, or agent seizes possession of or interferes with a tenant's access to a tenant's or household member's personal property in any manner not in accordance with G.S. 44A-2(e2), 42-25.9(d), 42-25.9(g), 42-25.9(h), or G.S. 42-36.2 the tenant or household member shall be entitled to recover possession of his personal property or compensation for the value of the personal property, and, in any action brought by a tenant or household member under this Article, the landlord shall be liable to the tenant or household member for actual damages, but not including punitive damages, treble damages or damages for emotional distress.

(c) The remedies created by this section are supplementary to all existing common-law and statutory rights and remedies.

(d) If any tenant abandons personal property of seven hundred fifty dollar ($750.00) value or less in the demised premises, or fails to remove such property at the time of execution of a writ of possession in an action for summary ejectment, the landlord may, as an alternative to the procedures provided in G.S. 42-25.9(g), 42-25.9(h), or 42-36.2, deliver the property into the custody of a nonprofit organization regularly providing free or at a nominal price clothing and household furnishings to people in need, upon that organization agreeing to identify and separately store the property for 30 days and to release the property to the tenant at no charge within the 30-day period. A landlord electing to use this procedure shall immediately post at the demised premises a notice containing the name and address of the property recipient, post the same notice for 30 days or more at the place where rent is received, and send the same notice by first-class mail to the tenant at the tenant's last known address. Provided, however, that the notice shall not include a description of the property.

(e) For purposes of subsection (d), personal property shall be deemed abandoned if the landlord finds evidence that clearly shows the premises has been voluntarily vacated after the paid rental period has expired and the landlord has no notice of a disability that caused the vacancy. A presumption of abandonment shall arise 10 or more days after the landlord has posted conspicuously a notice of suspected abandonment both inside and outside the premises and has received no response from the tenant.

(f) Any nonprofit organization agreeing to receive personal property under subsection (d) shall not be liable to the owner for a disposition of such property provided that the property has been separately identified and stored for release to the owner for a period of 30 days.

(g) Seven days after being placed in lawful possession by execution of a writ of possession, a landlord may dispose of personal property remaining on the premises in accordance with the provisions of this section and G.S. 42-36.2(b), except that in the case of the lease of a space for a manufactured home as defined in G.S. 143-143.9(6), G.S. 44A-2(e2) shall apply to the disposition of a manufactured home with a current value in excess of five hundred dollars ($500.00) and its contents by a landlord after being placed in lawful possession by execution of a writ of possession. During the seven-day period after being placed in lawful possession by execution of a writ of possession, a landlord may move for storage purposes, but shall not throw away, dispose of, or sell any items of personal property remaining on the premises unless otherwise provided for in this Chapter. Upon the tenant's request prior to the expiration of the seven-day period, the landlord shall release possession of the property to the tenant during regular business hours or at a time agreed upon. If the landlord elects to sell the property at public or private sale, the landlord shall give written notice to the tenant by first-class mail to the tenant's last known address at least seven days prior to the day of the sale. The seven-day notice of sale may run concurrently with the seven-day period which allows the tenant to request possession of the property. The written notice shall state the date, time, and place of the sale, and that any surplus of proceeds from the sale, after payment of unpaid rents, damages, storage fees, and sale costs, shall be disbursed to the tenant, upon request, within seven days after the sale, and will thereafter be delivered to the government of the county in which the rental property is located. Upon the tenant's request prior to the day of sale, the landlord shall release possession of the property to the tenant during regular business hours or at a time agreed upon. The landlord may apply the proceeds of the sale to the unpaid rents, damages, storage fees, and sale costs. Any surplus from the sale shall be disbursed to the tenant, upon request, within seven days of the sale and shall thereafter be delivered to the government of the county in which the rental property is located.

(h) If the total value of all property remaining on the premises at the time of execution of a writ of possession in an action for summary ejectment is less than five hundred dollars ($500.00), the property shall be deemed abandoned five days after the time of execution, and the landlord may throw away or dispose of the property. Upon the tenant's request prior to the expiration of the five-day period, the landlord shall release possession of the property to the tenant during regular business hours or at a time agreed upon. (1981, c. 566, s. 1; 1985, c. 612, ss. 1-4; 1995, c. 460, ss. 1-3; 1999-278, ss. 1, 2; 2012-17, s. 2(a), (b); 2013-334, s. 4.)

Article 3.

Summary Ejectment.

§ 42-26. Tenant holding over may be dispossessed in certain cases.

(a) Any tenant or lessee of any house or land, and the assigns under the tenant or legal representatives of such tenant or lessee, who holds over and continues in the possession of the demised premises, or any part thereof, without the permission of the landlord, and after demand made for its surrender, may be removed from such premises in the manner hereinafter prescribed in any of the following cases:

(1) When a tenant in possession of real estate holds over after his term has expired.

(2) When the tenant or lessee, or other person under him, has done or omitted any act by which, according to the stipulations of the lease, his estate has ceased.

(3) When any tenant or lessee of lands or tenements, who is in arrear for rent or has agreed to cultivate the demised premises and to pay a part of the crop to be made thereon as rent, or who has given to the lessor a lien on such crop as a security for the rent, deserts the demised premises, and leaves them unoccupied and uncultivated.

(b) An arrearage in costs owed by a tenant for water or sewer services pursuant to G.S. 62-110(g) or electric service pursuant to G.S. 62-110(h) shall not be used as a basis for termination of a lease under this Chapter. Any payment to the landlord shall be applied first to the rent owed and then to charges for electric service, or water or sewer service, unless otherwise designated by the tenant.

(c) In an action for ejectment based upon G.S. 42-26(a)(2), the lease may provide that the landlord's acceptance of partial rent or partial housing subsidy payment does not waive the tenant's breach for which the right of reentry was reserved, and the landlord's exercise of such a provision does not constitute a violation of Chapter 75 of the General Statutes. (4 Geo. II, c. 28; 1868-9, c. 156, s. 19; Code, ss. 1766, 1777; 1905, cc. 297, 299, 820; Rev., s. 2001; C.S., s. 2365; 2001-502, s. 3; 2004-143, s. 2; 2011-252, s. 1; 2012-17, s. 3.)

§ 42-26.1: Expired.

§ 42-27. Local: Refusal to perform contract ground for dispossession.

When any tenant or cropper who enters into a contract for the rental of land for the current or ensuing year willfully neglects or refuses to perform the terms of his contract without just cause, he shall forfeit his right of possession to the premises. This section applies only to the following counties: Alamance, Alexander, Alleghany, Anson, Ashe, Beaufort, Bertie, Bladen, Brunswick, Burke, Cabarrus, Camden, Carteret, Caswell, Chatham, Chowan, Cleveland, Columbus, Craven, Cumberland, Currituck, Davidson, Duplin, Edgecombe, Forsyth, Franklin, Gaston, Gates, Greene, Guilford, Halifax, Harnett, Hertford,

Hoke, Hyde, Jackson, Johnston, Jones, Lee, Lenoir, Martin, Mecklenburg, Montgomery, Moore, Nash, New Hanover, Northampton, Onslow, Pasquotank, Pender, Perquimans, Pitt, Polk, Randolph, Robeson, Rockingham, Rowan, Rutherford, Sampson, Stokes, Surry, Swain, Tyrrell, Union, Wake, Warren, Washington, Wayne, Wilson, Yadkin. (4 Geo. II, c. 28; 1868-9, c. 156, s. 19; Code, ss. 1766, 1777; 1905, cc. 297, 299, 820; Rev., s. 2001, subsec. 4; 1907, cc. 43, 153; 1909, cc. 40, 550; C.S., s. 2366; Pub. Loc. Ex. Sess. 1924, c. 66; 1931, cc. 50, 194, 446; 1933, cc. 86, 485; 1935, c. 39; 1943, cc. 69, 115, 459; 1951, c. 279; 1953, c. 271; c. 499, s. 2; 1955, c. 93; 1961, c. 25; 1995 (Reg. Sess., 1996), c. 566, s. 1.)

§ 42-28. Summons issued by clerk.

When the lessor or his assignee files a complaint pursuant to G.S. 42-26 or 42-27, and asks to be put in possession of the leased premises, the clerk of superior court shall issue a summons requiring the defendant to appear at a certain time and place not to exceed seven days from the issuance of the summons, excluding weekends and legal holidays, to answer the complaint. The plaintiff may claim rent in arrears, and damages for the occupation of the premises since the cessation of the estate of the lessee, not to exceed the jurisdictional amount established by G.S. 7A-210(1), but if he omits to make such claim, he shall not be prejudiced thereby in any other action for their recovery. (1868-9, c. 156, s. 20; 1869-70, c. 212; Code, s. 1767; Rev., s. 2002; C.S., s. 2367; 1971, c. 533, s. 4; 1973, c. 1267, s. 4; 1979, c. 144, s. 4; 1981, c. 555, s. 4; 1983, c. 332, s. 2; 1985, c. 329, s. 1; 1989, c. 311, s. 3; 1993, c. 553, s. 73(c); 1995, c. 460, s. 4.)

§ 42-29. Service of summons.

The officer receiving the summons shall mail a copy of the summons and complaint to the defendant no later than the end of the next business day or as soon as practicable at the defendant's last known address in a stamped addressed envelope provided by the plaintiff to the action. The officer may, within five days of the issuance of the summons, attempt to telephone the defendant requesting that the defendant either personally visit the officer to accept service, or schedule an appointment for the defendant to receive delivery of service from the officer. If the officer does not attempt to telephone the defendant or the attempt is unsuccessful or does not result in service to the defendant, the officer shall make at least one visit to the place of abode of the defendant within five days of the issuance of the summons, but at least two days prior to the day the defendant is required to appear to answer the complaint, excluding legal holidays, at a time reasonably calculated to find the defendant at the place of abode to attempt personal delivery of service. He then shall deliver a copy of the summons together with a copy of the complaint to the defendant, or leave copies thereof at the defendant's dwelling house or usual place of abode with some person of suitable age and discretion then residing therein. If such service cannot be made the officer shall affix copies to some conspicuous part of the premises claimed and make due return showing compliance with this section. (1868-9, c. 156, s. 21; Code, s. 1768; Rev., s. 2003; C.S., s. 2368; 1973, c. 87; 1983, c. 332, s. 1; 1985, c. 102; 1995, c. 460, s. 5; 2009-246, s. 1.)

§ 42-30. Judgment by confession, where plaintiff has proved case, or failure to appear.

The summons shall be returned according to its tenor, and if on its return it appears to have been duly served, and if (i) the plaintiff proves his case by a preponderance of the evidence, (ii) the defendant admits the allegations of the complaint, or (iii) the defendant fails to appear on the day of court, and the plaintiff requests in open court a judgment for possession based solely on the filed pleadings where the pleadings allege defendant's failure to pay rent as a breach of the lease for which reentry is allowed and the defendant has not filed a responsive pleading, the magistrate shall give judgment that the defendant be removed from, and the plaintiff be put in possession of, the demised premises; and if any rent or damages for the occupation of the premises after the cessation of the estate of the lessee, not exceeding the jurisdictional amount established by G.S. 7A-210(1), be claimed in the oath of the plaintiff as due and unpaid, the magistrate shall inquire thereof, and if supported by a preponderance of the evidence, give judgment as he may find the fact to be. (1868-9, c. 156, s. 22; Code, s. 1769; Rev., s. 2004; C.S., s. 2369; 1971, c. 533, s. 5; 1973, c. 10; c. 1267, s. 4; 1979, c. 144, s. 5; 1981, c. 555, s. 5; 1985, c. 329, s. 1; 1989, c. 311, s. 4; 1993, c. 553, s. 73(d); 2005-423, s. 10.)

§ 42-31. Trial by magistrate.

If the defendant by his answer denies any material allegation in the oath of the plaintiff, the magistrate shall hear the evidence and give judgment as he shall find the facts to be. (1868-9, c. 156, s. 23; Code, s. 1770; Rev., s. 2005; C.S., s. 2370; 1971, c. 533, s. 6.)

§ 42-32. Damages assessed to trial.

On appeal to the district court, the jury trying issues joined shall assess the damages of the plaintiff for the detention of his possession to the time of the trial in that court; and, if the jury finds that the detention was wrongful and that the appeal was without merit and taken for the purpose of delay, the plaintiff, in addition to any other damages allowed, shall be entitled to the amount of rent in arrears, or which may have accrued, to the time of trial in the district court. Judgment for the rent in arrears and for the damages assessed may, on motion, be rendered against the sureties to the appeal. (1868-9, c. 156, s. 28; Code, s. 1775; Rev., s. 2006; C.S., s. 2371; 1945, c. 796; 1971, c. 533, s. 7; 1979, c. 820, s. 7.)

§ 42-33. Rent and costs tendered by tenant.

If, in any action brought to recover the possession of demised premises upon a forfeiture for the nonpayment of rent, the tenant, before judgment given in such action, pays or tenders the rent due and the costs of the action, all further proceedings in such action shall cease. If the plaintiff further prosecutes his action, and the defendant pays into court for the use of the plaintiff a sum equal to that which shall be found to be due, and the costs, to the time of such payment, or to the time of a tender and refusal, if one has occurred, the defendant shall recover from the plaintiff all subsequent costs; the plaintiff shall be allowed to receive the sum paid into court for his use, and the proceedings shall be stayed. (4 Geo. II, c. 28, s. 4; 1868-9, c. 156, s. 26; Code, s. 1773; Rev., s. 2007; C.S., s. 2372.)

§ 42-34. Undertaking on appeal and order staying execution.

(a) Upon appeal to the district court, either party may demand that the case be tried at the first session of the court after the appeal is docketed, but the presiding judge, in his discretion, may first try any pending case in which the rights of the parties or the public demand it. If the case has not been previously continued in district court, the court shall continue the case for an appropriate period of time if any party initiates discovery or files a motion to allow further pleadings pursuant to G.S. 7A-220 or G.S. 7A-229, or for summary judgment pursuant to Rule 56 of the Rules of Civil Procedure.

(b) During an appeal to district court, it shall be sufficient to stay execution of a judgment for ejectment if the defendant appellant pays to the clerk of superior court any rent in arrears as determined by the magistrate and signs an undertaking that he or she will pay into the office of the clerk of superior court the amount of the tenant's share of the contract rent as it becomes due periodically after the judgment was entered and, where applicable, comply with subdivision (c) below. For the sole purpose of determining the amount of rent in arrears pursuant to a judgment for possession pursuant to G.S. 42-30(iii), the magistrate's determination shall be based upon (i) the available evidence presented to the magistrate or (ii) the amounts listed on the face of the filed Complaint in Summary Ejectment. Provided however, when the magistrate makes a finding in the record, based on evidence presented in court, that there is an actual dispute as to the amount of rent in arrears that is due and the magistrate specifies the specific amount of rent in arrears in dispute, in order to stay execution of a judgment for ejectment, the defendant appellant shall not be required to pay to the clerk of superior court the amount of rent in arrears found by the magistrate to be in dispute, even if the magistrate's judgment includes this amount in the amount of rent found to be in arrears. If a defendant appellant appeared at the hearing before the magistrate and the magistrate found an amount of rent in arrears that was not in dispute, and if an attorney representing the defendant appellant on appeal to the district court signs a pleading stating that there is evidence of an actual dispute as to the amount of rent in arrears, then the defendant appellant shall not be required to pay the rent in arrears alleged to be in dispute to stay execution of a judgment for ejectment pending appeal. Any magistrate, clerk, or district court judge shall order stay of execution upon the defendant appellant's paying the undisputed rent in arrears to the clerk and signing the undertaking. If either party disputes the amount of the payment or the due date in the undertaking, the aggrieved party may move for modification of the terms of the undertaking before the clerk of superior court or the district court. Upon such motion and upon notice to all interested parties, the clerk or court shall hold a hearing within 10 calendar days of the date the motion is filed and determine what modifications, if any, are appropriate. No writ of possession or other execution of the magistrate's judgment shall take place during the time the aggrieved party's motion for modification is pending before the clerk of court.

(c) In an ejectment action based upon alleged nonpayment of rent where the judgment is entered more than five working days before the day when the next rent will be due under the lease, the appellant shall make an additional undertaking to stay execution pending appeal. Such additional undertaking shall be the payment of the prorated rent for the days between the day that the judgment was entered and the next day when the rent will be due under the lease.

(c1) Notwithstanding the provisions of subsection (b) of this section, an indigent defendant appellant, as set forth in G.S. 1-110, who prosecutes his or her appeal as an indigent and who meets the requirement of G.S. 1-288 shall pay the amount of the contract rent as it becomes periodically due as set forth in subsection (b) of this section, but shall not be required to pay rent in arrears as set forth in subsection (b) of this section in order to stay execution pending appeal.

(d) The undertaking by the appellant and the order staying execution may be substantially in the following form:

"State of North Carolina,

"County of ____

"____, Plaintiff

vs.   Bond to

"____, Defendant   Stay Execution

On Appeal to

District Court

"Now comes the defendant in the above entitled action and respectfully shows the court that judgment for summary ejectment was entered against the defendant and for the plaintiff on the ____ day of ____, ____, by the Magistrate. Defendant has appealed the judgment to the District Court.

"Pursuant to the terms of the lease between plaintiff and defendant, defendant is obligated to pay rent in the amount of $____ per ____, due on the____ day of each ____.

"Where the payment of rent in arrears or an additional undertaking is required by G.S. 42-34, the defendant hereby tenders $____ to the Court as required.

"Defendant hereby undertakes to pay the periodic rent hereinafter due according to the aforesaid terms of the lease and moves the Court to stay execution on the judgment for summary ejectment until this matter is heard on appeal by the District Court.

"This the _____ day of _____, ____.

_____

                                                                                  Defendant

"Upon execution of the above bond, execution on said judgment for summary ejectment is hereby stayed until the action is heard on appeal in the District Court. If defendant fails to make any rental payment to the clerk's office within five days of the due date, upon application of the plaintiff, the stay of execution shall dissolve and the sheriff may dispossess the defendant.

"This the _____ day of _____, ____.

_____

                                                       Assistant Clerk of Superior Court."

(e)   Upon application of the plaintiff, the clerk of superior court shall pay to the plaintiff any amount of the rental payments paid by the defendant into the clerk's office which are not claimed by the defendant in any pleadings.

(f)   If the defendant fails to make a payment within five days of the due date according to the undertaking and order staying execution, the clerk, upon application of the plaintiff, shall issue execution on the judgment for possession.

(9) When it appears by stipulation executed by all of the parties or by final order of the court that the appeal has been resolved, the clerk of court shall disburse any accrued moneys of the undertaking remaining in the clerk's office according to the terms of the stipulation or order. (1868-9, c. 156, s. 25; 1883, c. 316; Code, s. 1772; Rev., s. 2008; C.S., s. 2373; 1921, c. 90; Ex. Sess., 1921, c. 17; 1933, c. 154; 1937, c. 294; 1949, c. 1159; 1971, c. 533, s. 8; 1979, c. 820, ss. 1-6; 1998-125, s. 1; 1999-456, s. 59; 2005-423, s. 11; 2009-279, s. 2.)

§ 42-34.1. Rent pending execution of judgment; post bond pending appeal.

(a) If the judgment in district court is against the defendant appellant, it shall be sufficient to stay execution of the judgment during the 30-day time period for taking an appeal provided for in Rule 3 of the North Carolina Rules of Appellate Procedure if the defendant appellant posts a bond as provided in G.S. 42-34(b), and no additional security under G.S. 1-292 is required. If the defendant appellant fails to make rental payments as provided in the undertaking within five days of the day rent is due under the terms of the residential rental agreement, the clerk of superior court shall, upon application of the plaintiff appellee, immediately issue a writ of possession, and the sheriff shall dispossess the defendant appellant as provided in G.S. 42-36.2.

(a1) If the judgment in district court is against the defendant appellant and the defendant appellant does not appeal the judgment, the defendant appellant shall pay rent to the plaintiff for the time the defendant appellant remains in possession of the premises after the judgment is given. Rent shall be prorated if the judgment is executed before the day rent would become due under the terms of the lease. The clerk of court shall disperse any rent in arrears paid by the defendant appellant in accordance with a stipulation executed by all parties or, if there is no stipulation, in accordance with the judge's order.

(b) If the judgment in district court is against the defendant appellant and the defendant appellant appeals the judgment, it shall be sufficient to stay execution of the judgment if the defendant appellant posts a bond as provided in G.S. 42-34(b), and no additional security under G.S. 1-292 is required. If the defendant appellant fails to perfect the appeal or the appellate court upholds the judgment of the district court, the execution of the judgment shall proceed. The clerk of court shall not disperse any rent in arrears paid by the defendant appellant until all appeals have been resolved. (1998-125, s. 2; 2012-17, s. 1.)

§ 42-35. Restitution of tenant, if case quashed, etc., on appeal.

If the proceedings before the magistrate are brought before a district court and quashed, or judgment is given against the plaintiff, the district or other court in which final judgment is given shall, if necessary, restore the defendant to the possession, and issue such writs as are proper for that purpose. (1868-9, c. 156, s. 27; Code, s. 1774; Rev., s. 2009; C.S., s. 2374; 1971, c. 533, s. 9.)

§ 42-36. Damages to tenant for dispossession, if proceedings quashed, etc.

If, by order of the magistrate, the plaintiff is put in possession, and the proceedings shall afterwards be quashed or reversed, the defendant may recover damages of the plaintiff for his removal. (1868-9, c. 156, s. 30; Code, s. 1776; Rev., s. 2010; C.S., s. 2375; 1971, c. 533, s. 10.)

§ 42-36.1. Lease or rental of manufactured homes.

The provisions of this Article shall apply to the lease or rental of manufactured homes, as defined in G.S. 143-145. (1971, c. 764; 1985, c. 487, s. 8.)

§ 42-36.1A. Judgments for possession more than 30 days old.

Prior to obtaining execution of a judgment that has been entered for more than 30 days for possession of demised premises, a landlord shall sign an affidavit stating that the landlord has neither entered into a formal lease with the defendant nor accepted rental money from the defendant for any period of time after entry of the judgment. (1995, c. 460, s. 7.)

§ 42-36.2. Notice to tenant of execution of writ for possession of property; storage of evicted tenant's personal property.

(a) When Sheriff May Remove Property. - Before removing a tenant's personal property from demised premises pursuant to a writ for possession of real property or an order, the sheriff shall give the tenant notice of the approximate time the writ will be executed. The time within which the sheriff shall have to execute the writ shall be no more than five days from the sheriff's receipt thereof. The sheriff shall remove the tenant's property, as provided in the writ, no earlier than the time specified in the notice, unless:

(1) The landlord, or his authorized agent, signs a statement saying that the tenant's property can remain on the premises, in which case the sheriff shall simply lock the premises; or

(2) The landlord, or his authorized agent, signs a statement saying that the landlord does not want to eject the tenant because the tenant has paid all court costs charged to him and has satisfied his indebtedness to the landlord.

Upon receipt of either statement by the landlord, the sheriff shall return the writ unexecuted to the issuing clerk of court and shall make a notation on the writ of his reasons. The sheriff shall attach a copy of the landlord's statement to the writ. If the writ is returned unexecuted because the landlord signed a statement described in subdivision (2) of this subsection, the clerk shall make an entry of satisfaction on the judgment docket. If the sheriff padlocks, the costs of the proceeding shall be charged as part of the court costs.

(b) Sheriff May Store Property. - When the sheriff removes the personal property of an evicted tenant from demised premises pursuant to a writ or order the tenant shall take possession of his property. If the tenant fails or refuses to take possession of his property, the sheriff may deliver the property to any storage warehouse in the county, or in an adjoining county if no storage warehouse is located in that county, for storage. The sheriff may require the landlord to advance the cost of delivering the property to a storage warehouse plus the cost of one month's storage before delivering the property to a storage warehouse. If a landlord refuses to advance these costs when requested to do so by the sheriff, the sheriff shall not remove the tenant's property, but shall return the writ unexecuted to the issuing clerk of court with a notation thereon of his reason for not executing the writ. Except for the disposition of manufactured homes and their contents as provided in G.S. 42-25.9(g) and G.S. 44A-2(e2), within seven days of the landlord's being placed in lawful possession by execution of a writ of possession and upon the tenant's request within that seven-day period, the landlord shall release possession of the property to the seven-day period after being placed in lawful possession by execution of a writ of possession, a landlord may move for storage purposes, but shall not throw away, dispose of, or sell any items of personal property remaining on the premises unless otherwise provided for in this Chapter. If, after being placed in lawful possession by execution of a writ, the landlord has offered to release the tenant's property and the tenant fails to retrieve such property during the landlord's regular business hours within seven days after execution of the writ, the landlord may throw away, dispose of, or sell the property in accordance with the provisions of G.S. 42-25.9(g). If the tenant does not request release of the property within seven days, all costs of summary ejectment, execution and storage proceedings shall be charged to the tenant as court costs and shall constitute a lien against the stored property or a claim against any remaining balance of the proceeds of a warehouseman's lien sale.

(c) Liability of the Sheriff. - A sheriff who stores a tenant's property pursuant to this section and any person acting under the sheriff's direction, control, or employment shall be liable for any claims arising out of the willful or wanton negligence in storing the tenant's property.

(d) Notice. - The notice required by subsection (a) shall, except in actions involving the lease of a space for a manufactured home as defined in G.S. 143-143.9(6), inform the tenant that failure to request possession of any property on the premises within seven days of execution may result in the property being thrown away, disposed of, or sold. Notice shall be made by one of the following methods:

(1) By delivering a copy of the notice to the tenant or his authorized agent at least two days before the time stated in the notice for serving the writ;

(2) By leaving a copy of the notice at the tenant's dwelling or usual place of abode with a person of suitable age and discretion who resides there at least two days before the time stated in the notice for serving the writ; or

(3) By mailing a copy of the notice by first-class mail to the tenant at his last known address at least five days before the time stated in the notice for serving the writ. (1983, c. 672, s. 1; 1995, c. 460, s. 6; 1999-278, ss. 3, 4; 2013-334, s. 5.)

personal property from the dwelling unit.

Notwithstanding any other provision of this Chapter, when a decedent who is the sole occupant of a dwelling unit dies leaving tangible personal property in the dwelling unit, the landlord may, instead of commencing a summary ejectment action, file an affidavit as provided in G.S. 28A-25-7. (2012-17, s. 9.)

Article 4.

Forms.

§ 42-37: Repealed by Session Laws 1971, c. 533, s. 11.

Article 4A.

Retaliatory Eviction.

§ 42-37.1. Defense of retaliatory eviction.

(a)   It is the public policy of the State of North Carolina to protect tenants and other persons whose residence in the household is explicitly or implicitly known to the landlord, who seek to exercise their rights to decent, safe, and sanitary housing. Therefore, the following activities of such persons are protected by law:

(1)   A good faith complaint or request for repairs to the landlord, his employee, or his agent about conditions or defects in the premises that the landlord is obligated to repair under G.S. 42-42;

(2)   A good faith complaint to a government agency about a landlord's alleged violation of any health or safety law, or any regulation, code, ordinance, or State or federal law that regulates premises used for dwelling purposes;

concerning premises rented by a tenant;

(4) A good faith attempt to exercise, secure or enforce any rights existing under a valid lease or rental agreement or under State or federal law; or

(5) A good faith attempt to organize, join, or become otherwise involved with, any organization promoting or enforcing tenants' rights.

(b) In an action for summary ejectment pursuant to G.S. 42-26, a tenant may raise the affirmative defense of retaliatory eviction and may present evidence that the landlord's action is substantially in response to the occurrence within 12 months of the filing of such action of one or more of the protected acts described in subsection (a) of this section.

(c) Notwithstanding subsections (a) and (b) of this section, a landlord may prevail in an action for summary ejectment if:

(1) The tenant breached the covenant to pay rent or any other substantial covenant of the lease for which the tenant may be evicted, and such breach is the reason for the eviction; or

(2) In a case of a tenancy for a definite period of time where the tenant has no option to renew the lease, the tenant holds over after expiration of the term; or

(3) The violation of G.S. 42-42 complained of was caused primarily by the willful or negligent conduct of the tenant, member of the tenant's household, or their guests or invitees; or

(4) Compliance with the applicable building or housing code requires demolition or major alteration or remodeling that cannot be accomplished without completely displacing the tenant's household; or

(5) The landlord seeks to recover possession on the basis of a good faith notice to quit the premises, which notice was delivered prior to the occurrence of any of the activities protected by subsections (a) and (b) of this section; or

(6) The landlord seeks in good faith to recover possession at the end of the tenant's term for use as the landlord's own abode, to demolish or make major alterations or remodeling of the dwelling unit in a manner that requires the

months the use of the property as a rental dwelling unit. (1979, c. 807.)

§ 42-37.2. Remedies.

(a)   If the court finds that an ejectment action is retaliatory, as defined by this Article, it shall deny the request for ejectment; provided, that a dismissal of the request for ejectment shall not prevent the landlord from receiving payments for rent due or any other appropriate judgment.

(b)   The rights and remedies created by this Article are supplementary to all existing common law and statutory rights and remedies. (1979, c. 807.)

§ 42-37.3. Waiver.

Any waiver by a tenant or a member of his household of the rights and remedies created by this Article is void as contrary to public policy. (1979, c. 807.)

Article 5.

Residential Rental Agreements.

§ 42-38. Application.

This Article determines the rights, obligations, and remedies under a rental agreement for a dwelling unit within this State. (1977, c. 770, s. 1.)

§ 42-39. Exclusions.

(a)   The provisions of this Article shall not apply to transient occupancy in a hotel, motel, or similar lodging subject to regulation by the Commission for Public Health.

into under Chapter 42A of the General Statutes.

(b) Nothing in this Article shall apply to any dwelling furnished without charge or rent. (1973, c. 476, s. 128; 1977, c. 770, ss. 1, 2; 1999-420, s. 3; 2007-182, s. 2.)

§ 42-40. Definitions.

For the purpose of this Article, the following definitions shall apply:

(1) "Action" includes recoupment, counterclaim, defense, setoff, and any other proceeding including an action for possession.

(2) "Premises" means a dwelling unit, including mobile homes or mobile home spaces, and the structure of which it is a part and facilities and appurtenances therein and grounds, areas, and facilities normally held out for the use of residential tenants.

(3) "Landlord" means any owner and any rental management company, rental agency, or any other person having the actual or apparent authority of an agent to perform the duties imposed by this Article.

(4) "Protected tenant" means a tenant or household member who is a victim of domestic violence under Chapter 50B of the General Statutes or sexual assault or stalking under Chapter 14 of the General Statutes. (1977, c. 770, s. 1; 1979, c. 880, ss. 1, 2; 1999-420, s. 2; 2005-423, s. 5.)

§ 42-41. Mutuality of obligations.

The tenant's obligation to pay rent under the rental agreement or assignment and to comply with G.S. 42-43 and the landlord's obligation to comply with G.S. 42-42(a) shall be mutually dependent. (1977, c. 770, s. 1.)

§ 42-42. Landlord to provide fit premises.

(a) The landlord shall:

(1) Comply with the current applicable building and housing codes, whether enacted before or after October 1, 1977, to the extent required by the operation of such codes; no new requirement is imposed by this subdivision (a)(1) if a structure is exempt from a current building code.

(2) Make all repairs and do whatever is necessary to put and keep the premises in a fit and habitable condition.

(3) Keep all common areas of the premises in safe condition.

(4) Maintain in good and safe working order and promptly repair all electrical, plumbing, sanitary, heating, ventilating, air conditioning, and other facilities and appliances supplied or required to be supplied by the landlord provided that notification of needed repairs is made to the landlord in writing by the tenant, except in emergency situations.

(5) Provide operable smoke alarms, either battery-operated or electrical, having an Underwriters' Laboratories, Inc., listing or other equivalent national testing laboratory approval, and install the smoke alarms in accordance with either the standards of the National Fire Protection Association or the minimum protection designated in the manufacturer's instructions, which the landlord shall retain or provide as proof of compliance. The landlord shall replace or repair the smoke alarms within 15 days of receipt of notification if the landlord is notified of needed replacement or repairs in writing by the tenant. The landlord shall ensure that a smoke alarm is operable and in good repair at the beginning of each tenancy. Unless the landlord and the tenant have a written agreement to the contrary, the landlord shall place new batteries in a battery-operated smoke alarm at the beginning of a tenancy and the tenant shall replace the batteries as needed during the tenancy, except where the smoke alarm is a tamper-resistant, 10-year lithium battery smoke alarm as required by subdivision (5a) of this subsection. Failure of the tenant to replace the batteries as needed shall not be considered as negligence on the part of the tenant or the landlord.

(5a) After December 31, 2012, when installing a new smoke alarm or replacing an existing smoke alarm, install a tamper-resistant, 10-year lithium battery smoke alarm. However, the landlord shall not be required to install a tamper-resistant, 10-year lithium battery smoke alarm as required by this subdivision in either of the following circumstances:

a. The dwelling unit is equipped with a hardwired smoke alarm with a battery backup.

b. The dwelling unit is equipped with a smoke alarm combined with a carbon monoxide alarm that meets the requirements provided in subdivision (7) of this section.

(6) If the landlord is charging for the cost of providing water or sewer service pursuant to G.S. 42-42.1 and has actual knowledge from either the supplying water system or other reliable source that water being supplied to tenants within the landlord's property exceeds a maximum contaminant level established pursuant to Article 10 of Chapter 130A of the General Statutes, provide notice that water being supplied exceeds a maximum contaminant level.

(7) Provide a minimum of one operable carbon monoxide alarm per rental unit per level, either battery-operated or electrical, that is listed by a nationally recognized testing laboratory that is OSHA-approved to test and certify to American National Standards Institute/Underwriters Laboratories Standards ANSI/UL2034 or ANSI/UL2075, and install the carbon monoxide alarms in accordance with either the standards of the National Fire Protection Association or the minimum protection designated in the manufacturer's instructions, which the landlord shall retain or provide as proof of compliance. A landlord that installs one carbon monoxide alarm per rental unit per level shall be deemed to be in compliance with standards under this subdivision covering the location and number of alarms. The landlord shall replace or repair the carbon monoxide alarms within 15 days of receipt of notification if the landlord is notified of needed replacement or repairs in writing by the tenant. The landlord shall ensure that a carbon monoxide alarm is operable and in good repair at the beginning of each tenancy. Unless the landlord and the tenant have a written agreement to the contrary, the landlord shall place new batteries in a battery-operated carbon monoxide alarm at the beginning of a tenancy, and the tenant shall replace the batteries as needed during the tenancy. Failure of the tenant to replace the batteries as needed shall not be considered as negligence on the part of the tenant or the landlord. A carbon monoxide alarm may be combined with smoke alarms if the combined alarm does both of the following: (i) complies with ANSI/UL2034 or ANSI/UL2075 for carbon monoxide alarms and ANSI/UL217 for smoke alarms; and (ii) emits an alarm in a manner that clearly differentiates between detecting the presence of carbon monoxide and the presence of smoke. This subdivision applies only to dwelling units having a fossil-fuel burning heater, appliance, or fireplace, and in any dwelling unit having

January 1, 2010, shall be deemed to be in compliance with this subdivision.

(8) Within a reasonable period of time based upon the severity of the condition, repair or remedy any imminently dangerous condition on the premises after acquiring actual knowledge or receiving notice of the condition. Notwithstanding the landlord's repair or remedy of any imminently dangerous condition, the landlord may recover from the tenant the actual and reasonable costs of repairs that are the fault of the tenant. For purposes of this subdivision, the term "imminently dangerous condition" means any of the following:

a. Unsafe wiring.

b. Unsafe flooring or steps.

c. Unsafe ceilings or roofs.

d. Unsafe chimneys or flues.

e. Lack of potable water.

f. Lack of operable locks on all doors leading to the outside.

g. Broken windows or lack of operable locks on all windows on the ground level.

h. Lack of operable heating facilities capable of heating living areas to 65 degrees Fahrenheit when it is 20 degrees Fahrenheit outside from November 1 through March 31.

i. Lack of an operable toilet.

j. Lack of an operable bathtub or shower.

k. Rat infestation as a result of defects in the structure that make the premises not impervious to rodents.

l. Excessive standing water, sewage, or flooding problems caused by plumbing leaks or inadequate drainage that contribute to mosquito infestation or mold.

section by the tenant's explicit or implicit acceptance of the landlord's failure to provide premises complying with this section, whether done before the lease was made, when it was made, or after it was made, unless a governmental subdivision imposes an impediment to repair for a specific period of time not to exceed six months. Notwithstanding the provisions of this subsection, the landlord and tenant are not prohibited from making a subsequent written contract wherein the tenant agrees to perform specified work on the premises, provided that said contract is supported by adequate consideration other than the letting of the premises and is not made with the purpose or effect of evading the landlord's obligations under this Article. (1977, c. 770, s. 1; 1995, c. 111, s. 2; 1998-212, s. 17.16(i); 2004-143, s. 3; 2008-219, ss. 2, 6; 2009-279, s. 3; 2010-97, s. 6(a); 2012-92, s. 1.)

§ 42-42.1. Water and electricity conservation.

(a) For the purpose of encouraging water and electricity conservation, pursuant to a written rental agreement, a landlord may charge for the cost of providing water or sewer service to tenants who occupy the same contiguous premises pursuant to G.S. 62-110(g) or electric service pursuant to G.S. 62-110(h).

(b) The landlord may not disconnect or terminate the tenant's electric service or water or sewer services due to the tenant's nonpayment of the amount due for electric service or water or sewer services. (2004-143, s. 4; 2011-252, s. 2.)

§ 42-42.2. Victim protection - nondiscrimination.

A landlord shall not terminate a tenancy, fail to renew a tenancy, refuse to enter into a rental agreement, or otherwise retaliate in the rental of a dwelling based substantially on: (i) the tenant, applicant, or a household member's status as a victim of domestic violence, sexual assault, or stalking; or (ii) the tenant or applicant having terminated a rental agreement under G.S. 42-45.1. Evidence provided to the landlord of domestic violence, sexual assault, or stalking may include any of the following:

(2) Documentation from a domestic violence or sexual assault program.

(3) Documentation from a religious, medical, or other professional. (2005-423, s. 6.)

§ 42-42.3. Victim protection - change locks.

(a) If the perpetrator of domestic violence, sexual assault, or stalking is not a tenant in the same dwelling unit as the protected tenant, a tenant of a dwelling may give oral or written notice to the landlord that a protected tenant is a victim of domestic violence, sexual assault, or stalking and may request that the locks to the dwelling unit be changed. A protected tenant is not required to provide documentation of the domestic violence, sexual assault, or stalking to initiate the changing of the locks, pursuant to this subsection. A landlord who receives a request under this subsection shall change the locks to the protected tenant's dwelling unit or give the protected tenant permission to change the locks within 48 hours.

(b) If the perpetrator of the domestic violence, sexual assault, or stalking is a tenant in the same dwelling unit as the victim, any tenant or protected tenant of a dwelling unit may give oral or written notice to the landlord that a protected tenant is a victim of domestic violence, sexual assault, or stalking and may request that the locks to the dwelling unit be changed. In these circumstances, the following shall apply:

(1) Before the landlord or tenant changes the locks under this subsection, the tenant must provide the landlord with a copy of an order issued by a court that orders the perpetrator to stay away from the dwelling unit.

(2) Unless a court order allows the perpetrator to return to the dwelling to retrieve personal belongings, the landlord has no duty under the rental agreement or by law to allow the perpetrator access to the dwelling unit, to provide keys to the perpetrator, or to provide the perpetrator access to the perpetrator's personal property within the dwelling unit once the landlord has been provided with a court order requiring the perpetrator to stay away from the dwelling. If a landlord complies with this section, the landlord is not liable for civil

dwelling unit or loss of use or damage to the perpetrator's personal property.

(3) The perpetrator who has been excluded from the dwelling unit under this subsection remains liable under the lease with any other tenant of the dwelling unit for rent or damages to the dwelling unit.

A landlord who receives a request under this subsection shall change the locks to the protected tenant's dwelling unit or give the protected tenant permission to change the locks within 72 hours.

(c) The protected tenant shall bear the expense of changing the locks. If a landlord fails to act within the required time, the protected tenant may change the locks without the landlord's permission. If the protected tenant changes the locks, the protected tenant shall give a key to the new locks to the landlord within 48 hours of the locks being changed. (2005-423, s. 6.)

§ 42-43. Tenant to maintain dwelling unit.

(a) The tenant shall:

(1) Keep that part of the premises that the tenant occupies and uses as clean and safe as the conditions of the premises permit and cause no unsafe or unsanitary conditions in the common areas and remainder of the premises that the tenant uses.

(2) Dispose of all ashes, rubbish, garbage, and other waste in a clean and safe manner.

(3) Keep all plumbing fixtures in the dwelling unit or used by the tenant as clean as their condition permits.

(4) Not deliberately or negligently destroy, deface, damage, or remove any part of the premises, nor render inoperable the smoke alarm or carbon monoxide alarm provided by the landlord, or knowingly permit any person to do so.

(5) Comply with any and all obligations imposed upon the tenant by current applicable building and housing codes.

(6) Be responsible for all damage, defacement, or removal of any property inside a dwelling unit in the tenant's exclusive control unless the damage, defacement or removal was due to ordinary wear and tear, acts of the landlord or the landlord's agent, defective products supplied or repairs authorized by the landlord, acts of third parties not invitees of the tenant, or natural forces.

(7) Notify the landlord, in writing, of the need for replacement of or repairs to a smoke alarm or carbon monoxide alarm. The landlord shall ensure that a smoke alarm and carbon monoxide alarm are operable and in good repair at the beginning of each tenancy. Unless the landlord and the tenant have a written agreement to the contrary, the landlord shall place new batteries in a battery-operated smoke alarm and battery-operated carbon monoxide alarm at the beginning of a tenancy and the tenant shall replace the batteries as needed during the tenancy, except where the smoke alarm is a tamper-resistant, 10-year lithium battery smoke alarm as required by G.S. 42-42(a)(5a). Failure of the tenant to replace the batteries as needed shall not be considered as negligence on the part of the tenant or the landlord.

(b) The landlord shall notify the tenant in writing of any breaches of the tenant's obligations under this section except in emergency situations. (1977, c. 770, s. 1; 1995, c. 111, s. 3; 1998-212, s. 17.16(j); 2008-219, s. 3; 2012-92, s. 2.)

§ 42-44. General remedies, penalties, and limitations.

(a) Any right or obligation declared by this Chapter is enforceable by civil action, in addition to other remedies of law and in equity.

(a1) If a landlord fails to provide, install, replace, or repair a smoke alarm under the provisions of G.S. 42-42(a)(5) or a carbon monoxide alarm under the provisions of G.S. 42-42(a)(7) within 30 days of having received written notice from the tenant or any agent of State or local government of the landlord's failure to do so, the landlord shall be responsible for an infraction and shall be subject to a fine of not more than two hundred fifty dollars ($250.00) for each violation. After December 31, 2012, if the landlord installs a new smoke alarm or replaces an existing smoke alarm, the smoke alarm shall be a tamper-resistant, 10-year lithium battery smoke alarm, except as provided in G.S. 42-42(a)(5a). The landlord may temporarily disconnect a smoke alarm or carbon monoxide activities when such activities are likely to activate the smoke alarm or carbon monoxide alarm or make it inactive.

(a2)   If a smoke alarm or carbon monoxide alarm is disabled or damaged, other than through actions of the landlord, the landlord's agents, or acts of God, the tenant shall reimburse the landlord the reasonable and actual cost for repairing or replacing the smoke alarm or carbon monoxide alarm within 30 days of having received written notice from the landlord or any agent of State or local government of the need for the tenant to make such reimbursement. If the tenant fails to make reimbursement within 30 days, the tenant shall be responsible for an infraction and subject to a fine of not more than one hundred dollars ($100.00) for each violation. The tenant may temporarily disconnect a smoke alarm or carbon monoxide alarm in a dwelling unit to replace the batteries or when it has been inadvertently activated.

(b)   Repealed by Session Laws 1979, c. 820, s. 8.

(c)   The tenant may not unilaterally withhold rent prior to a judicial determination of a right to do so.

(d)   A violation of this Article shall not constitute negligence per se. (1977, c. 770, s. 1; 1979, c. 820, s. 8; 1998-212, s. 17.16(k); 2008-219, s. 4; 2012-92, s. 3.)

§ 42-45. Early termination of rental agreement by military personnel, surviving family members, or lawful representative.

(a)   Any member of the Armed Forces of the United States who (i) is required to move pursuant to permanent change of station orders to depart 50 miles or more from the location of the dwelling unit, or (ii) is prematurely or involuntarily discharged or released from active duty with the Armed Forces of the United States, may terminate the member's rental agreement for a dwelling unit by providing the landlord with a written notice of termination to be effective on a date stated in the notice that is at least 30 days after the landlord's receipt of the notice. The notice to the landlord must be accompanied by either a copy of the official military orders or a written verification signed by the member's commanding officer.

with a military unit for a period of not less than 90 days may terminate the member's rental agreement for a dwelling unit by providing the landlord with a written notice of termination. The notice to the landlord must be accompanied by either a copy of the official military orders or a written verification signed by the member's commanding officer. Termination of a lease pursuant to this subsection is effective 30 days after the first date on which the next rental payment is due or 45 days after the landlord's receipt of the notice, whichever is shorter, and payable after the date on which the notice of termination is delivered.

(a2) Upon termination of a rental agreement under this section, the tenant is liable for the rent due under the rental agreement prorated to the effective date of the termination payable at such time as would have otherwise been required by the terms of the rental agreement. The tenant is not liable for any other rent or damages due to the early termination of the tenancy except the liquidated damages provided in subsection (b) of this section. If a member terminates the rental agreement pursuant to this section 14 or more days prior to occupancy, no damages or penalties of any kind shall be due.

(a3) If a member of the Armed Forces of the United States dies while on active duty, then an immediate family member, or a lawful representative of the member's estate, may terminate the member's rental agreement for a dwelling unit by providing the landlord with a written notice of termination to be effective on the date described in subsection (a1) of this section. A copy of the death certificate, official military personnel casualty report, or letter from the commanding officer verifying the member's death must accompany the notice for this subsection to be effective. Termination of the member's lease obligations under this subsection shall also terminate the lease obligations of any cotenants who are immediate family members. If the member was a cotenant with a person who is not an immediate family member, then the termination shall relate only to the obligation of the member under the rental agreement. The prorated charges in subsection (a2) of this section and the liquidated damages provisions of subsection (b) of this section shall apply to any claims against the member's estate.

(b) In consideration of early termination of the rental agreement, the tenant is liable to the landlord for liquidated damages provided the tenant has completed less than nine months of the tenancy and the landlord has suffered actual damages due to loss of the tenancy. The liquidated damages shall be in an amount no greater than one month's rent if the tenant has completed less half of one month's rent if the tenant has completed at least six but less than nine months of the tenancy as of the effective date of termination.

(c) The provisions of this section may not be waived or modified by the agreement of the parties under any circumstances. Nothing in this section shall affect the rights established by G.S. 42-3. (1987, c. 478, s. 1; 2005-445, s. 4.1; 2011-183, s. 29(a), (b); 2012-64, s. 1.)

§ 42-45.1. Early termination of rental agreement by victims of domestic violence, sexual assault, or stalking.

(a) Any protected tenant may terminate his or her rental agreement for a dwelling unit by providing the landlord with a written notice of termination to be effective on a date stated in the notice that is at least 30 days after the landlord's receipt of the notice. The notice to the landlord shall be accompanied by either: (i) a copy of a valid order of protection issued by a court pursuant to Chapter 50B or 50C of the General Statutes, other than an ex parte order, (ii) a criminal order that restrains a person from contact with a protected tenant, or (iii) a valid Address Confidentiality Program card issued pursuant to G.S. 15C-4 to the victim or a minor member of the tenant's household. A victim of domestic violence or sexual assault must submit a copy of a safety plan with the notice to terminate. The safety plan, dated during the term of the tenancy to be terminated, must be provided by a domestic violence or sexual assault program which substantially complies with the requirements set forth in G.S. 50B-9 and must recommend relocation of the protected tenant.

(b) Upon termination of a rental agreement under this section, the tenant who is released from the rental agreement pursuant to subsection (a) of this section is liable for the rent due under the rental agreement prorated to the effective date of the termination and payable at the time that would have been required by the terms of the rental agreement. The tenant is not liable for any other rent or fees due only to the early termination of the tenancy. If, pursuant to this section, a tenant terminates the rental agreement 14 days or more before occupancy, the tenant is not subject to any damages or penalties.

(c) Notwithstanding the release of a protected tenant from a rental agreement under subsection (a) of this section, or the exclusion of a perpetrator of domestic violence, sexual assault, or stalking by court order, if there are any those tenants. The perpetrator who has been excluded from the dwelling unit under court order remains liable under the lease with any other tenant of the dwelling unit for rent or damages to the dwelling unit.

(d)   The provisions of this section may not be waived or modified by agreement of the parties. (2005-423, s. 7.)

§ 42-45.2. Early termination of rental agreement by military and tenants residing in certain foreclosed property.

Any tenant who resides in residential real property containing less than 15 rental units that is being sold in a foreclosure proceeding under Article 2A of Chapter 45 of the General Statutes may terminate the rental agreement for the dwelling unit after receiving notice pursuant to G.S. 45-21.17(4) by providing the landlord with a written notice of termination to be effective on a date stated in the notice that is at least 10 days after the date of the notice of sale. Upon termination of a rental agreement under this section, the tenant is liable for the rent due under the rental agreement prorated to the effective date of the termination payable at the time that would have been required by the terms of the rental agreement. The tenant is not liable for any other rent or damages due only to the early termination of the tenancy. (2007-353, s. 3.)

§ 42-46. Authorized fees.

(a)   In all residential rental agreements in which a definite time for the payment of the rent is fixed, the parties may agree to a late fee not inconsistent with the provisions of this subsection, to be chargeable only if any rental payment is five days or more late. If the rent:

(1)   Is due in monthly installments, a landlord may charge a late fee not to exceed fifteen dollars ($15.00) or five percent (5%) of the monthly rent, whichever is greater.

(2)   Is due in weekly installments, a landlord may charge a late fee not to exceed four dollars ($4.00) or five percent (5%) of the weekly rent, whichever is greater.

(3) Repealed by Session Laws 2009-279, s. 4, effective October 1, 2009, and applicable to leases entered into on or after that date.

(b) A late fee under subsection (a) of this section may be imposed only one time for each late rental payment. A late fee for a specific late rental payment may not be deducted from a subsequent rental payment so as to cause the subsequent rental payment to be in default.

(c) Repealed by Session Laws 2009-279, s. 4, effective October 1, 2009, and applicable to leases entered into on or after that date.

(d) A lessor shall not charge a late fee to a lessee pursuant to subsection (a) of this section because of the lessee's failure to pay for water or sewer services provided pursuant to G.S. 62-110(g).

(e) Complaint-Filing Fee. - Pursuant to a written lease, a landlord may charge a complaint-filing fee not to exceed fifteen dollars ($15.00) or five percent (5%) of the monthly rent, whichever is greater, only if the tenant was in default of the lease, the landlord filed and served a complaint for summary ejectment and/or money owed, the tenant cured the default or claim, and the landlord dismissed the complaint prior to judgment. The landlord can include this fee in the amount required to cure the default.

(f) Court-Appearance Fee. - Pursuant to a written lease, a landlord may charge a court-appearance fee in an amount equal to ten percent (10%) of the monthly rent only if the tenant was in default of the lease; the landlord filed, served, and prosecuted successfully a complaint for summary ejectment and/or monies owed in the small claims court; and neither party appealed the judgment of the magistrate.

(g) Second Trial Fee. - Pursuant to a written lease, a landlord may charge a second trial fee for a new trial following an appeal from the judgment of a magistrate. To qualify for the fee, the landlord must prove that the tenant was in default of the lease and the landlord prevailed. The landlord's fee may not exceed twelve percent (12%) of the monthly rent in the lease.

(h) Limitations on Charging and Collection of Fees.

section is entitled to charge and retain only one of the above fees for the landlord's complaint for summary ejectment and/or money owed.

(2) A landlord who earns a fee under subsections (e) through (g) of this section may not deduct payment of that fee from a tenant's subsequent rent payment or declare a failure to pay the fee as a default of the lease for a subsequent summary ejectment action.

(3) It is contrary to public policy for a landlord to put in a lease or claim any fee for filing a complaint for summary ejectment and/or money owed other than the ones expressly authorized by subsections (e) through (g) of this section, and a reasonable attorney's fee as allowed by law.

(4) Any provision of a residential rental agreement contrary to the provisions of this section is against the public policy of this State and therefore void and unenforceable.

(5) If the rent is subsidized by the United States Department of Housing and Urban Development, by the United States Department of Agriculture, by a State agency, by a public housing authority, or by a local government, any fee charged pursuant to this section shall be calculated on the tenant's share of the contract rent only, and the rent subsidy shall not be included. (1987, c. 530, s. 1; 2001-502, s. 4; 2003-370, s. 1; 2004-143, s. 5; 2009-279, s. 4.)

§§ 42-47 through 42-49: Reserved for future codification purposes.

Article 6.

Tenant Security Deposit Act.

§ 42-50. Deposits from the tenant.

Security deposits from the tenant in residential dwelling units shall be deposited in a trust account with a licensed and insured bank or savings institution located from an insurance company licensed to do business in North Carolina. The security deposits from the tenant may be held in a trust account outside of the State of North Carolina only if the landlord provides the tenant with an adequate bond in the amount of said deposits. The landlord or his agent shall notify the tenant within 30 days after the beginning of the lease term of the name and address of the bank or institution where his deposit is currently located or the name of the insurance company providing the bond. (1977, c. 914, s. 1.)

§ 42-51. Permitted uses of the deposit.

(a)   Security deposits for residential dwelling units shall be permitted only for the following:

(1)   The tenant's possible nonpayment of rent and costs for water or sewer services provided pursuant to G.S. 62-110(g) and electric service pursuant to G.S. 62-110(h).

(2)   Damage to the premises, including damage to or destruction of smoke alarms or carbon monoxide alarms.

(3)   Damages as the result of the nonfulfillment of the rental period, except where the tenant terminated the rental agreement under G.S. 42-45, G.S. 42-45.1, or because the tenant was forced to leave the property because of the landlord's violation of Article 2A of Chapter 42 of the General Statutes or was constructively evicted by the landlord's violation of G.S. 42-42(a).

(4)   Any unpaid bills that become a lien against the demised property due to the tenant's occupancy.

(5)   The costs of re-renting the premises after breach by the tenant, including any reasonable fees or commissions paid by the landlord to a licensed real estate broker to re-rent the premises.

(6)   The costs of removal and storage of the tenant's property after a summary ejectment proceeding.

(7)   Court costs.

(b) The security deposit shall not exceed an amount equal to two weeks' rent if a tenancy is week to week, one and one-half months' rent if a tenancy is month to month, and two months' rent for terms greater than month to month. These deposits must be fully accounted for by the landlord as set forth in G.S. 42-52. (1977, c. 914, s. 1; 1983, c. 672, s. 3; 2001-502, s. 5; 2004-143, s. 6; 2011-252, s. 3; 2012-17, s. 4; 2012-194, s. 59(a), (b).)

§ 42-52. Landlord's obligations.

Upon termination of the tenancy, money held by the landlord as security may be applied as permitted in G.S. 42-51 or, if not so applied, shall be refunded to the tenant. In either case the landlord in writing shall itemize any damage and mail or deliver same to the tenant, together with the balance of the security deposit, no later than 30 days after termination of the tenancy and delivery of possession of the premises to the landlord. If the extent of the landlord's claim against the security deposit cannot be determined within 30 days, the landlord shall provide the tenant with an interim accounting no later than 30 days after termination of the tenancy and delivery of possession of the premises to the landlord and shall provide a final accounting within 60 days after termination of the tenancy and delivery of possession of the premises to the landlord. If the tenant's address is unknown the landlord shall apply the deposit as permitted in G.S. 42-51 after a period of 30 days and the landlord shall hold the balance of the deposit for collection by the tenant for at least six months. The landlord may not withhold as damages part of the security deposit for conditions that are due to normal wear and tear nor may the landlord retain an amount from the security deposit which exceeds his actual damages. (1977, c. 914, s. 1; 2009-279, s. 5.)

§ 42-53. Pet deposits.

Notwithstanding the provisions of this section, the landlord may charge a reasonable, nonrefundable fee for pets kept by the tenant on the premises. (1977, c. 914, s. 1.)

Upon termination of the landlord's interest in the dwelling unit in question, whether by sale, assignment, death, appointment of receiver or otherwise, the landlord or his agent shall, within 30 days, do one of the following acts, either of which shall relieve him of further liability with respect to such payment or deposit:

(1) Transfer the portion of such payment or deposit remaining after any lawful deductions made under this section to the landlord's successor in interest and thereafter notify the tenant by mail of such transfer and of the transferee's name and address; or

(2) Return the portion of such payment or deposit remaining after any lawful deductions made under this section to the tenant. (1977, c. 914, s. 1.)

§ 42-55. Remedies.

If the landlord or the landlord's successor in interest fails to account for and refund the balance of the tenant's security deposit as required by this Article, the tenant may institute a civil action to require the accounting of and the recovery of the balance of the deposit. The willful failure of a landlord to comply with the deposit, bond, or notice requirements of this Article shall void the landlord's right to retain any portion of the tenant's security deposit as otherwise permitted under G.S. 42-51. In addition to other remedies at law and equity, the tenant may recover damages resulting from noncompliance by the landlord; and upon a finding by the court that the party against whom judgment is rendered was in willful noncompliance with this Article, such willful noncompliance is against the public policy of this State and the court may award attorney's fees to be taxed as part of the costs of court. (1977, c. 914, s. 1; 2009-279, s. 6.)

§ 42-56. Application of Article.

The provisions of this Article shall apply to all persons, firms, or corporations engaged in the business of renting or managing residential dwelling units, excluding single rooms, on a weekly, monthly or annual basis. (1977, c. 914, s. 2.)

§ 42-57. Reserved for future codification purposes.

§ 42-58. Reserved for future codification purposes.

Article 7.

Expedited Eviction of Drug Traffickers and Other Criminals.

§ 42-59. Definitions.

As used in this Article:

(1) "Complete eviction" means the eviction and removal of a tenant and all members of the tenant's household.

(2) "Criminal activity" means (i) activity that would constitute a violation of G.S. 90-95 other than a violation of G.S. 90-95(a)(3), or a conspiracy to violate any provision of G.S. 90-95 other than G.S. 90-95(a)(3); or (ii) other criminal activity that threatens the health, safety, or right of peaceful enjoyment of the entire premises by other residents or employees of the landlord.

(3) "Entire premises" or "leased residential premises" means a house, building, mobile home, or apartment, whether publicly or privately owned, which is leased for residential purposes. These terms include the entire building or complex of buildings or mobile home park and all real property of any nature appurtenant thereto and used in connection therewith, including all individual rental units, streets, sidewalks, and common areas. These terms do not include a hotel, motel, or other guest house or part thereof rented to a transient guest.

Carolina law.

(5) "Guest" means any natural person who has been given express or implied permission by a tenant, a member of the tenant's household, or another guest of the tenant to enter an individual rental unit or any portion of the entire premises.

(6) "Individual rental unit" means an apartment or individual dwelling or accommodation which is leased to a particular tenant, whether or not it is used or occupied or intended to be used or occupied by a single family or household.

(7) "Landlord" means a person, entity, corporation, or governmental authority or agency who or which owns, operates, or manages any leased residential premises.

(8) "Partial eviction" means the eviction and removal of specified persons from a leased residential premises.

(9) "Resident" means any natural person who lawfully resides in a leased residential premises who is not a signatory to a lease or otherwise has no contractual relationship to a landlord. The term includes members of the household of a tenant.

(10) "Tenant" means any natural person or entity who is a named party or signatory to a lease or rental agreement, and who occupies, resides in, or has a legal right to possess and use an individual rental unit. (1995, c. 419, s. 1.)

§ 42-59.1. Statement of Public Policy.

The General Assembly recognizes that the residents of this State have the right to the peaceful, safe, and quiet enjoyment of their homes. The General Assembly further recognizes that these rights, as well as the health, safety, and welfare of residents, are often jeopardized by the criminal activity of other residents of rented residential property, but that landlords are often unable to remove those residents engaged in criminal activity. In order to ensure that residents of this State can have the peaceful, safe, and quiet enjoyment of their homes, the provisions of this Article are deemed to apply to all residential rental agreements in this State. (1995, c. 419, s. 1.)

§ 42-60. Nature of actions and jurisdiction.

The causes of action established in this Article are civil actions to remove tenants or other persons from leased residential premises. These actions shall be brought in the district court of the county where the individual rental unit is located. If the plaintiff files the complaint as a small claim, the parties shall not be entitled to discovery from the magistrate. However, if such a case is filed originally in the district court or is appealed from the judgment of a magistrate for a new trial in the district court, all of the procedures and remedies in this Article shall be applicable. (1995, c. 419, s. 1.)

§ 42-61. Standard of proof.

The civil causes of action established in this Article shall be proved by a preponderance of the evidence, except as otherwise expressly provided in G.S. 42-64. (1995, c. 419, s. 1.)

§ 42-62. Parties.

(a)   Who May Bring Action. - A civil action pursuant to this Article may be brought by the landlord of a leased residential premises, or the landlord's agent, as provided for in G.S. 1-57 of the General Statutes and in Article 3 of this Chapter.

(b)   Defendants to the Action. - A civil action pursuant to this Article may be brought against any person within the jurisdiction of the court, including a tenant, adult or minor member of the tenant's household, guest, or resident of the leased residential premises. If any defendant's true name is unknown to the plaintiff, process may issue against the defendant under a fictitious name, stating it to be fictitious and adding an appropriate description sufficient to identify him or her.

Article shall be served in the same manner as serving complaints in civil actions pursuant to G.S. 1A-1, Rule 4 and G.S. 42-29. (1995, c. 419, s. 1.)

§ 42-63. Remedies and judicial orders.

(a)   Grounds for Complete Eviction. - Subject to the provisions of G.S. 42-64 and pursuant to G.S 42-68, the court shall order the immediate eviction of a tenant and all other residents of the tenant's individual unit where it finds that:

(1)   Criminal activity has occurred on or within the individual rental unit leased to the tenant; or

(2)   The individual rental unit leased to the tenant was used in any way in furtherance of or to promote criminal activity; or

(3)   The tenant, any member of the tenant's household, or any guest has engaged in criminal activity on or in the immediate vicinity of any portion of the entire premises; or

(4)   The tenant has given permission to or invited a person to return or reenter any portion of the entire premises, knowing that the person has been removed and barred from the entire premises pursuant to this Article or the reasonable rules and regulations of a publicly assisted landlord; or

(5)   The tenant has failed to notify law enforcement or the landlord immediately upon learning that a person who has been removed and barred from the tenant's individual rental unit pursuant to this Article has returned to or reentered the tenant's individual rental unit.

(b)   Grounds for Partial Eviction and Issuance of Removal Orders. - The court shall, subject to the provisions of G.S. 42-64, order the immediate removal from the entire premises of any person other than the tenant, including an adult or minor member of the tenant's household, where the court finds that such person has engaged in criminal activity on or in the immediate vicinity of any portion of the leased residential premises. Persons removed pursuant to this section shall be barred from returning to or reentering any portion of the entire premises.

court finds that a member of the tenant's household or a guest of the tenant has engaged in criminal activity on or in the immediate vicinity of any portion of the leased residential premises, but such person has not been named as a party defendant, has not appeared in the action or otherwise has not been subjected to the jurisdiction of the court, a conditional eviction order issued pursuant to subsection (b) of this section shall be directed against the tenant, and shall provide that as an express condition of the tenancy, the tenant shall not give permission to or invite the barred person or persons to return to or reenter any portion of the entire premises. The tenant shall acknowledge in writing that the tenant understands the terms of the court's order, and that the tenant further understands that the failure to comply with the court's order will result in the mandatory termination of the tenancy pursuant to G.S. 42-68. (1995, c. 419, s. 1.)

§ 42-64. Affirmative defense or exemption to a complete eviction.

(a)   Affirmative Defense. - The court shall refrain from ordering the complete eviction of a tenant pursuant to G.S. 42-63(a) where the tenant has established that the tenant was not involved in the criminal activity and that:

(1)   The tenant did not know or have reason to know that criminal activity was occurring or would likely occur on or within the individual rental unit, that the individual rental unit was used in any way in furtherance of or to promote criminal activity, or that any member of the tenant's household or any guest has engaged in criminal activity on or in the immediate vicinity of any portion of the entire premises; or

(2)   The tenant had done everything that could reasonably be expected under the circumstances to prevent the commission of the criminal activity, such as requesting the landlord to remove the offending household member's name from the lease, reporting prior criminal activity to appropriate law enforcement authorities, seeking assistance from social service or counseling agencies, denying permission, if feasible, for the offending household member to reside in the unit, or seeking assistance from church or religious organizations.

Notwithstanding the court's denial of eviction of the tenant, if the plaintiff has proven that an evictable offense under G.S. 42-63 was committed by someone other than the tenant, the court shall order such other relief as the court deems

G.S. 42-63(b) and conditional eviction orders under G.S. 42-63(c).

(b) Subsequent Affirmative Defense to a Complete Eviction. - The affirmative defense set forth in subsection (a) of this section shall not be available to a tenant in a subsequent action brought pursuant to this Article unless the tenant can establish by clear and convincing evidence that no reasonable person could have foreseen the occurrence of the subsequent criminal activity or that the tenant had done everything reasonably expected under the circumstances to prevent the commission of the second criminal activity.

(c) Exemption. - Where the grounds for a complete eviction have been established, the court shall order the eviction of the tenant unless, taking into account the circumstances of the criminal activity and the condition of the tenant, the court is clearly convinced that immediate eviction or removal would be a serious injustice, the prevention of which overrides the need to protect the rights, safety, and health of the other tenants and residents of the leased residential premises. The burden of proof for the exemption set forth shall be by clear and convincing evidence. (1995, c. 419, s. 1.)

§ 42-65. Obstructing the execution or enforcement of a removal or eviction order.

Any person who knowingly violates any order issued pursuant to this Article or who knowingly interferes with, obstructs, impairs, or prevents any law enforcement officer from enforcing or executing any order issued pursuant to this Article, shall be subject to criminal contempt under Article 1 of Chapter 5A of the General Statutes. Nothing in this section shall be construed in any way to preclude or preempt prosecution for any other criminal offense. (1995, c. 419, s. 1.)

§ 42-66. Motion to enforce eviction and removal orders.

service of the motion.

(b) Mandatory Eviction. - The court shall order the immediate eviction of the tenant where it finds that:

(1) The tenant has given permission to or invited any person removed or barred from the leased residential premises pursuant to this Article to return to or reenter any portion of the premises; or

(2) The tenant has failed to notify appropriate law enforcement authorities or the landlord immediately upon learning that any person who had been removed and barred pursuant to this Article has returned to or reentered the tenant's individual rental unit; or

(3) The tenant has otherwise knowingly violated an express term or condition of any order issued by court pursuant to this Article. (1995, c. 419, s. 1.)

§ 42-67. Impermissible defense.

It shall not be a defense to an action brought pursuant to this Article that the criminal activity was an isolated incident or otherwise has not recurred. Nor is it a defense that the person who actually engaged in the criminal activity no longer resides in the tenant's individual rental unit. However, evidence of such facts may be admissible if offered to support affirmative defenses or grounds for an exemption pursuant to G.S. 42-64. (1995, c. 419, s. 1.)

§ 42-68. Expedited proceedings.

Where the complaint is filed as a small claim, the expedited process for summary ejectment, as provided in Article 3 of this Chapter and Chapter 7A of the General Statutes, applies. Where the complaint is filed initially in the district court or a judgment by the magistrate is appealed to the district court, the procedure in G.S. 42-34(b) through (g), if applicable, and the following procedures apply:

(1) Expedited Hearing. - When a complaint is filed initiating an action pursuant to this Article, the court shall set the matter for a hearing which shall be held on an expedited basis and within the first term of court falling after 30 days from the service of the complaint on all defendants or from service of notice of appeal from a magistrate's judgment, unless either party obtains a continuance. However, where a defendant files a counterclaim, the court shall reset the trial for the first term of court falling after 30 days from the defendant's service of the counterclaim.

(2) Standards for Continuances. - The court shall not grant a continuance, nor shall it stay the civil proceedings pending the disposition of any related criminal proceedings, except as required to complete permitted discovery, to have the plaintiff reply to a counterclaim, or for compelling and extraordinary reasons or on application of the district attorney for good cause shown.

(3) When Presented. - The defendant in an action brought in district court pursuant to this Article shall serve an answer within 20 days after service of the summons and complaint, or within 20 days after service of the appeal to district court when the action was initially brought in small claims court. The plaintiff shall serve a reply to a counterclaim in the answer within 20 days after service of the answer.

(4) Extensions of Time for Filing. - The parties to an action brought pursuant to this Article shall not be entitled to an extension of time for completing an act required by subdivision (3) of this section, except for compelling and extraordinary reasons.

(5) Default. - A party to an action brought pursuant to this Article who fails to plead in accordance with the time periods in subdivision (3) of this section shall be subject to the provisions of G.S. 1A-1, Rule 55.

(6) Rules of Civil Procedure. - Unless otherwise provided for in this Article, G.S. 1A-1, the Rules of Civil Procedure, shall apply in the district court to all actions brought pursuant to this Article. (1995, c. 419, s. 1.)

§ 42-69. Relation to criminal proceedings.

or, if commenced, has not yet been concluded or has terminated without a conviction or adjudication of delinquency shall not preclude a civil action or the issuance of any order pursuant to this Article.

(b)   Effect of Conviction or Adjudication. - Where a criminal prosecution involving the criminal activity results in a final criminal conviction or adjudication of delinquency, such adjudication or conviction shall be considered in the civil action as conclusive proof that the criminal activity occurred.

(c)   Admissibility of Criminal Trial Recordings or Transcripts. - Any evidence or testimony admitted in the criminal proceeding, including recordings or transcripts of the adult or juvenile criminal proceedings, whether or not they have been transcribed, may be admitted in the civil action initiated pursuant to this Article.

(d)   Use of Sealed Criminal Proceeding Records. - In the event that the evidence or records of a criminal proceeding which did not result in a conviction or adjudication of delinquency have been sealed by court order, the court in a civil action brought pursuant to this Article may order such evidence or records, whether or not they have been transcribed, to be unsealed if the court finds that such evidence or records would be relevant to the fair disposition of the civil action. (1995, c. 419, s. 1.)

§ 42-70. Discovery.

(a)   The parties to an action brought pursuant to this Article shall be entitled to conduct discovery, if the action is filed originally in or appealed to the district court, only in accordance with this section.

(b)   Any defendant must initiate all discovery within the time allowed by this Article for the filing of an answer or counterclaim.

(c)   The plaintiff must initiate all discovery within 20 days of service of an answer or counterclaim by a defendant.

shall serve their responses within 20 days.

(e) Upon application by the plaintiff, or agreement of the parties, the court shall issue a preliminary injunction against all alleged illegal activity by the defendant or other identified parties who are residents of the individual rental unit or guests of defendants, pending the completion of discovery and any other wait before the trial has occurred. (1995, c. 419, s. 1.)

§ 42-71. Protection of threatened witnesses or affiants.

If proof necessary to establish the grounds for eviction depends, in whole or in part, upon the affidavits or testimony of witnesses who are not peace officers, the court may, upon a showing of prior threats of violence or acts of violence by any defendant or any other person, issue orders to protect those witnesses, including the nondisclosure of the name, address, or any other information which may identify those witnesses. (1995, c. 419, s. 1.)

§ 42-72. Availability of law enforcement resources to plaintiffs or potential plaintiffs.

A law enforcement agency may make available to any person or entity authorized to bring an action pursuant to this Article any police report or edited portion thereof, or forensic laboratory report or edited portion thereof, concerning criminal activity committed on or in the immediate vicinity of the leased residential premises. A law enforcement agency may also make any officer or officers available to testify as a fact witness or expert witness in a civil action brought pursuant to this Article. The agency shall not disclose such information where, in the agency's opinion, such disclosure would jeopardize an investigation, prosecution, or other proceeding, or where such disclosure would violate any federal or State statute. (1995, c. 419, s. 1.)

§ 42-73. Collection of rent.

constituting a waiver of the alleged defaults. (1995, c. 419, s. 1.)

§ 42-74. Preliminary or emergency relief.

The district court shall have the authority at any time to issue a temporary restraining order, grant a preliminary injunction, or take such other actions as the court deems necessary to enjoin or prevent the commission of criminal activity on or in the immediate vicinity of leased residential premises, or otherwise to protect the rights and interests of all tenants and residents. A violation of any such duly issued order or preliminary relief shall subject the violator to civil or criminal contempt. (1995, c. 419, s. 1.)

§ 42-75. Cumulative remedies.

The causes of action and remedies authorized by this Article shall be cumulative with each other and shall be in addition to, not in lieu of, any other causes of action or remedies which may be available at law or equity, including causes of action and remedies based on express provisions of the lease not contrary to this Article. (1995, c. 419, s. 1.)

§ 42-76. Civil immunity.

Any person or organization who, in good faith, institutes, participates in, or encourages a person or entity to institute or participate in a civil action brought pursuant to this Article, or who in good faith provides any information relied upon by any person or entity in instituting or participating in a civil action pursuant to this Article shall have immunity from any civil liability that might otherwise be incurred or imposed. Any such person or organization shall have the same immunity from civil liability with respect to testimony given in any judicial proceeding conducted pursuant to this Article. (1995, c. 419, s. 1.)

Chapter 42A.

Article 1.

Vacation Rentals.

§ 42A-1. Title.

This Chapter shall be known as the North Carolina Vacation Rental Act. (1999-420, s. 1.)

§ 42A-2. Purpose and scope of act.

The General Assembly finds that the growth of the tourism industry in North Carolina has led to a greatly expanded market of privately owned residences that are rented to tourists for vacation, leisure, and recreational purposes. Rental transactions conducted by the owners of these residences or licensed real estate brokers acting on their behalf present unique situations not normally found in the rental of primary residences for long terms, and therefore make it necessary for the General Assembly to enact laws regulating the competing interests of landlords, real estate brokers, and tenants. (1999-420, s. 1.)

§ 42A-3. Application; exemptions.

(a) The provisions of this Chapter shall apply to any person, partnership, corporation, limited liability company, association, or other business entity who acts as a landlord or real estate broker engaged in the rental or management of residential property for vacation rental as defined in this Chapter.

(b) The provisions of this Chapter shall not apply to:

(1) Lodging provided by hotels, motels, tourist camps, and other places subject to regulation under Chapter 72 of the General Statutes.

(2) Rentals to persons temporarily renting a dwelling unit when traveling away from their primary residence for business or employment purposes.

(4) Rentals for which no more than nominal consideration is given. (1999-420, s. 1.)

§ 42A-4. Definitions.

The following definitions apply in this Chapter:

(1) Real estate broker. - A real estate broker as defined in G.S. 93A-2(a).

(2) Residential property. - An apartment, condominium, single-family home, townhouse, cottage, or other property that is devoted to residential use or occupancy by one or more persons for a definite or indefinite period.

(3) Vacation rental. - The rental of residential property for vacation, leisure, or recreation purposes for fewer than 90 days by a person who has a place of permanent residence to which he or she intends to return.

(4) Vacation rental agreement. - A written agreement between a landlord or his or her real estate broker and a tenant in which the tenant agrees to rent residential property belonging to the landlord for a vacation rental. (1999-420, s. 1.)

§§ 42A-5 through 42A-9. Reserved for future codification purposes.

Article 2.

Vacation Rental Agreements.

§ 42A-10. Written agreement required.

(a) A landlord or real estate broker and tenant shall execute a vacation rental agreement for all vacation rentals subject to the provisions of this

(1) The tenant's signature on the agreement.

(2) The tenant's payment of any monies to the landlord or real estate broker after the tenant's receipt of the agreement.

(3) The tenant's taking possession of the property after the tenant's receipt of the agreement.

(b) Any real estate broker who executes a vacation rental agreement that does not conform to the provisions of this Chapter or fails to execute a vacation rental agreement shall be guilty of an unfair trade practice in violation of G.S. 75-1.1, and shall be prohibited from commencing an expedited eviction proceeding as provided in Article 4 of this Chapter. (1999-420, s. 1.)

§ 42A-11. Vacation rental agreements.

(a) A vacation rental agreement executed under this Chapter shall contain the following notice on its face which shall be set forth in a clear and conspicuous manner that distinguishes it from other provisions of the agreement: "THIS IS A VACATION RENTAL AGREEMENT UNDER THE NORTH CAROLINA VACATION RENTAL ACT. THE RIGHTS AND OBLIGATIONS OF THE PARTIES TO THIS AGREEMENT ARE DEFINED BY LAW AND INCLUDE UNIQUE PROVISIONS PERMITTING THE DISBURSEMENT OF RENT PRIOR TO TENANCY AND EXPEDITED EVICTION OF TENANTS. YOUR SIGNATURE ON THIS AGREEMENT, OR PAYMENT OF MONEY OR TAKING POSSESSION OF THE PROPERTY AFTER RECEIPT OF THE AGREEMENT, IS EVIDENCE OF YOUR ACCEPTANCE OF THE AGREEMENT AND YOUR INTENT TO USE THIS PROPERTY FOR A VACATION RENTAL."

(b) The vacation rental agreement shall contain provisions separate from the requirements of subsection (a) of this section which shall describe the following as permitted or required by this Chapter:

(1) The manner in which funds shall be received, deposited, and disbursed in advance of the tenant's occupancy of the property.

(2a) Any cleaning fee permitted under G.S. 42A-17(d).

(3) The rights and obligations of the landlord and tenant under G.S. 42A-17(b).

(4) The applicability of expedited eviction procedures.

(5) The rights and obligations of the landlord or real estate broker and the tenant upon the transfer of the property.

(6) The rights and obligations of the landlord or real estate broker and the tenant under G.S. 42A-36.

(7) Any other obligations of the landlord and tenant. (1999-420, s. 1; 2012-17, s. 5.)

§§ 42A-12 through 42A-14. Reserved for future codification purposes.

Article 3.

Handling and Accounting of Funds.

§ 42A-15. Trust account uses.

A landlord or real estate broker may require a tenant to pay all or part of any required rent, security deposit, or other fees permitted by law in advance of the commencement of a tenancy under this Chapter if these payments are expressly authorized in the vacation rental agreement. If the tenant is required to make any advance payments, other than a security deposit, whether the payment is denominated as rent or otherwise, the landlord or real estate broker shall deposit these payments in a trust account in an insured bank or savings and loan association in North Carolina no later than three banking days after the rental agreement that the payments may be deposited in an interest-bearing account. The landlord and tenant shall also provide in the agreement to whom the accrued interest shall be disbursed. (1999-420, s. 1.)

§ 42A-16. Advance payments uses.

(a) A landlord or real estate broker shall not disburse prior to the occupancy of the property by the tenant an amount greater than fifty percent (50%) of the total rent except as permitted pursuant to this subsection. A landlord or real estate broker may disburse prior to the occupancy of the property by the tenant any fees owed to third parties to pay for goods, services, or benefits procured by the landlord or real estate broker for the benefit of the tenant, including administrative fees permitted by G.S. 42A-17(c), if the disbursement is expressly authorized in the vacation rental agreement. The funds remaining after any disbursement permitted under this subsection shall remain in the trust account and may not be disbursed until the occurrence of one of the following:

(1) The commencement of the tenancy, at which time the remaining funds may be disbursed in accordance with the terms of the agreement.

(2) The tenant commits a material breach, at which time the landlord may retain an amount sufficient to defray the actual damages suffered by the landlord as a result of the breach.

(3) The landlord or real estate broker refunds the money to the tenant.

(4) The funds in the trust account are transferred in accordance with G.S. 42A-19(b) upon the termination of the landlord's interest in the property.

(b) Funds collected for sales or occupancy taxes and tenant security deposits shall not be disbursed from the trust account prior to termination of the tenancy or material breach of the agreement by the tenant, except as a refund to the tenant.

(c) The tenant's execution of a vacation rental agreement in which he or she agrees to the advance disbursement of payments shall not constitute a waiver

§ 42A-17. Accounting; reimbursement.

(a)   A vacation rental agreement shall identify the name and address of the bank or savings and loan association in which the tenant's security deposit and other advance payments are held in a trust account, and the landlord and real estate broker shall provide the tenant with an accounting of such deposit and payments if the tenant makes a reasonable request for an accounting prior to the tenant's occupancy of the property.

(b)   Except as provided in G.S. 42A-36, if, at the time the tenant is to begin occupancy of the property, the landlord or real estate broker cannot provide the property in a fit and habitable condition or substitute a reasonably comparable property in such condition, the landlord and real estate broker shall refund to the tenant all payments made by the tenant.

(c)   A vacation rental agreement may include administrative fees, the amounts of which shall be provided in the agreement, reasonably calculated to cover the costs of processing the tenant's reservation, transfer, or cancellation of a vacation rental.

(d)   A vacation rental agreement may include a cleaning fee, the amount of which shall be provided in the agreement, reasonably calculated to cover the costs of cleaning the residential property upon the termination of the tenancy. (1999-420, s. 1; 2005-292, s. 1; 2012-17, s. 6.)

§ 42A-18. Applicability of the Residential Tenant Security Deposit Act.

(a)   Except as may otherwise be provided in this Chapter, all funds collected from a tenant and not identified in the vacation rental agreement as occupancy or sales taxes, fees, or rent payments shall be considered a tenant security deposit and shall be subject to the provisions of the Residential Tenant Security Deposit Act, as codified in Article 6 of Chapter 42 of the General Statutes. Funds collected as a tenant security deposit in connection with a vacation rental shall be deposited into a trust account as required by G.S. 42-50. The landlord uses of tenant security deposit monies as provided in G.S. 42-51, a landlord or real estate broker may, after the termination of a tenancy under this Chapter, deduct from any tenant security deposit the amount of any long distance or per call telephone charges and cable television charges that are the obligation of the tenant under the vacation rental agreement and are left unpaid by the tenant at the conclusion of the tenancy. The landlord or real estate broker shall apply, account for, or refund tenant security deposit monies as provided in G.S. 42-51 within 45 days following the conclusion of the tenancy.

(b) A vacation rental agreement shall not contain language compelling or permitting the automatic forfeiture of all or part of a tenant security deposit in case of breach of contract by the tenant, and no such forfeiture shall be allowed. The vacation rental agreement shall provide that a tenant security deposit may be applied to actual damages caused by the tenant as permitted under Article 6 of Chapter 42 of the General Statutes. (1999-420, s. 1.)

§ 42A-19. Transfer of property subject to a vacation rental agreement.

(a) The grantee of residential property voluntarily transferred by a landlord who has entered into a vacation rental agreement for the use of the property shall take title to the property subject to the vacation rental agreement if the vacation rental is to end not later than 180 days after the grantee's interest in the property is recorded in the office of the register of deeds. If the vacation rental is to end more than 180 days after the recording of the grantee's interest, the tenant shall have no right to enforce the terms of the agreement unless the grantee has agreed in writing to honor those terms, but the tenant shall be entitled to a refund of payments made by him or her, as provided in subsection (b) of this section.

Prior to entering into any contract of sale, the landlord shall disclose to the grantee the time periods that the property is subject to a vacation rental agreement. Not later than 10 days after transfer of the property, the landlord shall disclose to the grantee each tenant's name and address and shall provide the grantee with a copy of each vacation rental agreement. In lieu of providing the grantee a copy of each vacation rental agreement, where the landlord or the landlord's agent utilizes a standard form vacation rental agreement, the landlord may provide the grantee with a copy of the part of each vacation rental the standard form vacation rental agreement. However, the landlord shall not be required to provide the grantee with copies of the vacation rental agreements if in anticipation of acquiring the property the grantee has engaged the landlord's rental agent to continue to manage the property after the transfer and the landlord authorizes the rental agent to provide the information to the grantee and the grantee approves. Not later than 20 days after transfer of the property, the grantee or the grantee's agent shall:

(1) Notify each tenant in writing of the property transfer, the grantee's name and address, and the date the grantee's interest was recorded.

(2) Advise each tenant whether he or she has the right to occupy the property subject to the terms of the vacation rental agreement and the provisions of this section.

(3) Advise each tenant of whether he or she has the right to receive a refund of any payments made by him or her.

Notwithstanding any other provision of this section, if the grantee engages as the grantee's broker and rental agent for the property the broker who procured the tenant's vacation rental agreement for the landlord, the grantee shall have no obligation under subdivisions (1), (2), and (3) of this subsection with regard to those tenants whose vacation rental agreements must be honored under this section or with regard to those tenants whose vacation rental agreements the grantee has agreed in writing to honor.

(b) Except as otherwise provided in this subsection, upon termination of the landlord's interest in the residential property subject to a vacation rental agreement, whether by sale, assignment, death, appointment of receiver or otherwise, the landlord or the landlord's agent, or the real estate broker, shall, within 30 days, transfer all advance rent paid by the tenant, and the portion of any fees remaining after any lawful deductions made under G.S. 42A-16, to the landlord's successor in interest and thereafter notify the tenant by mail of such transfer and of the transferee's name and address. For vacation rentals that end more than 180 days after the recording of the interest of the landlord's successor in interest, unless the landlord's successor in interest has agreed in writing to honor the vacation rental agreement, the landlord or the landlord's agent, or the real estate broker, shall, within 30 days, transfer all advance rent paid by the tenant, and the portion of any fees remaining after any lawful respect to any payment of rent or fees. Funds held as a security deposit shall be disbursed in accordance with G.S. 42A-18.

(c) Repealed by Session Laws 2000-140, s. 41, effective July 21, 2000.

(d) The failure of a landlord to comply with the provisions of this section shall constitute an unfair trade practice in violation of G.S. 75-1.1. A landlord who complies with the requirements of this section shall have no further obligations to the tenant. (1999-420, s. 1; 2000-140, s. 41; 2005-292, s. 2.)

§§ 42A-20 through 42A-22. Reserved for future codification purposes.

Article 4.

Expedited Eviction Proceedings.

§ 42A-23. Grounds for eviction.

(a) Any tenant who leases residential property subject to a vacation rental agreement under this Chapter for 30 days or less may be evicted and removed from the property in an expedited eviction proceeding brought by the landlord, or real estate broker as agent for the landlord, as provided in this Article if the tenant does one of the following:

(1) Holds over possession after his or her tenancy has expired.

(2) Has committed a material breach of the terms of the vacation rental agreement that, according to the terms of the agreement, results in the termination of his or her tenancy.

(3) Fails to pay rent as required by the agreement.

(4) Has obtained possession of the property by fraud or misrepresentation.

proceeding. All other issues related to the rental of the residential property shall be presented in a separate civil action. (1999-420, s. 1.)

§ 42A-24. Expedited eviction.

(a) Before commencing an expedited eviction proceeding, the landlord or real estate broker shall give the tenant at least four hours' notice, either orally or in writing, to quit the premises. If reasonable efforts to personally give oral or written notice have failed, written notice may be given by posting the notice on the front door of the property.

(b) An expedited eviction proceeding shall commence with the filing of a complaint and issuance of summons in the county where the property is located. If the office of the clerk of superior court is closed, the complaint shall be filed with, and the summons issued by, a magistrate. The service of the summons and complaint for expedited eviction shall be made by a sworn law enforcement officer on the tenant personally or by posting a copy of the summons and complaint on the front door of the property. The officer, upon service, shall promptly file a return therefor. A hearing on the expedited eviction shall be held before a magistrate in the county where the property is located not sooner than 12 hours after service upon the tenant and no later than 48 hours after such service. To the extent that the provisions of this Article are in conflict with the Rules of Civil Procedure, Chapter 1A of the General Statutes, with respect to the commencement of an action or service of process, this Article controls.

(c) The complaint for expedited eviction shall allege and the landlord or real estate broker shall prove the following at the hearing:

(1) The vacation rental is for a term of 30 days or less.

(2) The tenant entered into and accepted a vacation rental agreement that conforms to the provisions of this Chapter.

(3) The tenant committed one or more of the acts listed in G.S. 42A-23(a) as grounds for eviction.

The rules of evidence shall not apply in an expedited eviction proceeding, and the court shall allow any reasonably reliable and material statements, documents, or other exhibits to be admitted as evidence. The provisions of G.S. 7A-218, 7A-219, and 7A-220, except any provisions regarding amount in controversy, shall apply to an expedited eviction proceeding held before the magistrate. These provisions shall not be construed to broaden the scope of an expedited eviction proceeding to issues other than the right to possession.

(d) If the court finds for the landlord or real estate broker, the court shall immediately enter a written order granting the landlord or real estate broker possession and stating the time when the tenant shall vacate the property. In no case shall this time be less than 2 hours or more than 8 hours after service of the order on the tenant. The court's order shall be served on the tenant at the hearing. If the tenant does not appear at the hearing or leaves before the order is served, the order shall be served by delivering the order to the tenant or by posting the order on the front door of the property by any sworn law enforcement officer. The officer, upon service, shall file a return therefor.

If the court finds for the landlord or real estate broker, the court shall determine the amount of the appeal bond that the tenant shall be required to post should the tenant seek to appeal the court order. The amount of the bond shall be an estimate of the rent that will become due while the tenant is prosecuting the appeal and reasonable damages that the landlord may suffer, including damage to property and damages arising from the inability of the landlord or real estate broker to honor other vacation rental agreements due to the tenant's possession of the property. (1999-420, s. 1.)

§ 42A-25. Appeal.

A tenant or landlord may appeal a court order issued pursuant to G.S. 42A-24(d) to district court for a trial de novo. A tenant may petition the district court to stay the eviction order and shall post a cash or secured bond with the court in the amount determined by the court pursuant to G.S. 42A-24(d). (1999-420, s. 1.)

If a tenant fails to remove personal property from a residential property subject to a vacation rental after the court has entered an order of eviction, the landlord or real estate broker shall have the same rights as provided in G.S. 42-36.2(b) as if the sheriff had not removed the tenant's property. The failure of a tenant or the guest of a tenant to vacate a residential property in accordance with a court order issued pursuant to G.S. 42A-24(d) shall constitute a criminal trespass under G.S. 14-159.13. (1999-420, s. 1.)

§ 42A-27. Penalties for abuse.

A landlord or real estate broker shall undertake to evict a tenant pursuant to an expedited eviction proceeding only when he or she has a good faith belief that grounds for eviction exists under the provisions of this Chapter. Otherwise, the landlord or real estate broker shall be guilty of an unfair trade practice under G.S. 75-1.1 and a Class 1 misdemeanor. (1999-420, s. 1.)

§§ 42A-28 through 42A-30. Reserved for future codification purposes.

Article 5.

Landlord and Tenant Duties.

§ 42A-31. Landlord to provide fit premises.

A landlord of a residential property used for a vacation rental shall:

(1) Comply with all current applicable building and housing codes.

(2) Make all repairs and do whatever is reasonably necessary to put and keep the property in a fit and habitable condition.

(3) Keep all common areas of the property in safe condition.

repair all electrical, plumbing, sanitary, heating, ventilating, and other facilities and major appliances supplied by him or her upon written notification from the tenant that repairs are needed.

(5) Provide operable smoke detectors. The landlord shall replace or repair the smoke detectors if the landlord is notified by the tenant in writing that replacement or repair is needed. The landlord shall annually place new batteries in a battery-operated smoke detector, and the tenant shall replace the batteries as needed during the tenancy. Failure of the tenant to replace the batteries as needed shall not be considered negligence on the part of the tenant or landlord.

These duties shall not be waived; however, the landlord and tenant may make additional covenants not inconsistent herewith in the vacation rental agreement. (1999-420, s. 1.)

§ 42A-32. Tenant to maintain dwelling unit.

The tenant of a residential property used for a vacation rental shall:

(1) Keep that part of the property which he or she occupies and uses as clean and safe as the conditions of the property permit and cause no unsafe or unsanitary conditions in the common areas and remainder of the property that he or she uses.

(2) Dispose of all ashes, rubbish, garbage, and other waste in a clean and safe manner.

(3) Keep all plumbing fixtures in the property or used by the tenant as clean as their condition permits.

(4) Not deliberately or negligently destroy, deface, damage, or remove any part of the property or render inoperable the smoke detector provided by the landlord or knowingly permit any person to do so.

(5) Comply with all obligations imposed upon the tenant by current applicable building and housing codes.

defacement, or removal was due to ordinary wear and tear, acts of the landlord or his or her agent, defective products supplied or repairs authorized by the landlord, acts of third parties not invitees of the tenant, or natural forces.

(7) Notify the landlord of the need for replacement of or repairs to a smoke detector. The landlord shall annually place new batteries in a battery-operated smoke detector, and the tenant shall replace the batteries as needed during the tenancy. Failure of the tenant to replace the batteries as needed shall not be considered negligence on the part of the tenant or the landlord.

These duties shall not be waived; however, the landlord and tenant may make additional covenants not inconsistent herewith in the vacation rental agreement. (1999-420, s. 1.)

§§ 42A-33 through 42A-35. Reserved for future codification purposes.

Article 6.

General Provisions.

§ 42A-36. Mandatory evacuations.

If State or local authorities, acting pursuant to Article 1A of Chapter 166A of the General Statutes, order a mandatory evacuation of an area that includes the residential property subject to a vacation rental, the tenant under the vacation rental agreement, whether in possession of the property or not, shall comply with the evacuation order. Upon compliance, the tenant shall be entitled to a refund from the landlord of the rent, taxes, and any other payments made by the tenant pursuant to the vacation rental agreement as a condition of the tenant's right to occupy the property prorated for each night that the tenant is unable to occupy the property because of the mandatory evacuation order. The tenant shall not be entitled to a refund if: (i) prior to the tenant taking possession of the property, the tenant refused insurance offered by the landlord or real estate broker that would have compensated the tenant for losses or damages resulting from loss of use of the property due to a mandatory evacuation order; or (ii) the by the North Carolina Department of Insurance, and the cost of the insurance shall not exceed eight percent (8%) of the total amount charged for the vacation rental to the tenant less the amount paid by the tenant for a security deposit. (1999-420, s. 1; 2005-292, s. 3; 2009-245, s. 2; 2012-12, s. 2(h).)

§§ 42A-37 through 42A-40. Reserved for future codification purposes.

Chapter 43.

Land Registration.

Article 1.

Nature of Proceeding.

§ 43-1. Jurisdiction in superior court.

For the purpose of enabling all persons owning real estate within this State to have the title thereto settled and registered, as prescribed by the provisions of this Chapter, the superior court of the county in which the land lies in the State shall have exclusive original jurisdiction of all petitions and proceedings had thereupon, under the rules of practice and procedure prescribed for special proceedings except as herein otherwise provided. (1913, c. 90, s. 1; C.S., s. 2377.)

§ 43-2. Proceedings in rem; vests title.

The proceedings under any petition for the registration of land, and all proceedings in the court in relation to registered land, shall be proceedings in rem against the land, and the decrees of the court shall operate directly on the land, and vest and establish title thereto in accordance with the provisions of this Chapter. (1913, c. 90, s. 2; C.S., s. 2378.)

The Attorney General, with the approval of the Supreme Court, shall from time to time make, change, revise and revoke rules of practice in the superior court for the administration of this Chapter. He shall in like manner prescribe forms for use in such court, and in the notation of the registry of titles of memorials, claims, liens, lis pendens, and all other involuntary charges upon and to such registered lands. Whenever a question shall arise in the administration of this Chapter as to the proper method of protecting or asserting any right or interest under the law, and the method of procedure is in doubt, it shall be the duty of the clerk or register of deeds to notify the Attorney General, who, with the approval of the Supreme Court, shall prescribe a rule covering such case. (1913, c. 90, s. 31; C.S., s. 2379.)

Article 2.

Officers and Fees.

§ 43-4. Examiners appointed by clerk.

The clerk of the superior court of each county shall appoint three or more examiners of titles, who shall be licensed attorneys-at-law, residing in the State of North Carolina. They shall qualify by taking oath before the clerk to faithfully discharge the duties of such office, which oath shall be filed in the office of the clerk. The term of office shall be two years. Examiners of titles shall have and exercise the jurisdiction and perform the duties hereinafter prescribed, and receive the fees herein provided. They shall not appear in or have any connection with any proceeding instituted under the provisions of this Chapter, and they shall be subject to removal at will by such clerk or judge of the superior court. (1913, c. 90, s. 3; 1917, c. 63; C.S., s. 2380.)

§ 43-5. Fees of officers.

The examiner provided for in G.S. 43-4 shall be compensated as provided in G.S. 1-408. All plats required by this Chapter shall comply with G.S. 47-30 and shall be recorded in the office of the register of deeds, and the recording fee shall be that specified in G.S. 161-10 for recording plats. The fee for recording certificates under this Chapter shall be that specified in G.S. 161-10 for issuing certified copies. The fee for noting the entries or memorandum required and for the entries noting the cancellation of mortgages and all other entries, if any, herein provided for shall be that specified in G.S. 161-10 for recording instruments in general.

There shall be no other fees allowed of any nature except as herein provided, and the bonds of the register and clerk shall be liable in case of any mistake, malfeasance, or misfeasance as to the duties imposed upon them by this Chapter in as full a manner as such bond is now liable by law. (1913, c. 90, s. 30; C.S., s. 2381; 1971, c. 1185, s. 1; 1977, c. 774; 1999-59, s. 1.)

Article 3.

Procedure for Registration.

§ 43-6. Who may institute proceedings.

Any person, firm, or corporation, including the State of North Carolina or any political subdivision thereof, being in the peaceable possession of land within the State and claiming an estate of inheritance therein, may prosecute a special proceeding in rem against all the world in the superior court for the county in which such land is situate, to establish his title thereto, to determine all adverse claims and have the title registered. Any number of the separate parcels of land claimed by the petitioner may be included in the same proceeding, and any one parcel may be established in several parts, each of which shall be clearly and accurately described and registered separately, and the decree therein shall operate directly upon the land and establish and vest an indefeasible title thereto. Any person in like possession of lands within the State, claiming an interest or estate less than the fee therein, may have his title thereto established under the provisions of this Chapter, without the registration and transfer features herein provided. (1913, c. 90, s. 4; C.S., s. 2382; 1963, c. 946, s. 1.)

§ 43-7. Land lying in two or more counties.

situated partly in one county and partly in another, or is situated in two or more counties, that is to say, when an entire tract, or two or more entire tracts, are situated in two or more counties (but not separate or several tracts in different counties) it shall be competent to institute the proceedings before the clerk of the superior court of any county in which any part of such tract lying in two or more counties is situated, and said clerk shall have jurisdiction both of the parties and of the subject matter as fully as if said land was situated wholly in his county; but upon the entry of a final decree of registration of title, the clerk by or before whom the same was rendered shall certify a copy thereof to the register of deeds of every county in which said land or any part thereof is situated, and the same shall be there filed and recorded; and every such register of deeds, upon demand of the person entitled and payment of requisite fees therefor, shall issue and deliver a certificate of title for that part of said land situated in his county. This section shall apply and become effective in all cases or proceedings heretofore conducted before any clerk of the superior court of this State for registration of title, as in this Chapter authorized, when the land described in the petition as an entire tract was situated in two or more counties, as aforesaid; and upon the filing and recording of a certified copy of the final decree or decree of registration therein, the register of deeds shall issue and deliver a certificate of title to the present owner or person entitled to the same, for that part of the land situated in his county, as aforesaid, upon payment or tender of proper fees therefor. (1919, c. 82, s. 1; C.S., s. 2383.)

§ 43-8. Petition filed; contents; State to be named as respondent; service on State.

Suit for registration of title shall be begun by a petition to the court by the persons claiming, singly or collectively, to own or have the power of appointing or disposing of an estate in fee simple in any land, whether subject to liens or not. Infants and other persons under disability may sue by guardian or trustee, as the case may be, and corporations as in other cases now provided by law; but the person in whose behalf the petition is made shall always be named as petitioner. The petition shall be signed and sworn to by each petitioner, and shall contain a full description of the land to be registered as hereinafter provided, together with a plot of same by metes and bounds, corners to be marked by permanent markers of iron, stone or cement; it shall show when, how and from whom it was acquired, and whether or not it is now occupied, and if so, and addresses, if known, of all persons who may be interested by marriage or otherwise, including adjoining owners and occupants, shall be given. If any person shall be unable to state the metes and bounds, the clerk may order a preliminary survey.

Except when the State of North Carolina is the petitioner, all special proceedings filed pursuant to this Article shall name the State of North Carolina as a respondent to the action. Service of process upon the State shall be made in accordance with G.S. 1A-1, Rule 4(j)(3). (1913, c. 90, s. 5; C.S., s. 2384; 1979, c. 73, s. 1.)

§ 43-9. Summons issued and served; disclaimer.

Summons shall be issued and shall be returnable as in other cases of special proceedings, except that the return shall be at least 60 days from the date of the summons. The summons shall be served at least 10 days before the return thereof and the return recorded in the same manner as in other special proceedings; and all parties under disabilities shall be represented by guardian, either general or ad litem. If the persons named as interested are not residents of the State of North Carolina, and their residence is known, which must appear by affidavit, the summons must be served on such nonresidents as is now prescribed by law for service of summons on nonresidents.

Any party defendant to such proceeding may file a disclaimer of any claim or interest in the land described in the petition, which shall be deemed an admission of the allegations of the petition, and the decree shall bar such party and all persons thereafter claiming under him, and such party shall not be liable for any costs or expenses of the proceeding except such as may have been incurred by reason of his delay in pleading. (1913, c. 90, s. 6; C.S., s. 2385; 1967, c. 954, s. 3.)

§ 43-10. Notice of petition published.

In addition to the summons issued, prescribed in the foregoing section [§ 43-9], the clerk of the court shall, at the time of issuing such summons, publish a of the land and the relief demanded, in some secular newspaper published in the county wherein the land is situate, and having general circulation in the county; and if there be no such paper, then in a newspaper in the county nearest thereto and having general circulation in the county wherein the land lies, once a week for eight issues of such paper. The notice shall set forth the title of the cause and in legible or conspicuous type the words "To whom it may concern," and shall give notice to all persons of the relief demanded and the return day of the summons: Provided, that no final order or judgment shall be entered in the cause until there is proof and adjudication of publication as in other cases of publication of notice of summons. The provisions of this section, in respect to the issuing and service of summons and the publication of the notice, shall be mandatory and essential to the jurisdiction of the court to proceed in the cause: Provided, that the recital of the service of summons and publication in the decree or in the final judgment in the cause, and in the certificate issued to the petitioner as hereinafter provided, shall be conclusive evidence thereof. The clerk of the court shall also record a copy of said notice in the lis pendens docket of his office and cross-index same as other notices of lis pendens and shall also certify a copy thereof to the superior court of each county in which any part of said land lies, and the clerk thereof shall record and cross-index same in the lis pendens records of his office as other notices of lis pendens are recorded and cross-indexed. (1913, c. 90, s. 7; 1915, c. 128, s. 1; 1919, c. 82, s. 2; C.S., s. 2386; 1925, c. 287.)

§ 43-11. Hearing and decree.

(a)   Referred to Examiner. - Upon the return day of the summons the petition shall be set down for hearing upon the pleadings and exhibits filed. If any person claiming an interest in the land described in the petition, or any lien thereon, shall file an answer, the petition and answer, together with all exhibits filed, shall be referred to the examiner of titles, who shall proceed, after notice to the petitioner and the persons who have filed answer or answered, to hear the cause upon such parol or documentary evidence as may be offered or called for and taken by him, and in addition thereto make such independent examination of the title as may be necessary. Upon his request the clerk shall issue a commission under the seal of the court for taking such testimony as shall be beyond the jurisdiction of such examiner.

report of his conclusions of law and fact, setting forth the state of such title, any liens or encumbrances thereon, by whom held, amount due thereon, together with an abstract of title to the lands and any other information in regard thereto affecting its validity.

(c) Exceptions to Report. - Any of the parties to the proceeding may, within 20 days after such report is filed, file exceptions, either to the conclusions of law or fact. Whereupon the clerk shall transmit the record to the judge of the superior court for his determination thereof; such judge may on his own motion certify any issue of fact arising upon any such exceptions to the superior court of the county in which the proceeding is pending, for a trial of such issue by jury, and he shall so certify such issue of fact for trial by jury upon the demand of any party to the proceeding. If, upon consideration of such record, or the record and verdict of issues to be certified and tried by jury, the title be found in the petitioner, the judge shall enter a decree to that effect, ascertaining all limitations, liens, etc., declaring the land entitled to registration accordingly, and the same, together with the record, shall be docketed by the clerk of the court as in other cases, and a copy of the decree certified to the register of deeds of the county for registration as hereinafter provided. Any of the parties may appeal from such judgment to the appellate division, as in other special proceedings.

(d) No Judgment by Default. - No judgment in any proceeding under this Chapter shall be given by default, but the court must require an examination of the title in every instance except as respects the rights of parties who, by proper pleadings, admit the petitioner's claim. If, upon the return day of the summons and the day upon which the petition is set down for hearing, no answer be filed, the clerk shall refer the same to the examiner of titles, who shall, after notice to the petitioner, proceed to examine the title, together with all liens or encumbrances set forth or referred to in the petition and exhibits, and shall examine the registry of deeds, mortgages, wills, judgments, mechanic liens and other records of the county, and upon such examination he shall, as hereinbefore provided, report to the clerk the condition of the title, with a notice of liens or encumbrances thereon. The examiner shall have power to take and call for evidence in such case as fully as if the application were being contested. If the title shall be found to be in the petitioner, the clerk shall enter a decree to that effect and declaring the land entitled to registration, with entry of any limitations, liens, etc., and shall certify the same for registration, as hereinbefore provided, after approval by the judge of the superior court. (1913, c. 90, s. 8; C.S., s. 2387; 1969, c. 44, s. 48.)

§ 43-12. Effect of decree; approval of judge.

Every decree rendered as hereinbefore provided shall bind the land and bar all persons and corporations claiming title thereto or interest therein; quiet the title thereto, and shall be forever binding and conclusive upon and against all persons and corporations, whether mentioned by name in the order of publication, or included under the general description, "to whom it may concern"; and every such decree so rendered, or a duly certified copy thereof, as also the certificate of title issued thereon to the person or corporation therein named as owner, or to any subsequent transferee or purchaser, shall be conclusive evidence that such person or corporation is the owner of the land therein described, and no other evidence shall be required in any court of this State of his, her, or its right or title thereto. It shall not be an exception to such conclusiveness that a person is a minor, is incompetent, or is under any disability, but such person may have recourse upon the indemnity fund hereinafter provided for, for any loss the person may suffer by reason of being so concluded. Notwithstanding the provisions of G.S. 43-10, such decrees shall not be binding on and include the State of North Carolina or any of its agencies unless the State of North Carolina is made a party to the proceeding and notice of said proceeding and copy of petition, etc., are served upon the State of North Carolina as provided in this Chapter. Such decrees shall, in addition to being signed by the clerk of the court, be approved by the judge of the superior court, who shall review the whole proceeding and have power to require any reformation of the process, pleading, decrees or entries. (1913, c. 90, s. 9; 1919, c. 82, s. 3; C.S., s. 2388; 1925, c. 263; 1979, c. 73, s. 2; 2011-29, s. 4.)

Article 4.

Registration and Effect.

§ 43-13. Manner of registration.

(a) The register of deeds shall register and index, as hereinafter provided, the decree of title before mentioned and all subsequent transfers of title, and note all voluntary and involuntary transactions in any wise affecting the title to the land, authorized to be entered thereon in the real property records and estate no. _____" and on the grantee index in the name of the registered owner. If the title be subject to trust, condition, encumbrance or the like, the words "in trust," "upon condition," "subject to encumbrance," "life estate," or like appropriate insertion shall indicate the fact and fix any person dealing with such certificate with notice of the particulars of such limitations upon the title as appears upon the registry, and no new or additional certificate number shall be issued in such circumstances. No erasure, alteration, or amendment shall be made upon the registry after entry and issuance of a certificate of title except by order of a court of competent jurisdiction.

(b) When a voluntary or involuntary transaction is entered on a certificate of title, the certificate with the new entry shall be copied and recorded and indexed in the real property records and indexes. The copied certificate shall be indexed on the grantor index in the name "Registered estate no. _____" and on the grantee index in the name of the registered owner. (1913, c. 90, s. 10; 1919, c. 236, s. 1; C.S., s. 2389; 1999-59, s. 2.)

§ 43-14. Cross-indexing of lands by registers of deeds.

Where any land is brought into the Torrens System and under said System is registered in the public records of the register's office, said register shall cross-index the registration in the general cross index for deeds in his office. (1931, c. 286, s. 2.)

§ 43-15. Certificate issued.

Upon the registration of such decree the register of deeds shall issue an owner's certificate of title, under the seal of his office, which shall be delivered to the owner or his agent duly authorized, and shall be substantially as follows:

State of North Carolina - County of _____

The certificate of _____

situate in said county and State, described as follows: (Here describe land as in decree.)

Estate _____ (here name the estate and any limitation or encumbrance thereon, as fee simple, upon condition, in trust, subject to encumbrance, and the like).

Under decree of the land court of _____ county, entitled _____.

Registered No. ____, Book No. ____, page ____.

Witness my hand and seal, at office at _____ this _____ day of _____, A.D. _____

(Seal)_____

                                              Register of Deeds

(1913, c. 90, s. 10; C.S., s. 2390; 1999-456, s. 59.)

§ 43-16. Certificates numbered; entries thereon.

All certificates of title to land in the county shall be numbered consecutively, which number shall be retained as long as the boundaries of the land remain unchanged, and a separate page or more, with appropriate space for subsequent entries, shall be devoted to each title in the registration of titles book for the county. Every entry made upon any certificate of title in such book or upon the owner's certificate, under any of the provisions of this Chapter, shall be signed by the register of deeds and minutely dated in conformity with the dates shown by the entry book. (1913, c. 90, s. 11; C.S., s. 2391.)

Whenever an owner's certificate of title is lost or destroyed, the owner or his personal representative may petition the court for the issuance of a new certificate. Notice of such petition shall be published once a week for four successive weeks, under the direction of the court, in some convenient newspaper, and noted upon the registry of titles, and upon satisfactory proof having been exhibited before it that the certificate has been lost or destroyed the court may direct the issuance of a new certificate, which shall be appropriately designated and take the place of the original, but at least 30 full days shall elapse between the filing of the petition and making the decree for such new certificate. (1913, c. 90, s. 24; C.S., s. 2392.)

§ 43-17.1. Issuance of certificate upon death of registered owner; petition and contents; dissolution of corporation; certificate lost or not received by grantee.

Upon the death of any person who is the registered owner of any estate or interest in land which has been brought under this Chapter, a petition may be filed with the clerk of the superior court of the county in which the title to such land is registered by anyone having any estate or interest in the land, or any part thereof, the title to which has been registered under the terms of this Chapter, attaching thereto the registered certificate of title issued to the deceased holder and setting forth the nature and character of the interest or estate of such petitioner in said land, the manner in which such interest or estate was acquired by the petitioner from the deceased person - whether by descent, by will, or otherwise, and setting forth the names and addresses of any and all other persons, firms or corporations which may have any interest or estate therein, or any part thereof, and the names and addresses of all persons known to have any claims or liens against the said land; and setting forth the changes which are necessary to be made in the registered certificate of title to land in order to show the true owner or owners thereof occasioned by the death of the registered owner of said certificate. Such petition shall contain all such other information as is necessary to fully inform the court as to the status of the title and the condition as to all liens and encumbrances against said land existing at the time the petition is filed, and shall contain a prayer for such relief as the petitioner may be entitled to under the provisions hereof. Such petition shall be duly verified.

In the event the registered certificate of title has been lost and after due diligence cannot be found, and this fact is made to appear by allegation in the petition, such registered certificate of title need not be attached to the petition as hereinabove required, but the legal representatives of the deceased registered owner shall be made parties to the proceeding. If such persons are unknown or, if known cannot after due diligence be found within the State, service of summons upon them may be made by publication of the notice prescribed in G.S. 43-17.2. In case the registered owner is a corporation which has been dissolved, service of summons upon such corporation and any others who may have or claim any interest in such land thereunder shall be made by publication of the notice containing appropriate recitals as required by G.S. 43-17.2.

If any registered owner has by writing conveyed or attempted to convey a title to any registered land without the surrender of the certificate of title issued to him, the person claiming title to said lands under and through said registered owner by reason of his or its conveyance may file a petition with the clerk of the superior court of the county in which the land is registered and in the proceeding under which the title was registered praying for the cancellation of the original certificate and the issuance of the new certificate. Upon the filing of such petition notice shall be published as prescribed in G.S. 43-17.2. The clerk of the superior court with whom said petition is filed shall by order determine what additional notice, if any, shall be given to registered owners. If the registered owner is a natural person, deceased, or a corporation dissolved the court may direct what additional notice, if any, shall be given. The clerk shall hear the evidence, make findings of fact, and if found as a fact that the original certificate of the registered owner has been lost and cannot be found, shall enter his order directing the register of deeds to cancel the same and to issue a new certificate to such person or persons as may be entitled thereto, subject to such claims or liens as the court may find to exist.

Any party within 10 days from the rendition of such judgment or order by the clerk of superior court of the county in which said land is registered may appeal to the superior court during a session of court, where the cause shall be heard de novo by the judge, unless a jury trial be demanded, in which event the issues of fact shall be submitted to a jury. From any order or judgment entered by the superior court during a session of court an appeal may be taken to the appellate

§ 43-17.2. Publication of notice; service of process.

Upon the filing of such duly verified petition, the petitioner shall cause to be published once a week for four weeks, in some newspaper having a general circulation in the county in which the land is situated, a notice signed by the clerk of the superior court, setting forth in substance the nature of the petition, a description of the land affected thereby, and the relief therein prayed for, and notifying all persons having or claiming any interest or estate in the land to appear at a time therein specified, which shall be at least 30 days after the first publication of said notice, to show cause, if any exists, why the relief prayed for in the petition should not be granted. An affidavit shall be filed by the publisher with the clerk of the court, showing a full compliance of this requirement. Upon a filing of said petition, the petitioner shall cause the summons, with a copy of the petition, to be served upon all persons, firms or corporations known to have any interest or estate in the lands referred to in the petition, and the personal representative, the devisees, if any, and all heirs at law of the deceased registered owner of said land. In the event any of the persons upon whom service of summons is to be made are nonresidents of the State of North Carolina, service may be made by publication in the manner prescribed by law for the service of summons in special proceedings. (1943, c. 466, s. 1.)

§ 43-17.3. Answer by person claiming interest.

Any person asserting a claim or any interest in such registered land may, at any time prior to the hearing provided for in G.S. 43-17.4, file such answer or other pleadings as may be proper, asserting his rights or claims to the property referred to in the petition. (1943, c. 466, s. 1.)

§ 43-17.4. Hearing by clerk of superior court; orders and decrees; cancellation of old certificate and issuance of new certificate.

the facts as ascertained and determined by the court. The court is authorized and empowered to order and direct that the outstanding registered certificate of title to the land shall be surrendered and cancelled in the office of the register of deeds, and that a new certificate of title shall be issued, showing therein the owner or owners of the land described in the original certificate and the nature and character of such ownership: Provided, the clerk of the superior court shall not authorize the issuance of the new certificate of title until the fees provided in G.S. 43-49 have been paid. Upon the surrender and cancellation by the register of deeds of the outstanding certificate of title, the new certificate of title shall be registered and cross-indexed in the same manner provided for the registration of the original certificate, and the register of deeds shall issue a new certificate of title in the same manner and form as provided for the original certificate. The said new certificate shall have the same force and effect as the original certificate of title and shall be subject to the same provisions of law with reference thereto. (1943, c. 466, s. 1.)

§ 43-17.5. Issuance of new certificate validated.

Whenever heretofore any registered certificate of title has been surrendered by the heirs or devisees of any deceased registered owner of any registered title and the registered certificate of title of such deceased owner has been surrendered and canceled and a new certificate of title issued to a purchaser or to such heirs or devisees, the same is hereby validated and confirmed and made effectual to the same extent as though such new certificate had been issued in compliance with the provisions of this Chapter. (1943, c. 466, s. 1.)

§ 43-18. Registered owner's estate free from adverse claims; exceptions.

Every registered owner of any estate or interest in land brought under this Chapter shall, except in cases of fraud to which he is a party or in which he is a privy, without valuable consideration paid in good faith, and except when any registration has been procured through forgery, hold the land free from any and all adverse claims, rights or encumbrances not noted on the certificate of title, except of the United States which the statutes of this State cannot require to appear of record under registry laws;

(2) Taxes and assessments thereon due the State or any county, city or town therein, but not delinquent;

(3) Any lease for a term not exceeding three years, under which the land is actually occupied. (1913, c. 90, s. 25; C.S., s. 2393.)

§ 43-19. Adverse claims existing at initial registry; affidavit; limitation of action.

Any person making any claim to or asserting any lien or charge upon registered land, existing at the initial registry of the same and not shown upon the register or adverse to the title of the registered owner, and for which no other provision is herein made for asserting the same in the registry of titles, may make an affidavit thereof setting forth his interest, right, title, lien or demand, and how and under whom derived, and the character and nature thereof. The affidavit shall state his place of residence and designate a place at which all notices relating thereto may be served. Upon the filing of such affidavit in the office of the clerk of the superior court, the clerk shall order a note thereof as in the case of charges or encumbrances, and the same shall be entered by the register of deeds. Action shall be brought upon such claim within six months after the entry of such note, unless for cause shown the clerk shall extend the time. Upon failure to commence such action within the time prescribed therefor, the clerk shall order a cancellation of such note. If any person shall wantonly or maliciously or without reasonable cause procure such notation to be entered upon the registry of titles, having the effect of a cloud upon the registered owner's title, he shall be liable for all damages the owner may suffer thereby. (1913, c. 90, s. 25; C.S., s. 2394.)

§ 43-20. Decree and registration run with the land.

The obtaining of a decree of registration and the entry of a certificate of title shall be construed as an agreement running with the land, and the same shall

§ 43-21. No right by adverse possession.

No title to nor right or interest in registered land in derogation of that of the registered owner shall be acquired by prescription or adverse possession. (1913, c. 90, s. 27; C.S., s. 2396.)

§ 43-22. Jurisdiction of courts; registered land affected only by registration.

Except as otherwise specially provided by this Chapter, registered land and ownership therein shall be subject to the jurisdiction of the courts in the same manner as if it had not been registered; but the registration shall be the only operative act to transfer or affect the title to registered land, and shall date from the time the writing, instrument or record to be registered is duly filed in the office of the register of deeds, subject to the provisions of this Chapter; no voluntary or involuntary transaction shall affect the title to registered lands until registered in accordance with the provisions of this Chapter: Provided, that all mortgages, deeds, surrendered and canceled certificates, when new certificates are issued for the land so deeded, the other paper-writings, if any, pertaining to and affecting the registered estate or estates herein referred to, shall be filed by the register of deeds for reference and information, but the consolidated real property records shall be and constitute sole and conclusive legal evidence of title, except in cases of mistake and fraud, which shall be corrected in the methods now provided for the correction of papers authorized to be registered. (1913, c. 90, s. 28; C.S., s. 2397; 2000-140, s. 42(a).)

§ 43-23. Priority of right.

In case of conflicting claims between the registered owners the right, title or estate derived from or held under the older certificate of title shall prevail. (1913, c. 90, s. 29; C.S., s. 2398.)

When the provisions of this Chapter have been complied with, all conveyances, deeds, contracts to convey or leases shall be considered duly registered, as against creditors and purchasers, in the same manner and as fully as if the same had been registered in the manner heretofore provided by law for the registration of conveyances. (1913, c. 90, s. 32; C.S., s. 2399.)

§ 43-25. Release from registration.

Whenever the record owner of any estate in lands, the title to which has been registered or attempted to be registered in accordance with the provisions of this Chapter, desires to have such estate released from the provisions of said Chapter insofar as said Chapter relates to the form of conveyance, so that such estate may ever thereafter be conveyed, either absolutely or upon condition or trust, by the use of any desired form of conveyance other than the certificate of title prescribed by said Chapter, such owner may present his owner's certificate of title to such registered estate to the register of deeds of the county wherein such land lies, with a memorandum or statement written by him on the margin thereof in the words following, or words of similar import, to wit: "I (or we),_____ , being the owner (or owners) of the registered estate evidenced by this certificate of title, do hereby release said estate from the provisions of Chapter 43 of the General Statutes of North Carolina insofar as said Chapter relates to the form of conveyance, so that hereafter the said estate may, and shall be forever until again hereafter registered in accordance with the provisions of said Chapter and acts amendatory thereof, conveyed, either absolutely or upon condition or trust, by any form of conveyance other than the certificate of title prescribed by said Chapter, and in the same manner as if said estate had never been registered." Which said memorandum or statement shall further state that it is made pursuant to the provisions of this section, and shall be signed by such record owner and attested by the register of deeds under his hand and official seal, and a like memorandum or statement so entered, signed and attested upon the margin of the record of the said owner's certificate of title in the consolidated real property records in said register's office, with the further notation made and signed by the register of deeds on the margin of the certificate of title in the consolidated real property records showing that such entry has been made upon the owner's certificate of title; and thereafter any conveyance of such registered estate, or any part thereof, by such owner, his to the same extent as if such estate had never been so registered. (Ex. Sess. 1924, c. 40; 2000-140, s. 42(b).)

Article 5.

Adverse Claims and Corrections after Registration.

§ 43-26. Limitations.

No decree of registration heretofore entered, and no certificate of title heretofore issued pursuant thereto, shall be adjudged invalid, revoked, or set aside, unless the action or proceeding in which the validity of such decree of registration or certificate of title issued pursuant thereto is attacked or called in question be commenced or the defense alleging the invalidity thereof be interposed within 12 months from March 10, 1919.

No decree of registration hereafter entered and no certificate of title hereafter issued pursuant thereto shall be adjudged invalid or revoked or set aside, unless the action or proceeding in which the validity of such decree or of the certificate of title issued pursuant thereto is attacked or called in question be commenced or the defense alleging the invalidity thereof be interposed within 12 months from the date of such decree.

No action or proceeding for the recovery of any right, title, interest, or estate in registered land adverse to the title established and adjudicated by any decree of registration heretofore entered shall be maintained unless such action or proceeding be commenced within 12 months from the date last mentioned; and no action or proceeding for the recovery of any right, title, interest, estate in registered land, adverse to the right established by any decree of registration hereafter shall be maintained unless such action or proceeding be commenced within 12 months from the date of such decree.

No action or proceeding for the enforcement or foreclosure of any lien upon or charge against registered land which existed at the date when any decree of registration was heretofore entered, and which was not recognized or established by such decree, shall be maintained, unless such action or registration hereafter entered, and which is not recognized and established by such decree, shall be maintained, unless such action or proceeding be commenced within 12 months from the date of such decree. (1919, c. 236, s. 1; C.S., s. 2400.)

§ 43-27. Adverse claim subsequent to registry; affidavit of claim prerequisite to enforcement; limitation.

Any person claiming any right, title, or interest in registered land adverse to the registered owner thereof, arising subsequent to the date of the original decree of registration, may, if no other provision is made for registering the same, file with the register of deeds of the county in which such decree was rendered or certificate of title thereon was issued, a verified statement in writing, setting forth fully the right, title, or interest so claimed, how or from whom it was acquired, and a reference to the number, book, and page of the certificate of title of the registered owner, together with a description of the land by metes and bounds, the adverse claimant's place of residence and his post-office address, and, if a nonresident, he shall designate or appoint the said register of deeds to receive all notices directed to or to be served upon such adverse claimant in connection with the claim by him made, and such statement shall be noted and filed by said register of deeds as an adverse claim; but no action or proceeding to enforce such adverse claim shall be maintained unless the same be commenced within six months of the filing of the statement thereof. (1919, c. 236, s. 1; C.S., s. 2401.)

§ 43-28. Suit to enforce adverse claim; summons and notice necessary.

Upon the institution of any action or proceeding to enforce such adverse claim, notice thereof shall be served upon the register of deeds, who shall enter upon the registry a memorandum that suit has been brought or proceeding instituted to determine the validity of such adverse claim; and summons or notice shall be served upon the holder or claimant of the registered title or certificate or other person against whom such adverse claim is alleged, as provided by law for the institution of suits or proceedings in the courts of this State.

registered title or certificate, or other person, as aforesaid, within seven months from the date of filing the statement of adverse claim, the register of deeds shall cancel upon the registry the adverse claim so filed and make a memorandum setting out that no notice of suit or proceeding to enforce the same had been served upon him within seven months as herein required, and that such adverse claim was therefore canceled; and thereafter no action or proceeding shall be begun or maintained to enforce such adverse claim in any of the courts of this State. (1919, c. 236, s. 1; C.S., s. 2402.)

§ 43-29. Judgment in suit to enforce adverse claim; register to file.

The court shall certify its judgment to the register of deeds; if such adverse claim be held valid, the register of deeds shall make such entry upon the registry and upon the owner's certificate of title as may be directed by the court, or he may file and record a certified copy of the judgment or order of the court thereon; if such adverse claim be held invalid the register of deeds shall cancel such adverse claim upon the registry, noting thereon that the same was done by order or judgment of the court, or he may file and record a certified copy of the judgment or order of the court thereon. (1919, c. 236, s. 1; C.S., s. 2403.)

§ 43-30. Correction of registered title; limitation of adverse claims.

Any registered owner or other claimant under the registered title may at any time apply to the court in which the original decree was entered, by petition, setting out that registered interests of any description, whether vested, contingent, expectant or inchoate, have terminated and ceased, or that new interests have arisen or been created which do not appear upon the certificate, or that any error or omission was made in entering or issuing the certificate or any duplicate thereof, or that the name of any person on the certificate has been changed, or that the registered owner had married or, if registered as married, that the marriage has been terminated, or that a corporation which owned registered lands has been dissolved, without conveying the same or transferring its certificate within three years after the dissolution, or any other reasonable and proper ground of correction or relief; and such court may hear and decree of registration which was entered more than 12 months prior to the filing of such petition, and nothing shall be done or ordered by the court to divest or impair the title or other interest of a purchaser who holds a transfer or certificate of title for value and in good faith. No action or proceeding shall be commenced or maintained to set up or establish any right, claim, interest or estate adverse to the order or decree or certificate of title issued thereon made or entered upon any petition or other proceeding authorized by this section, unless the same shall be brought and instituted within six months from the date of such order or decree authorized by this section. (1919, c. 236, s. 1; C.S., s. 2404.)

Article 6.

Method of Transfer.

§ 43-31. When whole of land conveyed.

Whenever the whole of any registered estate is transferred or conveyed the same shall be done by a transfer or conveyance attached to the certificate substantially as follows:

The owners (giving the names of the parties owning land described in the certificate) hereby, in consideration of _____ dollars, sell and convey to the purchaser (giving name of purchaser) the lot or tract of land, as the case may be, described in the certificate of title hereto attached. The transfer shall be indexed on the grantor and grantee indexes in the same manner as deeds are indexed.

The same shall be signed and properly acknowledged by the parties and shall have the full force and effect of a deed in fee simple: Provided, that if the sale shall be in trust, upon condition, with power to sell or other unusual form of conveyance, the same shall be set out in the transfer, and shall be entered upon the consolidated real property records as hereinafter provided; that upon presentation of the transfer, together with the certificate of title, to the register of deeds, the transaction shall be duly noted and registered in accordance with the provisions of this Chapter, and certificate of title so presented shall be canceled and a new certificate with the same number issued to the purchaser thereof,

§ 43-32. Conveyance of part of registered land.

The transfer of any part of a registered estate, either of an undivided interest therein or of a separate lot or parcel thereof, shall be made by an instrument of the transfer or conveyance similar in form to that herein provided for the transfer of the whole of any registered estate, to which shall be attached the certificate of title of such registered estate. In case of the transfer of an undivided interest in a registered estate, such instrument of transfer or conveyance shall accurately specify and describe the extent and amount of the interest transferred and of the interest retained, respectively. In case of a transfer of a separate lot or parcel of a registered estate, such instrument of transfer or conveyance shall describe the lot or parcel transferred either by metes and bounds or by reference to the map or plat attached thereto, and shall in every case be accompanied by a map or plat having clearly indicated thereon the boundaries of the whole of the registered estate and of the lot or parcel to be transferred, but a new survey of the original registered estate shall not be required. The transfer shall be indexed on the grantor and grantee indexes in the same manner as deeds are indexed. (1919, c. 82, s. 4; C.S., s. 2406; 1999-59, s. 4.)

§ 43-33. Duty of register of deeds upon part conveyance.

Upon presentation to the register of deeds of an instrument of transfer or conveyance of an undivided interest in a registered estate, in proper form as above prescribed, it shall be his duty to cancel the certificate of title attached thereto and to issue to each owner a new certificate of title, each bearing the same number as the original certificate of title and accurately specifying and describing the extent and the amount of the interest retained or of the interest transferred, as the case may be. Upon presentation to the register of deeds of an instrument of transfer or conveyance of a separate lot or parcel of a registered estate, in proper form as above prescribed, it shall be his duty to cancel the certificate of the title attached thereto and to issue to each owner a new certificate of title bearing a new number and describing the separate lot or parcel retained or transferred, as the case may be, either by metes and bounds accuracy of any description. (1919, c. 82, s. 4; C.S., s. 2407; 1999-59, s. 5.)

§ 43-34. Subdivision of registered estate.

Any owner of a registered estate who may desire to subdivide the same may make application in writing to the register of deeds for the issuance of a new certificate of title for each subdivision, to which application shall be attached a map or plat having clearly indicated thereon the boundaries of the whole of the registered estate in question and of each lot or parcel for which he desires a new certificate of title. Thereupon it shall be the duty of the register of deeds, upon payment by such applicant of necessary surveyor's fees, if any are required, and of the amount herein provided for issuing the certificates of title and recording the map, to cancel the certificate of title attached to said application and to issue to such owner new certificates of title, each bearing a new number, for each lot or parcel shown upon the said map, describing such lot or parcel in such certificates either by metes and bounds or by reference to a map or plat attached thereto. (1919, c. 82, s. 4; C.S., s. 2408.)

§ 43-35. References and cross references entered on register.

In all cases the register of deeds shall place upon the consolidated real property records and upon the certificate of title of such registered estate therein, references and cross references to the new certificates issued as above provided, in accordance with the provisions of this Article, and the new certificates issued shall fully refer by number and by name of the holder to the canceled certificate in place of which they are issued. (1919, c. 82, s. 4; C.S., s. 2409; 2000-140, s. 42(d).)

§ 43-36. When land conveyed as security.

A.B. and wife (giving names of all owners or holders of certificates and their wives) hereby transfer to C.D. the tract or lot of land described as No. _____ in registration of titles book for _____ County, a certificate for the title for same being hereto attached, to secure a debt of _____ dollars, due to _____, of _____ County and State, on the _____ day of _____, _____, evidenced by bond (or otherwise as the case may be) dated the _____ day of _____, _____. In case of default in payment of said debt with accrued interest, _____ days notice of sale required.

The same shall be signed and properly acknowledged by the parties making same, and shall be presented, together with the owner's certificate, to the register of deeds, whose duty it shall be to note upon the owner's certificate and upon the certificate of title in the consolidated real property records the name of the trustee, the amount of debt, and the date of maturity of same.

(b) Part of Land Conveyed. - When a part of the registered estate shall be so conveyed, the register of deeds shall note upon the consolidated real property records and owner's certificate the part so conveyed, and if the same be required and the proper fee paid by the trustee, shall issue what shall be known as a partial certificate, over his hand and seal, setting out the portion so conveyed.

(c) Effect of Transfer. - All transfers by such short form shall convey the power of sale upon due advertisement at the county courthouse and in some newspaper published in the county, or adjoining county, in the same manner and as fully as is now provided by law in the case of mortgages and deeds of trust and default therein.

(d) Other Encumbrances Noted. - All registered encumbrances, rights or adverse claims affecting the estate represented thereby shall continue to be noted, not only upon the certificate of title in the consolidated real property records, but also upon the owner's certificate, until same shall have been released or discharged. And in the event of second or other subsequent voluntary encumbrances the holder of the certificate may be required to produce such certificate for the entry thereon or attachment thereto of the note of such subsequent charge or encumbrance as provided in this Article.

or any part of the same, as security for a debt by deed of trust or mortgage in any form which may be agreed upon between the parties thereto, and having such deed of trust or mortgage recorded in the office of the register of deeds as other deeds of trust and mortgages are recorded: Provided, that the book and page of the record at which such deed of trust or mortgage is recorded shall be entered by the register of deeds upon the owner's certificate and also on the consolidated real property records.

(f) Sale under Lien; New Certification. - Upon foreclosure of such deed of trust or mortgage, or sale under execution for taxes or other lien on the land, the fact of such foreclosure or sale shall be reported by the trustee, mortgagee or other person authorized to make the same, to the register of deeds of the county in which the land lies, and, upon satisfactory evidence thereof, it shall be his duty to call in and cancel the outstanding certificate of title for the land, so sold, and to issue a new certificate in its place to the purchaser or other person entitled thereto; and the production of such outstanding certificate and its surrender by the holder thereof may be compelled, upon notice to him, by motion before and order of the clerk of the superior court in the original proceeding or the clerk of the superior court of the county in which the land lies; but the right of appeal from such order may be exercised and shall be allowed as in other special proceedings, and pending any such appeal the rights of all parties shall be preserved. (1913, c. 90, s. 14; 1915, c. 245; 1919, c. 82, s. 5; C.S., s. 2410; 1999-456, s. 59; 2000-140, s. 42(e).)

§ 43-37. Owner's certificate presented with transfer.

In voluntary transactions the owner's certificate of title must be presented along with the writing or instrument conveying or effecting the sale, and thereupon and not otherwise the register shall be authorized to register the conveyance or other transaction upon proof of payment of all delinquent taxes or liens, if any, or if such payment be not shown the entry and new certificate shall note such taxes or liens as having priority thereto. (1913, c. 90, s. 15; C.S., s. 2411.)

§ 43-38. Transfers probated; partitions; contracts.

boundary by partition, subtraction or addition of land there shall be an accurate survey and permanent marking of boundaries and accurate plots, showing the courses, distances and markings of every portion thereof, which shall be duly proved and registered as upon the initial registration. Such transfers shall be presented to the register of deeds for entry upon the consolidated real property records and upon the owner's certificate within 30 days from the date thereof, or become subject to any rights which may accrue to any other person by a prior registration. All leases or contracts affecting land for a period exceeding three years shall be in writing, duly proved before the clerk of the superior court, recorded in the register's office, and noted upon the registry and upon the owner's certificate. (1913, c. 90, ss. 15, 32; C.S., s. 2412; 2000-140, s. 42(f).)

§ 43-39. Certified copy of order of court noted.

In voluntary transactions a certificate from the proper State, county or court officer, or certified copy of the order, decree or judgment of any court of competent jurisdiction shall be authority for him to order a proper notation thereof upon the consolidated real property records, and for the register of deeds to note the transaction under the direction of the court. (1913, c. 90, s. 16; C.S., s. 2413; 2000-140, s. 42(g).)

§ 43-40. Production of owner's certificate required.

Whenever owner's certificate is not presented to the register along with any writing, instrument or record filed for registration under this Chapter, he shall forthwith send notice by registered mail to the owner of such certificate, requesting him to produce the same in order that a memorial of the transaction may be made thereon; and such production may be required by subpoena duces tecum or by other process of the court, if necessary. (1913, c. 90, s. 17; C.S., s. 2414.)

§ 43-41. Registration notice to all persons.

office of the proper register as the case may be, and not otherwise, be notice to all persons from the time of such registration, and operate, in accordance with law and the provisions of this Chapter, upon any registered land in the county of such registration. (1913, c. 90, s. 18; C.S., s. 2415.)

§ 43-42. Conveyance of registered land in trust.

Whenever a writing, instrument or record is filed for the purpose of transferring registered land in trust, or upon any equitable condition or limitation expressed therein, or for the purpose of creating or declaring a trust or other equitable interest in such land, the particulars of the trust, condition, limitation or other equitable interest shall not be entered on the certificate, but it shall be sufficient to enter in the consolidated real property records and upon the certificates a memorial thereof by the terms "in trust" or "upon condition" or in other apt words, and to refer by number to the writing, instrument or record authorizing or creating the same. And if express power is given to sell, encumber or deal with the land in any manner, such power shall be noted upon the certificates by the term "with power to sell" or "with power to encumber," or by other apt words. (1913, c. 90, s. 19; C.S., s. 2416; 2000-140, s. 42(h).)

§ 43-43. Authorized transfer of equitable interests registered.

No writing or instrument for the purpose of transferring, encumbering or otherwise dealing with equitable interests in registered land shall be registered unless the power thereto enabling has been expressly conferred by or has been reserved in the writing or instrument creating such equitable instrument, or has been declared to exist by the decree of some court of competent jurisdiction, which decree must also be registered. (1913, c. 90, s. 20; C.S., s. 2417.)

§ 43-44. Validating conveyance by entry on margin of certificate.

made any conveyance of such estate, or any portion thereof, by any form of conveyance sufficient in law to pass the title thereto if the title to said lands had not been so registered, the record owner and holder of the certificate of title covering such registered estate may enter upon the margin of his certificate of title in the consolidated real property records a memorandum showing that such registered estate, or a portion thereof, has been so conveyed, and further showing the name of the grantee or grantees and the number of the book and the page thereof where such conveyance is recorded in the office of the register of deeds, and make a like entry upon the owner's certificate of title held by him, both of such entries to be signed by him and witnessed by the register of deeds, and attested by the seal of office of the register of deeds upon said owner's certificate, with the further notation made and signed by the register of deeds on the margin of the certificate of title in the consolidated real property records showing that such entry has been made upon the owner's certificate of title, and thereupon such conveyance shall become and be as valid and effectual to pass such estate of the owner according to the tenor and purport of such conveyance as if the title to said lands had never been so registered, whether such conveyance be in form absolute or upon condition of trust; and in all cases where such conveyance has been made before August 21, 1924, upon the making of the entries herein authorized by the record owner and holder of such owner's certificate of title, the grantee and his heirs and assigns shall thereafter have the same right to convey the said estate or any part of the same in all respects as if the title to said lands had never been so registered. (Ex. Sess. 1924, c. 41; 2000-140, s. 42(i).)

Article 7.

Liens upon Registered Lands.

§ 43-45. Docketed judgments.

Whenever any judgment of the superior court of the county in which the registered estate is situated shall be duly docketed in the office of the clerk of the superior court, or any lien or notice of lis pendens is filed in the office of the clerk of the superior court, it shall be the duty of the clerk, upon the request of any interested party, to certify the same to the register of deeds. The register of debtor, and the register of deeds is authorized to recover the certificate of title pursuant to G.S. 43-40. The register of deeds shall also enter notice of the judgment, lien, or lis pendens on the record copy of the certificate of title, and the encumbrance is valid against the registered estate from the time it is noted on the record copy. (1913, c. 90, s. 22; C.S., s. 2418; 1999-59, s. 6.)

§ 43-46. Notice of delinquent taxes filed.

It shall be the duty of the tax collector of each taxing unit, not later than June 30 following the date the taxes became delinquent, to file an exact memorandum of the delinquency, if any, of any registered land for the nonpayment of the taxes or assessments thereon, including interest, in the office of the register of deeds for registration; and if such officer fails to perform such duty, and there shall be subsequent to such day a transfer of the land as hereinbefore provided, the grantee shall acquire a good title free from any lien for such taxes and assessments, and the collector and his sureties shall be liable for the payment of the taxes and assessments with the interest thereon. The register of deeds shall enter the notice of delinquency on the record copy of the certificate of title, and the tax lien shall be valid against the registered estate from the time it is noted on the record copy. The register of deeds shall enter the notice of cancellation of the tax lien on the record copy of the certificate of title upon presentation of satisfactory evidence of payment. (1913, c. 90, s. 21; C.S., s. 2419; 1999-59, s. 7; 2000-140, s. 9.)

§ 43-47: Repealed by Session Laws 1999-59, s. 8.

§ 43-48. Foreclosure of tax lien.

The lien for ad valorem taxes may be foreclosed and the property sold pursuant to G.S. 105-375. A note of the sale under this section shall be duly registered, and a certificate shall be entered and an owner's certificate issued in favor of the purchaser in whom title shall be thereby vested as registered owner, in the default of the tenant for life in paying the taxes or assessments thereon. (1913, c. 90, s. 23; C.S., s. 2421; 1999-59, s. 9.)

Article 8.

Assurance Fund.

§ 43-49. Assurance fund provided; investment.

Upon the original registration of land and also upon the entry of certificate showing the title as registered owners in heirs or devisees, there shall be paid to the clerk of the court one tenth of one percent (0.1%) of the assessed value of the land for taxes, as an assurance fund, which shall be paid over to the State Treasurer, who shall be liable therefor upon his official bond as for other moneys received by him in his official capacity. He shall keep all the principal and interest of such fund invested, except as required for the payment of indemnities, in bonds and securities of the United States, of this State, or of counties and other municipalities within the State. Such investment shall be made upon the advice and concurrence of the Governor and Council of State, and he shall make report of such funds and the investment thereof to the General Assembly biennially. When registration involves the State of North Carolina or any political subdivision thereof, the local tax collector shall assess the value of the land involved as if for tax purposes and the amount to be paid to the clerk shall be an amount equal to one tenth of one percent (0.1%) of such assessed value; provided, however, that no taxes shall be levied upon such land while title thereto remains in the State of North Carolina or any political subdivision thereof. (1913, c. 90, s. 33; C.S., s. 2422; 1963, c. 946, s. 2.)

§ 43-50. Action for indemnity.

Any person who, without negligence on his part, sustains loss or damage or is deprived of land, or of any estate or interest therein, through fraud or negligence or in consequence of any error, omission, mistake, misfeasance, or misdescription in any certificate of title or in any entry or memorandum in the of the county in which the land is situate for the recovery of compensation for such loss or damage from the assurance fund. Such action shall be against the State Treasurer and all other persons who may be liable for the fraud, negligence, omission, mistake or misfeasance; but if such claimant has the right of action or other remedy for the recovery of the land, or of the estate or interest therein, or of the claim upon same, he shall exhaust such remedy before resorting to the assurance fund. (1913, c. 90, s. 34; C.S., s. 2423.)

§ 43-51. Satisfaction by third person or by Treasurer.

If there are defendants other than the State Treasurer, and judgment is rendered in favor of the plaintiff and against the Treasurer and some or all of the other defendants, execution shall first be issued against the other defendants, and if such execution is returned unsatisfied in whole or in part, and the officer returning the same shall certify that it cannot be collected from the property and effects of the other defendants, or if the judgment be against the Treasurer only, the clerk of the court shall certify the amount due on the execution to the State Treasurer, and the same shall be paid. In all such cases the Treasurer may employ counsel who shall receive reasonable compensation for his services from the assurance fund. (1913, c. 90, s. 35; C.S., s. 2424; 1993, c. 257, s. 1.)

§ 43-52. Payment by Treasurer, if assurance fund insufficient.

If the assurance fund shall be insufficient at any time to meet the amount called for by any such certificate, the Treasurer shall pay the same from any funds in the treasury not otherwise appropriated; and in such case any amount thereafter received by the Treasurer on account of the assurance fund shall be transferred to the general funds of the treasury until the amount advanced shall have been paid. (1913, c. 90, s. 36; C.S., s. 2425.)

§ 43-53. Treasurer subrogated to right of claimant.

trustee, or by the improper exercise of any power of sale in benefit of the assurance fund. (1913, c. 90, s. 37; C.S., s. 2426.)

§ 43-54. Assurance fund not liable for breach of trust; limit of recovery.

The assurance fund shall not be liable to pay any loss, damage or deprivation occasioned by a breach of trust, whether expressed, constructive or implied, by any registered owner who is a trustee, or by the improper exercise of any power of sale in a mortgage or deed of trust. Nor shall any plaintiff recover as compensation under the provisions of this Chapter more than the fair market value of the land at the time when he suffered the loss, damage or deprivation thereof. (1913, c. 90, s. 38; C.S., s. 2427.)

§ 43-55. Statute of limitation as to assurance fund.

Action for compensation from the assurance fund shall be begun within three years from the time the cause of action accrued. In cases of infancy or other disability now recognized by law, persons under such disability shall have one year after the removal of such disability within which to begin the action. (1913, c. 90, s. 39; C.S., s. 2428.)

Article 9.

Removal of Land from Operation of Torrens Law.

§ 43-56. Proceedings.

Any land brought under the provisions and operation of this Chapter before April 16, 1931, may be removed and excluded therefrom by a motion in writing filed in the original cause wherein said land was brought under the provisions and operation of said Chapter, and upon the filing of a petition therein showing the names of all persons owning an interest in said land and of all lien holders, citation and upon the hearing of said motion, the said clerk of the superior court may enter a decree in said cause removing and excluding said land from the provisions and operation of this Chapter, and transfer and conveyance of said land may be made thereafter as other common-law conveyances. (1931, c. 286, s. 1.)

§ 43-57. Existing liens unaffected.

Nothing in G.S. 43-56 shall be construed to impair or remove any lien or encumbrance existing against said land. (1931, c. 286, s. 3.)

§§ 43-58 through 43-62. Reserved for future codification purposes.

Article 10.

Instruments Describing Party as Trustee or Agent.

§ 43-63. When instrument describing party as trustee or agent not to operate as notice of limitation upon powers of such party.

When any instrument affecting title to real estate describes a party as trustee or agent, or otherwise indicates that a party is or may be acting as trustee or agent, but does not indicate any beneficial interest, set forth his powers or specify some other recorded instrument setting forth such powers and the place in the public records where it is recorded, and there is no recorded instrument in the record chain of title to such real estate setting forth such powers, then the description or indication shall not be notice to any person thereafter dealing with the real estate of any limitation upon the powers of the party nor require any inquiry or investigation as to such trust or agency. Such trustee or agent shall be deemed to have full power to convey or otherwise dispose of the real estate; and no person interested under such trust or agency shall be entitled to make any claim against the real estate based upon notice given by such description or

§ 43-64. Application of Article; filing notice of claim; application of § 47B-6.

This Article shall apply to instruments recorded before or after May 15, 1975, but shall not bar any claim based on notice given by any instrument if, within one year after May 15, 1975, a written notice of the claim is recorded, identifying the place in the public records where the reference to a fiduciary may be found, stating the powers of such fiduciary, and naming the person who is then the record owner of the real estate affected. Such notice of claim shall be signed and acknowledged by the person executing the same, and may be executed by any person interested under such trust or agency, or by his attorney, agent, guardian, conservator, parent, or any other person acting on his behalf, if for any reason he is unable to act. The notice of claim shall be recorded and indexed under the name of the person declared therein to be the record owner.

Registrations hereunder shall be subject to the provisions and penalties imposed by G.S. 47B-6. (1975, c. 181, ss. 2, 3.)

Fax Orders:	1-980-299-5965
Phone Orders:	1-704-898-0770
E-mail Orders:	www.visionbooks.org
Mail Orders:	Vision Books, LLC P.O. Box 42406 Charlotte, NC 28215

Shipp To:
Name_____
Address_____
City_____State_____Zip_____
Phone_____Fax_____
Email_____@_____

Bill To: We can bill a third party on your behalf.
Name_____
Address_____
City_____State_____Zip_____
Phone___(_____)_____Fax_____
Email_____@_____

Pamphlet Number ($15.00 Each)	Qty	Total Cost
_____	_____	_____
_____	_____	_____
_____	_____	_____
_____	_____	_____
_____	_____	_____
_____	_____	_____
_____	_____	_____
Full Volume Set 1-92	92 Pamphlets	1,380.00

Free Shipping Shipping & Handling on Full Volume Orders
Add $1.00 Shipping & Handling per pamphlet $_____

Total Cost $_____
        Thank You for Your Support. Management!

been fasely imprisoned, we would like to hear your story. If the 'North Carolina Criminal Law and Procedure' has had an effect in your life or if you have suggestions, we would like to hear from you. Send your letters to:

Vision Books, LLC
Attn: Staff Writers
P.O. Box 42406
Charlotte, NC 28215
Email: staff@visionbooks.org

Order Additional Copies:

Fax Orders: 1-980-299-5965

Phone Orders: 1-704-898-0770

E-mail Orders: www.visionbooks.org

Mail Orders: Vision Books, LLC
                    P.O. Box 42406
                    Charlotte, NC 28215

www.ingramcontent.com/pod-product-compliance
Lightning Source LLC
Chambersburg PA
CBHW051627170526
45167CB00001B/88